Piracy in the Eastern Mediterranean

Piracy in the Eastern Mediterranean

Maritime Marauders in the Greek and Ottoman Aegean

Leonidas Mylonakis

I.B. TAURIS
LONDON • NEW YORK • OXFORD • NEW DELHI • SYDNEY

I.B. TAURIS
Bloomsbury Publishing Plc
50 Bedford Square, London, WC1B 3DP, UK
1385 Broadway, New York, NY 10018, USA
29 Earlsfort Terrace, Dublin 2, Ireland

BLOOMSBURY, I.B. TAURIS and the I.B. Tauris logo are
trademarks of Bloomsbury Publishing Plc

First published in Great Britain 2021
This paperback edition published 2023

Copyright © Leonidas Mylonakis, 2021

Leonidas Mylonakis has asserted his right under the Copyright, Designs
and Patents Act, 1988, to be identified as Author of this work.

For legal purposes the Acknowledgments on p. x constitute an
extension of this copyright page.

Cover design by Adriana Brioso
Cover image: The Battle of Navarino, 20 October 1827, oil on canvas,
by Ambroise-Louis Garneray (1783–1857). (© Bridgeman Images)

All rights reserved. No part of this publication may be reproduced or transmitted
in any form or by any means, electronic or mechanical, including photocopying,
recording, or any information storage or retrieval system, without prior
permission in writing from the publishers.

Bloomsbury Publishing Plc does not have any control over, or responsibility for, any
third-party websites referred to or in this book. All internet addresses given in
this book were correct at the time of going to press. The author and publisher
regret any inconvenience caused if addresses have changed or sites have
ceased to exist, but can accept no responsibility for any such changes.

A catalogue record for this book is available from the British Library.

A catalog record for this book is available from the Library of Congress.

ISBN:	HB:	978-0-7556-0669-6
	PB:	978-0-7556-4360-8
	ePDF:	978-0-7556-0671-9
	eBook:	978-0-7556-0670-2

Typeset by Integra Software Services Pvt. Ltd.

To find out more about our authors and books visit www.bloomsbury.com
and sign up for our newsletters.

To Anna

Contents

List of Figures	viii
List of Maps	ix
Acknowledgments	x
Note on Transliteration and Dates	xiii
Maps	xiv
1 Introduction: Piracy Enters the Modern Era	1
2 Piracy during the Ottoman Civil Wars	27
3 A New Age of Piracy	47
4 Paris, Patrols, and Persistent Piracy	65
5 Currants, Capital, and Declining Piracy	85
6 Piracy during the 1897 Greco-Ottoman War	97
Epilogue: Why Was This All Forgotten?	119
Appendix	125
Notes	129
Bibliography	172
Index	187

List of Figures

1.1 Number of pages per year concerning piracy, YE   20
1.2 Average number of pages per three-year period concerning piracy, YE   20
1.3 Frequency of *"Korsan"* in BOA, 1096(1685) to 1343(1924), All Seas   22
1.4 Number of documents concerning Mediterranean piracy, BOA and YE   22
4.1 Comparison of documents pertaining to piracy in BOA and YE over fourteen-year periods   67
5.1 Quantity and revenue of raisin exports in İzmir. Raisin export quantity and calculated value in İzmir based off Table A5 in Kasaba, Reşat   93
5.2 Annual average value of exports from İzmir to Britain. Based off data in Roger Owen   94
6.1 The cannon drill on the Imperial Ironclad Frigate Mes'udiye. Abdullah Freres, photographers. "[The cannon drill on the Imperial Ironclad Frigate Mes'udiye]/Constantinople, Abdullah Freres"   101

List of Maps

1 The Ottoman Empire and its dependencies, 1800 xiv
2 Territorial expansion of Greece in the Aegean Sea over the nineteenth century xv

Acknowledgments

This book is the result of a decade of research that began during my doctoral program in history at the University of California San Diego. I owe a debt of gratitude to those who have helped me flourish academically and stood by my side on the path to completing this work.

I would like to thank my committee for standing by me from the conception of this project. I must begin by thanking Thomas Gallant, my PhD advisor who inspired me during my undergraduate years to head to graduate school to study modern Greek and Mediterranean history. The unwavering support he has given has helped me get through the most trying times of the graduate program. He has truly gone above and beyond. Mark Hanna has graciously guided my scholarship once I selected to focus on piracy and has been a great aid in connecting me with others interested in the topic. Hasan Kayalı has shown me the same attention as his own advisees, helping me learn the scholarship of the Ottoman Empire and guiding me toward resources in my study of both modern and Ottoman Turkish. Michael Provence has been a diligent editor, and his advice remains a whisper in my ear when considering word choice. Lastly, Gary Fields has helped me gain a stronger grasp on the theories useful when studying violence and social boundaries in borderland regions.

I would also like to issue a special thank-you to the late John Marino. It was in his research seminar on Early Modern Europe that I first began to gain interest in piracy. He graciously accommodated the fluidity between Europe and the Middle East that is so necessary when studying the Mediterranean world and genuinely aided each of his students who were mostly selecting topics outside of our modern-era specializations. He is sorely missed.

Many others have helped me flourish in academia. Denise Demetriou and Edward Watts have been critical in running the Center for Hellenic Studies. They have offered me much intellectual and moral support. I warmly thank Cynthia Truant, Patrick Patterson, Jeremy Prestholdt, Pamela Radcliff, Matthew Herbst, and Eberly Mareci for their instruction and friendship. Begüm Yılmaz and Efsun Pektaş were both wonderful Turkish-language instructors at Tömer İstanbul. My Fulbright advisor, Maria Christina Chatziioannou, helped me navigate Greek academia and brought scholarship I had not before seen to my attention. I am grateful to the staff at Fulbright Greece, especially Nicholas Tourides and Artemis Zenetou, for having offered me the honor to conduct research in Greece and the personal warmth and charisma each of them displayed. I thank the staff at I.B. Tauris, especially Yasmin Garcha, Rory Gormley, and my anonymous reviewers, for their help with bringing this book into fruition.

Over the years my research has taken me to several libraries and archives. Without the help of the staff in Greece at the General State Archives, archives of the Ministry of Foreign Affairs, regional archives in Herakleion, Chania, Rhodes, the Gennadius Library and the National Research Institute, and in Turkey at the Ottoman Prime Ministry Archives and İSAM, I would not have been able to gather the primary and secondary source materials needed to complete my research. I extend my gratitude to University of California San Diego's own Geisel library, whose support staff and interlibrary loan department have eased my research while stateside.

Several research groups at University of California San Diego have brought together scholars from various disciplines to talk about certain themes. I thank all the co-participants of the piracy and borderlands groups. I would like to single out John Alaniz as the man who stepped up to the plate and held the piracy research group together when faculty became too busy to manage it. I warmly recall our conversations both in and outside of those groups. I thank the countless individuals who have offered feedback on my work at conferences, particularly Will Smiley, Ali Atabey, Ceren Abi, Christin Zurbach, Joshua White, Gillian Weiss, Daniel Hershenzon, Fariba Zarinebaf, Benjamin Fortna, Christine Isom-Verhaaren, David Starkey, and Judith Tucker, to name only a few.

Over the years I have made many close friends. I began my graduate study of Ottoman history alongside Patrick Adamiak, who has not only been a great friend but also a great mentor. He has helped me bounce ideas off him, improve my Ottoman Turkish reading, and navigate the unrest on the streets of İstanbul during the summer of the Gezi Park protests. My cohorts in modern Greek history at University of California San Diego are both great friends and great scholars; I expect great things from Kalliopi Kefalas, Juan Carmona Zabala, David Idol, Dimitris Stergiopoulos, Emre Sunu, Aytek Soner Alpan, and Chris Theofilogiannakos. Same goes for my friends in Middle Eastern studies: Ben Smuin, Johanna Peterson, Nur Duru, Barış Taşyakan, Ted Falk, Nazar Bağcı, and Nadeen Kharputly. I cherished my time with these upcoming scholars in my field of specialization, and many others not yet listed, for brightening my days in San Diego.

When my mother, Helen, unexpectedly died in 1998, it was her dream that my brother and I would be the first in the family to earn doctoral degrees. My father, Anthony, has shown great strength in raising us and has offered unwavering support as we pursued our studies. I am so proud of my brother and close friend, Kyle, who has recently completed his doctorate in mathematics at University of California Santa Barbara. Finally, I want to thank my wife, Anna, for her endless love, support, and endurance. I look forward to spending all my years by her side. I dedicate this work to her.

Note on Transliteration and Dates

This book uses sources written in several Mediterranean languages that each requires different strategies to integrate them into an English-language text. Ottoman Turkish benefits from two primary transliteration systems in wide use. In lieu of the system offered by the *International Journal of Middle Eastern Studies*, I have adopted a modified version of the modern Turkish orthography. Thus, the name "Mehmed" with the final voiced syllable consistent with Ottoman usage will appear rather than the strictly modern Turkish "Mehmet." I have provided Greek names as provided in the source documents. Thus, the Greek name Γεώργιος appears as Georgios, Giorgios, Yorgo, and George.

Primary sources used four different calendrical systems. Ottoman documents primarily used the Hijri (Islamic) and Rumi (Islamic month/Julian year hybrid) lunar calendars. These dates have been converted to Gregorian system which is in widespread use today. During the nineteenth century, Greece used the Julian calendar which was at the time roughly two weeks out of sync with the Gregorian calendar. When discussing dates of major events such as treaties or combining sources from sources that use Julian and Gregorian dating, I convert dates to Gregorian. Otherwise, I retain the Julian system used in Greek archival documents for internal consistency.

Some notes on Turkish pronunciation:

- c = j, as in "jam"
- ç = ch, as in "chain"
- ı = i, as in "girl"
- ğ = silent gh, as in "though"
- j = zh, as in "gendarme"
- ş = sh, as in "shock"

Maps

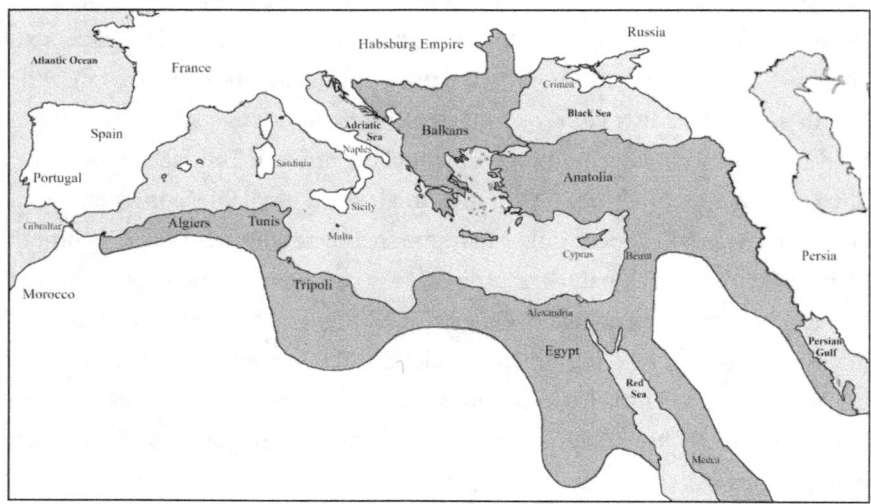

Map 1 The Ottoman Empire and its dependencies, 1800

Map 2 Territorial expansion of Greece in the Aegean Sea over the nineteenth century

1

Introduction: Piracy Enters the Modern Era

"You tell me Monte Cristo serves as a refuge for pirates, who are, it seems to me, a very different kind of game from goats."

"Yes, your excellency, and it is the truth."

"I knew there were smugglers, but I thought that since the capture of Algiers and the destruction of the regency, pirates existed only in the romances of Cooper and Captain Marryat."

"Your excellency is mistaken. There are pirates, like the bandits who were believed to have been exterminated by Pope Leo XII, and who yet rob travelers at the gates of Rome every day. Has not your excellency heard that the French *charge d'affaires* was robbed six months ago within five hundred paces of Velletri?"

"But of course."

"Well, if, like us, your excellency lived in Livorno, he would hear from time to time that a little boat loaded with goods, or a pretty English yacht, which was expected at Bastia, Porto Ferrejo, or Civita Vecchia has not arrived. No one knows what has become of it, and doubtless it will have been wrecked against some rock. Well, that rock it met was a low, narrow barge of six or eight men, who surprised and looted it on a dark and stormy night at the bend of some wild and uninhabited islet, like how bandits stop and loot a mail coach at the corner of a forest."

"But," said Franz, still stretched out in his boat, "Why do those who have such an accident not come to complain? Why do they not call down on these pirates the vengeance of the French, Sardinian, or Tuscan government?"

"Why not?" Gaetano said with a smile.

"Yes, why not?"

"Because, first of all, they carry off everything that is worth taking from the ship or yacht to their boat. They then bind the feet and hands of the crew, attach to each man's neck a cannonball of twenty-four, make a hole the size of a barrel in the keel of the captured ship, go back to the bridge, close the hatches and return to their own boat. After ten minutes, the vessel begins to creak and moan; gradually it sinks. First, one side plunges, then the other; it rises and plunges again, sinking ever further. Suddenly a noise like a cannon-shot sounds: air bursting through the bridge. Then the ship agitates like a drowned man who struggles, getting heavier with each movement. Soon the water, pressuring upon the cavities, rushes out of the openings, like the liquid columns which would be thrown by the vents of some gigantic sperm whale. Finally, it utters a last rattle, makes a last turn on itself, and rushes into the deep by digging a vast funnel that swirls for a moment, fills up little by little and eventually completely fade away; so that at the end of five minutes it would take the eye of God himself to go to the bottom of this calm sea to retrieve the missing ship."

"Do you understand now," added the boss, smiling, "why the vessel does not enter the port, and how the crew does not file a complaint?"[1]

By the time Alexandre Dumas wrote his masterpiece *The Count of Monte Cristo* in 1844, the only pirate ships that were supposed to be in the Mediterranean were either wrecks upon the sea floor or fictitious ones that were imagined memories of a romanticized past. For a novel set largely in France and Italy, the connection to an orientalized Eastern Mediterranean was strong. The protagonist's mistress was none other than the fictional daughter of Ali Pasha Tepedelenli, the Lion of Ioannina whose roar commenced the Greek revolution and whose head later adorned a silver platter presented to Sultan Mahmud II. It was those uprisings in the Near East that advanced the plot while Edmond Dantes rotted his youth away in prison, creating the conditions for his rival to hone his military edge and his outlaw allies to thread the line of legality and make their way as smugglers. Dumas expected his reader to believe these to be romanticized characters of a past that no longer existed, making an exciting last hurrah in times when absolutism had returned to crush the dreams in which lower-class figures could rise to prominence.[2]

Whether or not pirates actually roved the eastern seas was of little concern to Dumas. *The Count of Monte Cristo* is a work of orientalist literature, more concerned with using an imagined Other to reflect on developments closer to home than accurately describing faraway lands.[3] It was widely accepted in France and the rest of Western Europe that maritime marauders were no more, that they only belonged to the realm of fiction. As it turns out, they were wrong. Piracy did not end with the conquest of Algiers and the demise of the Barbary corsairs. In the Aegean, piracy persisted and would do so into the following century.

After British, French, and Russian gunboats sailed into the Eastern Mediterranean flying the banner of civilization and security, piracy in the region was believed to have vanished along with its legally permissible equivalents, corsairing and privateering. Ottoman, Greek, and other archival sources show this to be inaccurate. Piracy carried on well past the installation of the Bavarian monarchy in Greece and the French colonization of Algiers in 1830 that brought an end to Mediterranean corsairs and the 1856 Treaty of Paris which formally outlawed privateering. Pirates continued raiding Greek and Ottoman waters into the early twentieth century. The nascent Kingdom of Greece viewed these marauders alternatingly as a menace and as nationalist martyrs revolting against the Ottomans as Greek rebels did earlier in the century.

This book charts the changing rates and nature of transnational piracy during the nineteenth century and considers the factors that shaped it. These range from political reforms to changes in the regional economy caused by the accelerated integration of the Mediterranean into the expanding global economy. Imperial power struggles, ecological phenomena, shifting maritime trade routes, revisions in international maritime law, and changes in the regional and world economy contributed to fluctuations in extrajudicial violence at sea. State decisions to label non-state naval raiders as illegitimate pirates or legitimate insurgents in a popular national uprising were central to claims over nationhood and sovereignty. Greece periodically protected pirates who pillaged neighboring seas and claimed them as rebels carrying out Greek irredentism. The Ottoman Empire struggled maintain its legitimacy as the Abode of Peace by effectively controlling piracy and exercising its monopoly on violence. Great Britain used the continued threat of piracy to international trade as a reason to maintain a strong naval presence in the region that did little on their own to mitigate the frequency of pirate raids. Maritime marauders only ceased to harry the Aegean coastline when both licit economic opportunities were available and, at the same time, local, regional, and international authorities dissuaded them from profiting through plunder.

Defining Piracy

The common understanding of piracy is violent theft originating from the sea carried out upon coastal settlements and transiting ships. Exact definitions of piracy vary by time, place, language, jurisdiction, legality, legitimacy, and social contexts. James Wadsworth recently proposed a definition of piracy that attempts to take a flexible approach to the topic: "Piracy is seaborne banditry that can manifest itself as parasitic, episodic, intrinsic or some combination of the above, given the specific historical and cultural context in which it was practiced."[4] There are some key differences that separate maritime piracy from terrestrial banditry. Piracy requires a ship, which is a sizable startup expense compared to that needed to commit banditry on land. It traditionally requires large numbers of people to crew said ship, especially if the goal is to overwhelm the intended target and to make resistance hopeless. Even smaller enterprises reliant on a handful of raiders on a caique must procure and maintain a vessel and a crew capable of operating it.

Another distinction is that piracy is a crime that takes place where borders are fluid and jurisdiction is murky. The boundary of international versus territorial waters also remains in flux. Over the centuries of its existence, the Ottoman Empire consistently expanded its maritime boundaries in an attempt to secure its island provinces from foreign interference.[5] The Sublime Porte considered islands and coastlines to be borderlands of its jurisdiction, a territorial littoral to be protected from foreign pirates, privateers, and the lawlessness of the open sea.[6] In the present day, we consider territorial water to be a certain distance from controlled land. Exactly how far that is has caused fierce debate and tension between Greece and Turkey, almost leading to war in the Aegean in several instances. The reach of territorial waters has been considered six, ten, or twelve nautical miles at various points over the twentieth and twenty-first centuries. Currently, further reach from the shoreline favors Greece as it controls almost all the Aegean islands.[7] Disagreement over these exact details leads to the grey and black spaces where pirates and smugglers can operate most effectively.

Non-state maritime marauders are typically divided into three or four sub-categories: pirate, privateer, corsair, and filibuster. The labeling of an action as piracy varies by context. Louis Sicking categorizes maritime military entrepreneurs upon two axes: first, whether they took orders from a state; and second, whether they were financed by a state. Navies and temporary war fleets both took orders and received funding from the state. Filibusters, such as those used for American expansion during the nineteenth century, were financed by but did not answer to the state; they were simply armed irregular soldiers who were set loose to make trouble for the enemy. Privateers answered to the state, but did not receive any funds, and instead were remunerated via captured booty. Lastly, pirates operated entirely outside of state control. They were unaffiliated opportunists who robbed whatever hapless victim they could. They were the enemy of any state claiming to provide security over their dominion. As with all forms of military entrepreneurship, the lines separating these naval forces were muddied and violated at a moment's notice. Naval officers would not turn down plunder and prizes out of hand, and even the most anarchic of pirates had some alibi should they come face to face with the law.[8]

Privateers were naval entrepreneurs who were given letters of marque to raid the shipping of enemy states. They were funded by capturing prizes which were regulated and assessed at tribunals. Thus, they operated in a similar manner as pirates, with the exception that they accepted one sovereign, rather than none. They were to abide by the alliances and regulations laid out by their patron state, but they operated with much more autonomy than regular naval forces. To their victims, there was often little difference if their assailant bore a letter of marque. States commissioned privateers to accomplish their general goals, as Britain hired privateers like Sir Francis Drake to raid Spanish bullion shipments, simultaneously weakening their imperial rival and bringing extra revenue into state coffers.

Corsairing and privateering are categorically the same thing, with *corso* being the Latin-based root meaning "pursuit" used for corsair in Mediterranean languages (French, Italian, Greek, Turkish, Arabic, etc.). The use of corsair for privateer arose in a distinct geography with historical baggage. Some historians describe Mediterranean corsairs and Caribbean privateers as the same, except the former are guided by religious ethos rather than the state.[9] This leads to discussion of corsairs to be reminiscent of the grand sectarian divisions laid out in Samuel Huntington's *The Clash of Civilizations*.[10] The narrative of piracy in this view takes on the undertones of crusade and jihad, two topics more often discussed with more passion than reason. Two groups dominate the history of corsairing. One was the order of the Knights of St. John, based in Malta, and the other was the Barbary corsairs of the Ottoman Empire's North African vassal states: Algeria, Tunis, and Tripoli. There were also other smaller groups, all based in the Mediterranean. In general, historians cast the conflict of corsairs in the Mediterranean as a struggle between a Christian northern shore against an Islamic southern one in need of complication.[11] When we take a critical view of Mediterranean corsairs as not only being motivated by religious conflict alongside a reminder that Atlantic privateers also participated in confessional conflicts, the two categories of raiders seem more alike despite their different historical contingencies.[12]

When discussing categories of maritime violence, note that the terms described above are used by Anglophone academics. Both Greek and Turkish authorities from the nineteenth century used different categories for piracy based on their mother tongues. In Ottoman Turkish, the term *korsan* encompasses all extrajudicial providers of maritime violence: pirates, privateers, and corsairs. Thus, when reading Ottoman documents referring to a *korsan*, pirate is only a correct translation when couched in proper context. Other Ottoman terms like *levend* (irregular), *ehl-i fesad* (people of malice), *eşkiya* (brigand), and *harami* (thief) could all refer to a pirate, but they are more general terms for outlawry that could also refer to terrestrial irregulars or brigands.[13] When appearing alongside *korsan*, such descriptors suggest that the sailors in question were pirates, not privateers. Nautical occupations like *firkateci* (frigateer) were frequently employed to refer to pirates, but those terms also covered licit sailors.[14] When the Ottomans saw a *korsan*, they saw a maritime military entrepreneur that could either be coopted to serve the state or labeled as an outlaw and hunted down. Either option acted to strengthen the state's claim to legitimacy by securing a monopoly on violence.

We need to pay close attention to attached adjectives and other contextual clues present in the documents if we are to understand the relations between these raiders and the state of Greece. Ottoman documents frequently described the raiders in one way or another as *Yunan korsanları*. The term *Yunan* was used specifically to refer to Greeks from the independent kingdom. Ottoman-Greeks were referred to as *Rum*.[15] Ottoman documents that dealt with piracy committed by Greeks indigenous to the empire either called them *Rum korsanı* or *ızbandut*, a specialized term specifically used for Ottoman-Greek pirates.[16] When the author used the term *Yunan*, it is clear that the Ottomans viewed these individuals as being foreigners encroaching into Ottoman space rather than rebellious *Rum*.

In the Greek language, there are two types of extra-state maritime military entrepreneurs. The term *peiratis* (πειρατής) is the root of the English term "pirate" and in modern times shares the same range of meaning.[17] In common parlance it carries all the ambiguities of its sub-categories and in academic parlance it carries the specificity of referring to those self-interested aquatic bandits acting without ties to any state. *Koursaros* (κουρσάρος) combines both the notion of corsair and privateer.

The denizens of the Eastern Mediterranean did not always separate themselves out into neat ethnic categories nor did they speak only purified forms of their languages. Many of them were polyglot, and many spoke hybridized versions of several languages. For example, interrogations of suspected pirates in the Kapodistrian naval courts were conducted in *Katharevousa*, a purified version of Greek used by the state, but the responses were in a version of the common demotic Greek that borrowed heavily from Turkish.[18] When the officials would ask for the suspect's profession, a common answer was "είμαι γεμιτζής," ["I am a sailor"] opting for the Turkish word for sailor, "*gemici*."[19] More uncommonly the suspects would respond in a pidgin, where the answers occasionally made use of Turkish grammar interwoven into the Greek: "*Ali Paşa'nın*" rather than "*tou Ali Pasa*" for the genitive case. Language was as fluid as the water upon which pirates sailed.

Pirates, like all other men of the sea, did not remain permanently adrift; they frequently touched land. And where they did, they formed connections: families, trading partners, suppliers, and the like. Outside the golden age of piracy in the early eighteenth-century Atlantic, only few thought of themselves as a pirate as a form of permanent identity. Instead, it was a temporary occupation, a means of making a living. For example, Sir Henry Morgan made his fortune from raiding Spanish shipping, and with his prize money bought several plantations, became Lieutenant Governor of Jamaica, and actively sought to suppress piracy in the Caribbean. Piracy was a means to gain wealth, not an end in itself.[20] Many historians either fall into the trap of romanticizing the freedoms that piracy offered or viewing all pirates as psychotic villains to be dealt with by the good landed men of the Royal Navy.[21] Pirates can be thought of as private military entrepreneurs. They primarily operated outside of the law, but they did not exit from society. Pirates maintained deep entanglements with landed society to be able to do things such as fence their goods, resupply, make social calls, and ultimately retire. Even when they took captives, pirates frequently gave an opportunity to their captives' loved ones to pay ransom to the appropriate people.[22] Hostages would fetch a higher price when paroled to their relations than when sold on the slave market. Whereas corsairs and privateers were bound by their sponsors' regulations concerning treatment of their captives, pirates were not, and as such they occasionally viewed it more in their interests to slay or otherwise dispose of their victims than to risk negotiating ransom to maximize their profits.

States and their representatives often labeled their enemies as "pirates," particularly when they wanted to cast them as illegitimate and not worth negotiating with. This usage goes back to ancient times, where in one example, Romans cast Mithridates Eupator VI of Pontus and his Cilician allies, Rome's rival in the Eastern Mediterranean, as being a "pirate king."[23] In the nineteenth century, British naval officers such as Sir Thomas Stamford Bingley Raffles labeled Malay nobles as "pirates" in order to justify taking naval action against them and by so doing to incorporate the Malay Peninsula into the British Empire.[24] Pirates were the enemy of all, *hostis humani generis*, and any modification of that category was meant to bring legitimacy to a profession that was usually cast as being outside the bounds of the law.

Hunting down outlaws was often ritualized to enhance state legitimacy beyond simply the act of monopolizing violence. State authorities often publicly displayed the corpses of captured outlaws. As traders and passengers were funneled past choke points in the natural geography, they would be confronted with the miserable fates of those deemed unacceptable to the state.[25] Whether it be the crucified bodies of rebellious gladiators lining the Appian Way or the rotting corpses of ungovernable pirates left hanging in Caribbean harbors, the message remained the same. The state decided what was illegal and it alone was responsible for exacting vengeance or showing mercy.

Geography

This book is primarily concerned with two states: the Ottoman Empire, and its first fully independent successor state—Greece. By the dawn of the nineteenth century, the Ottoman Empire was only just shy of its maximum historical territorial reach, having lost territory in central Europe and the northern Balkans as a result of the rout resulting from the failed 1683 Siege of Vienna and the 1699 Treaty of Karlowitz. After that retreat from Hungary and the other territories that fell to the Habsburgs, their European border remained relatively stable for over a century. The other major area of Ottoman territorial loss occurred on the northern shores of the Black Sea. After the 1710–11 war with Russia, the Danubian Principalities of Moldavia and Wallachia (present-day Romania) gained autonomy and the requirement to be governed by a Christian *voyvoda*. The Ottomans were also unable to defend their close ally, the Crimean Khanate, from Russian annexation in 1783.[26] These losses meant that the Black Sea, once in practice an Ottoman lake, became a contested sea. The conquest of Crimea granted Russia a warm-water port with which they could build a naval force potentially able to sail straight for the Dardanelles. The Black Sea would no longer only be trafficked by merchant ships. Once the domain of peace, the sea would now become a domain of war which would require the Sublime Porte to send its frigates northward—resources that would have been spent on their other vast coastal territories.

There were two Ottoman provinces that had "islands" in their name. The province of the Aegean and surrounding regions was the *Eyalet-i Cezayir-i Bahr-i Sefid,* or Province of the Islands of the White Sea, commonly referred to as the Archipelago Province.[27] Southwest of the Archipelago Province lays the other island province of the Ottomans: *Eyalet-i Cezayir-i Garb*, or Province of the Islands of the West, known today as Algeria.[28] Algeria was at the heart of piracy in the Mediterranean during the early modern era. Along with the other North African territories of Tunis and Tripoli, they retained a great deal of autonomy under the Ottoman Empire and made much of their income from taxing trade passing through their waters. Whereas the Archipelago Province was under İstanbul's direct control and fully integrated into Ottoman legal norms and could be considered as the "Ottoman Mediterranean," the North African corsair-states enjoyed a great deal of judicial autonomy and by the 1620s even began conducting their own foreign policy.[29]

In all its forms, the Aegean Sea has been composed primarily of two geographic features: islands and peninsulas. What little land states held was surrounded by sea. The waters could bring forth the bounties of trade, but they also simultaneously exposed the region's inhabitants to the ravages of maritime marauders.[30] Both powerful foreign navies and small-scale raiding enterprises were able to shape the archipelago's history. A single instance of piracy could provide a *casus belli* that would draw in larger fleet action. In 1645, pirates attacked an Ottoman pilgrim ship carrying the chief of the harem Sünbüllü Ağa in the vicinity of Venetian-controlled Crete. This affront provoked the wrath of the Sublime Porte and resulted in a war to conquer the island that lasted until 1669.[31] In the modern era, how the Ottoman Empire and Greece interacted with both the Great Powers and backwater pillagers would shape their alliances and security strategy. Greece was a small coastal state on the southern extremity of the Balkan Peninsula that was crippled in any instance, such as during the Crimean War, when it opposed Britain's fleet. The dominant British Royal Navy patrolled waters around the globe to protect its merchant fleet from pirates and privateers. How the states of the Eastern Mediterranean dealt with endemic sea-robbery played an important role in protecting their sovereignty from interference by foreign powers.

The Ottoman Empire was one of the largest states in history.[32] Despite reaching the Red Sea, Black Sea, Persian Gulf, Indian Ocean, Adriatic Sea, and much of the Mediterranean, most of the reports of piracy in both the Greek and Ottoman archives during the nineteenth century took place in the Aegean Sea. This is unsurprising when considering the island topography and surplus of trade routes and opportunities for ambush in the far-southern tip of the Balkan Peninsula and the nearby islands.[33] This is a land where mountains rise from the sea, intermingled as such that neither of these elements is ever more than twenty miles apart. Sailors could navigate the Aegean without ever losing sight of land.³⁴ Those on the islands and coastline had two options for how to build their settlements: they could either live by the shore and thus connect themselves to the bounties and perils of trade and piracy on the sea lanes, or they could build up in the mountains, isolating and protecting themselves.

The mountains and sea created two opposing forces upon Mediterranean societies: centrifugal and centripetal forces that would push people apart or bring them together. Mountains would isolate settlements from one another, even if they were relatively nearby. On the other hand, coastal settlements would be in close contact with all other coastal settlements throughout the Mediterranean and beyond. The sea offered a cheap way of shipping goods, people, and ideas across all ports upon its shores. Unlike shipping goods by lands, which would need to be trucked across a certain series of maintained land routes, the sea provided a multitude of routes, allowing options for bypassing certain choke points.

Traversing the Mediterranean by ship funnels travelers through certain areas. The two main entrances and exits to the Mediterranean are Gibraltar in the west, connecting to the Atlantic, and the Bosporus in the east, connecting to the Black Sea. The construction of the Suez Canal in 1869 added Port Said, Egypt to the last of gateways by adding access to the Red Sea. While the Archipelago Province of the Ottoman Empire did not include İstanbul, the great city on the Bosporus, it was also a necessary through point for maritime trade. Much as mountainous territory provided cover from which bandits could launch their ambushes, so too could pirates seek cover hiding in the coves and caves of these partially submerged mountain ranges of the Aegean Sea.³⁵

The final geography we must confront is political. The division of the world into discrete continents is a mythology used to make political, religious, cultural, and other claims over space.³⁶ The Mediterranean is often viewed as a watery boundary between continents that are in fact connected, separating Europe from Asia and Africa, Christianity from Islam, colonizer from colonized. Amedeo Policante has shown how the discourse of the pirate-state went from different, equal, conflicting, northern versus southern Mediterranean to unequal colonial relations imposing European culture on "rogue-" or "pirate-" states, and why this was done over the last two centuries.³⁷ He builds upon Lotfi ben Rejeb's scholarship that shows that the entire discourse of North Africa as "Barbary," and thus barbarian, was used as an orientalized, imagined contrast against what Europeans thought of themselves.[38] In the buildup to the 1801–5 Tripolitan War, America began viewing North African corsairs as uncivilized pirates conducting wanton raids rather than as privateers legally collecting tribute for passage through their territory.[39] The history of piracy is intimately entangled with broader hegemonic discourses of power.

The Traditional End of Piracy

As with most matters in history, Mediterranean piracy is generally associated with a certain time and place. Popular tales hark back to the sixteenth century and Barbarossa's fleet wreaking havoc upon his Frankish foes. The regencies on the North African coast, known to the Europeans as Barbary, continued plaguing European trade in the Mediterranean up until the nineteenth century. The Barbary corsairs and their Catholic foes in Malta totally dominated Western discussions of piracy in the Mediterranean.[40] Rather than summarize the entire history of piracy in the region, this section will simply trace each thread of piracy's historical yarn to where they have been cut off.

The populations of the Mediterranean were deeply connected by piracy and ransom networks during the early modern era. Historians of the region have given the moniker the "corrupting sea" or the "captive sea" to describe the region's deep interpersonal networks of population movement, communication, and exchange.[41] Mediterranean captivity and slavery was a single interrelated and asymmetrical system, where the predominately Christian West had set up a series of redemptive institutions which did not have a direct equivalent in the Muslim-dominated East.[42] These communities responded to the threat of enslavement largely through the establishment of sectarian funds for ransoming their captive comrades.[43] Ransom payments were also occasionally secured across sectarian lines.[44]

Nowhere had a more developed or widespread ransom network as the corsair states in North Africa and Malta. Each ransom negotiator sent to North Africa allowed for a dialogue between states that took each other's subjects captive. Hostage exchanges occurred, especially when a state was tight on funds.[45] The pirate regencies had an advantage though. They often sold off their captives in exchange for new weapons.[46] This made it more difficult for

European powers to effectively mount slave-raids upon the Barbary Coast.[47] Spaniards still attempted to take slaves in land raids upon North Africa, while Maltese and Tuscan corsairs continued targeting Muslim merchant ships at sea and in the Eastern Mediterranean.[48] The local government in Algiers organized a pious foundation, the *waqf al-haramayn*, to pay ransom. A portion of the booty seized from Christian ships provided funding for the foundation.[49]

One characteristic of early modern piracy was that their quarry often was isolated and unable to protect themselves. Pirates predated upon coastal communities and lone merchant ships as they plied uncertain trade routes in the Mediterranean. Rules set in place to protect Ottoman non-Muslims from enslavement were frequently ignored by North African corsairs who sought to increase profits by laundering their illegally taken, co-imperial captives at faraway slave markets.[50] French merchants had grown dominant over trade in the Eastern Mediterranean, but Greek shipping came to surpass the declining French trade in the Levant as the latter became embroiled in various wars in the late eighteenth century.[51] Military conflicts may reduce piracy by offering employment to military entrepreneurs, but they also employ seafaring merchants and create hostile conditions for maritime trade. In the tumultuous decades surrounding the French revolution, the only viable strategy for trade was to form large caravans escorted by naval vessels to ward off attackers.[52] Ottoman Greek merchant ships also traveled in heavily armed caravans and did so well into the nineteenth century.[53] As the Ottomans had conflicts with France and Russia during this time, they were subject to the predations of pirates and privateers given letters of marque by those two states. To help defend against these aggressions, they gradually extended their claims over maritime territory during the eighteenth century from being only the Aegean archipelago to including everything in the open sea east of the Peloponnese and Benghazi.[54]

On the northern shores of the Mediterranean, the Maltese corsairs, the Knights of St. John, were essentially either a criminal organization or a microstate unto themselves with their Grand Master afforded the rank of sovereign from the Pope.[55] Once the bloodthirsty crusader faction known as the Knights Hospitaller, the knights continued their crusade at sea after they were driven out of the Holy Land to Rhodes then Malta.[56] Molly Greene has shown how their supposedly faith-based raids were unconcerned with targeting only

Muslims. The knights did not hesitate to take prizes from Catholic Venetians or Orthodox Ottoman Greeks.[57] The Knights of St. John were opportunist pirates, not crusaders. Emrah Safa Gürkan has also questioned the degree to which North African ships were motivated to conflict by religion.[58] The regencies of North Africa turned their cannons on their rival Muslim states as often as they turned them upon Western ships and shores.

The knightly Order of St. John was the first pirate society to end in the nineteenth century. The French revolution is often pinned as the starting point of the modern era, and it is fitting that Napoleon brought about the first end to a corsairing society that had shaped the previous epoch.[59] The knights remained active raiding in the 1790s trying to supplement their income after Napoleon seized their French estates until he finally expelled them from the island in 1798.[60] Two years later, England captured Malta, and in 1807 banned slavery. Malta rapidly transformed from a corsair's castle to a British colonial naval base. When the Maltese corsairs were no more, the ransom networks built up during the early modern period gave way to more profitable British imperial trade networks as the island became a notable transit hub.[61] This is not to say that piracy did not bring Malta wealth. It most certainly did. But the entire industry of Malta was focused around corsairing. As *corso* became no longer profitable or sustainable, the island's economy stagnated until it became deeply integrated into the capitalist world economy under British suzerainty.[62]

Tunis, Tripoli, and Algiers began operating independently of Ottoman diplomacy in the early seventeenth century. They ignored treaties that foreign nations had set with İstanbul and seized the ships of France, England, Holland, and Venice as prizes. These states responded with a number of punitive expeditions before all but Venice decided to treat with the North African regencies independently from the Sublime Porte, negotiating tribute payments that were cheaper than the expense of naval security.[63] At the start of the nineteenth century political circumstances changed. Rather than paying tribute and acknowledging the sovereignty of Algiers, Tunis, and Tripoli over their own seas, Western powers chose war. The first was the United States, a fledgling country that found its trade routes with the Mediterranean were no longer protected by British tribute payments. Tripolitan ships began harassing American merchant ships in the Mediterranean beginning in the 1780s. In 1800, the US flagship *George Washington* was pressed into Algeria's service to act as a cargo freighter to send Algeria's tribute to İstanbul.⁶⁴ America began tributary payments to Algeria, but Tunis and Tripoli began demanding comparable payments for safe passage. After Algeria raised ransom and tribute demands to unreasonable levels, over $1,000,000 in 1800 dollars, President Thomas Jefferson lobbied for the formation of a federal navy, a controversial proposition in a divided Congress. In 1801 America sent over a small fleet to Tripoli, who had recently raised their ransom demands to the level of the larger and more dangerous Algeria. For three years the Tripolitans laughed off the American blockade which consisted of a handful of deep-water warships, unable to pursue the lighter Tripolitan gunboats into shallow water. In one episode of the war, a US warship ran aground some rocks and was captured by Tripoli. Rather than risking the warship's use by enemy forces, Jefferson appointed Stephen Decatur to lead a raid to demolish the ship in Tripoli's harbor.⁶⁵ The high-risk stealth mission succeeded without incident, leading to Decatur becoming a national hero, and solidifying his position in America's continued conflicts with the North African regencies.

In 1804, America returned with a larger fleet, containing proper gunboats, which was able to successfully block off Tripoli's port and capture Derna. The US ambassador to Tripoli negotiated a reduced annual tribute to Tripoli along with the release of Americans captured during and prior to hostilities. Concerned with budgetary spending, Congress downsized the navy. With the American military threat removed, Tripoli once again raised their tribute demand.

The Napoleonic Wars disrupted European commerce and opened the door for North African merchant ships to seek trade rather than tribute. There was a notable drop of North African corsairing expeditions in 1806 while British and French privateers carried on their war at sea. When Napoleon was first defeated in 1812 and European merchants were again able to edge out their African competition, the number of Tunisian corsairing expeditions tripled.⁶⁶ The drop in corsairing expeditions during this period can also be partially attributed to internecine warfare. In 1807, the North African Regencies of the Ottoman Empire began fighting among themselves. Tunis fought and defeated Algeria's army.⁶⁷ While North Africa was war weary, and Europe laid in ruins following the Napoleonic wars, the United States sought to end its tribute payments to the Barbary states once and for all.

The American Navy had dramatically expanded to fight against the British in the War of 1812, which ended in 1814. One year after those hostilities ended, the fleet sailed to North Africa to subdue the weakened regencies. Seeing the threat that the US Navy posed and weak from regional conflict, each regency quickly sued for peace and formally ended their tribute demands to the United States.[68]

After the two wars, the United States set a precedent showing that raiding off the North African coast could be prevented by military might, not simply through diplomacy. Following the American example, in 1816 British and Dutch fleets also bombarded Algiers to demand release from tribute payments and freedom for European captives. Most of the captives held were not English or French but overwhelmingly hailed from the various states of the Italian peninsula. The days of North African raiding were not yet over. As they had done repeatedly in the past, within two years Algiers reconstructed its fleet and resumed roving the sea for captives.[69] The Greek struggle for independence inspired France to turn against its Islamic Ottoman ally and send troops to the two island provinces of the Ottoman Empire: Greece and Algeria.[70] The republican opposition to the Bourbon royalists took up the cause of philhellenism and imbued it with rhetoric laced with race, faith, violence, and gender.

In 1830, France would pick up on the lesson from earlier bombardments that Barbary could be beaten and prepared an invasion under the gesture of proto-humanitarianism.[71] The Greek War of Independence helped fuel the French will to "liberate" North Africans from their "barbarian" nature. Like many Western observers, the French saw the war in certain lights. There was the ever-popular religious view, of Christendom and Islam being engaged in holy war. Another light was that of color, of "dark" North African pirates fighting and enslaving "white" Greek Christians. This viewpoint ignored the actual myriad skin tone present on both shores of the Mediterranean, and instead was simply a relabeling of the religious categories. Lastly, the Greeks striving for independence were portrayed in artwork as women seeking freedom from violent male oppression.[72] The root for all these categories laid in the religion of the people, but the employed rhetoric masked the religious categories as others that secular leaning French republicans would be keener to support.

Until 1827 the French monarch stood by his ally, Sultan Mahmud II. Unlike those with the sultan, French relations with the Algerian *Dey* Hussein leading up to then had been stretched since the 1790s. During its own revolution, France had borrowed exorbitant sums from two Jewish merchants in Algeria who were in the business of redeeming captives. France remained delinquent on this debt, creating tensions between the two states. When Hussein hit the French Consul Pierre Deval with a flyswatter in 1827, France (over)responded by sending a squadron to blockade Algeria's port until they received an official apology.[73] The blockade lasted until 1830, when King Charles X of France decided to invade.

The king's decision to forgo his alliance and side with the republican philhellenic opposition was part succumbing to unending republican rhetoric, part seeking a permanent solution to naval security, and part desire to set up a cash-crop industry to trade with in "liberated" Algeria. Whatever the justification for the invasion, within six days of the French fleet reaching the Algerian shore, the war was over. The *dey*'s fortifications crumbled and his palace prisons were torn open, revealing neither thousands of beaten Frenchmen nor harems filled with alabaster-skinned Christian women. Instead they found only about 200 Greek, Spanish, and Italian men who while happy to be set free did not exactly sate the French orientalist fantasy. Charles X of France's invasion of North Africa was based on fiscal, political, and diplomatic factors, but his public rhetoric was of liberation and expanding civilization to the region.[74] The French colonization of Algiers was the final form of Western intervention initiated by England and America in the southern coasts of the Mediterranean. Faced with the threat of violent coercion and hoping to retain their sovereignty, Tunis and Tripoli ceased granting letters of marque to corsairs.[75] From the Western viewpoint, Mediterranean piracy ends when gunboats arrived from the West flying sails of red, white, and blue; and blue, white, and red. Western powers deemed North African sailors, once renowned for their marked autonomy, to be "free" only when they were fettered under the shackles of colonialism.

Maritime Raiding by the Numbers

Digitization of archives in Greece and Turkey has made this book possible. The bulk of the primary sources used in this study was attained by keyword searches relating to piracy in the Greek Ministry of Foreign Affairs and

Ottoman Prime Ministry archives. These filters resulted in thousands of pages of relevant results, which were nestled among millions more pages of irrelevant documents. The bulk of the results was diplomatic correspondence which often included enclosures of supporting judicial or military reports. This section will go over the data-collection methodology and describe some general trends that are observable from metadata.

Both the Greek and Ottoman archives have been making large strides to digitizing their collections, but in these cases digitization efforts are aimed primarily at uploading facsimiles. This book draws upon previously unused archival documents in Greek, Ottoman Turkish, French, English, and Italian. Almost all the documents in the Greek and Ottoman archives are handwritten, which impedes efforts at performing optical character recognition (OCR) to create machine-readable files which would allow textual searches throughout entire documents. OCR researchers have made progress with creating programs to digitally transcribe some handwriting in the Latin script, but as of writing this book, there is no publicly available program that can decipher and transcribe handwriting in the Arabic or Greek scripts. While the Greek archives only provide facsimile scans of their collection, the Ottoman archives include keywords and a machine-readable summary which aid in parsing through their database. I have used metadata from these documents to trace the rates of piracy over the nineteenth century and delved deep into reading them to provide qualitative examples upon which to base my historical analysis.

The cases of piracy I have assembled across Greek and Ottoman diplomatic archives are adequately numerous to tell the story of piracy in the Eastern Mediterranean over the long nineteenth century, but many cases have slipped through my net. I was unable to attain access to the archives of the Ottoman and Hellenic navies while conducting research. Thus, this book does not claim to be a comprehensive history of piracy but a qualitative and quantitative analysis of the data on inter-state incidents. Since the main archives used in this study are diplomatic, the cases of piracy presented all have a transnational nature, be that involving crossed borders, international waters, or differing subjecthood of involved parties. The cases that caught the eyes of diplomats were fewer than entered the records of patrolling navies, but we can still infer much about the frequency of raids. When searching through the archives, I have erred on the side of being conservative on which cases to include as piracy, rejecting cases that did not explicitly contain maritime or illicit descriptors. I also removed documents which did not describe Mediterranean piracy, such as news of piracy elsewhere, mutinies, and intellectual piracy.[76]

The Greek Ministry of Foreign Affairs archives begin in 1826 and end in 1913, after which access is more tightly restricted. There are seventy-six document folders dealing with piracy spread over those eighty-seven years, so the average rate is just under one folder of documents reporting piracy a year. This rate holds roughly steady, with small spikes or remissions forming exceptions. Category 55/1 under the old classification system was reserved for piracy, but occasionally the archives returned cases of piracy in other folders for court proceedings. Only four folders concerning piracy were filed in the Greek Ministry of Foreign Affairs archives during the revolutionary 1820s. This lack of paper trail does more to highlight the nascence of the revolutionary government rather than correctly reflect the elevated level of piracy in and around the Aegean. For a folder on piracy to be present for a year, at least one case needed to be on record, and most folders contain several cases. Archival sources from the Ottoman Empire and Great Britain show that piratical incidences occurred at elevated levels during Greece's revolutionary decade.

Viewing these documents year-by-year helps to reveal precise periods of elevated or decreased piratical activities that can be tied to political or international events. In the five-year span from 1835 to 1839, ten cases were reported, doubling the general rate. There was also a small spike in 1843 and during the Crimean War in the 1850s. The year 1858 was the first year that there were no reports of piracy in the Greek Ministry of Foreign Affairs archives, and from 1861 to 1913, a fifty-two-year span, there were only thirty-one cases reported, with a spike observable in 1893.

Looking at the proliferation of page count dedicated to piracy for each year can also offer some valuable insights, with the caveat that as the bureaucracy grew over the century, so too did the length of reports. For example, by the 1880s and 1890s, the page count for piracy spiked without an actual spike in the number of reports. Smoothing the data by taking three-year averages (Figure 1.2) allows for a quicker understanding of the general trends by reducing the seeming jaggedness of the graph.[77] Tracking the page count in each folder allows us to get a sense of both the number and complexity of

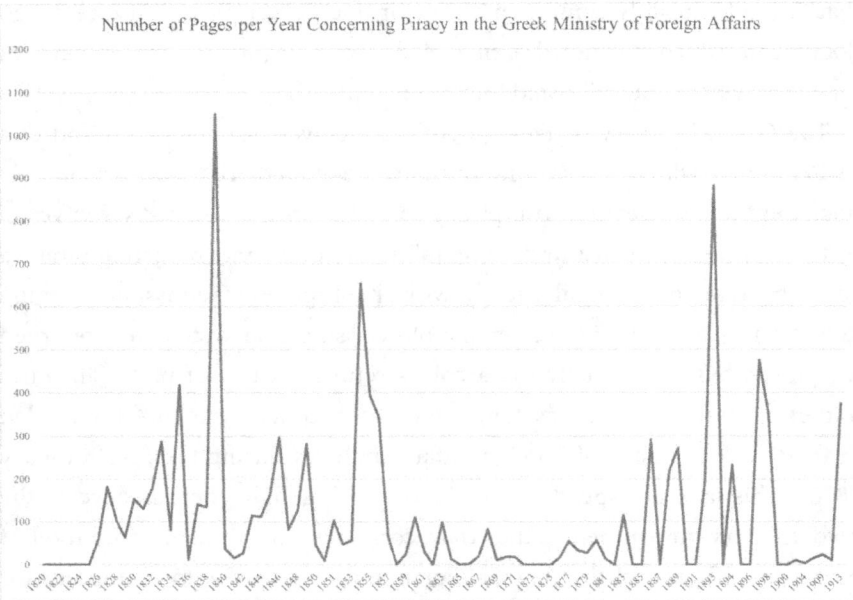

Figure 1.1 Number of pages per year concerning piracy, YE

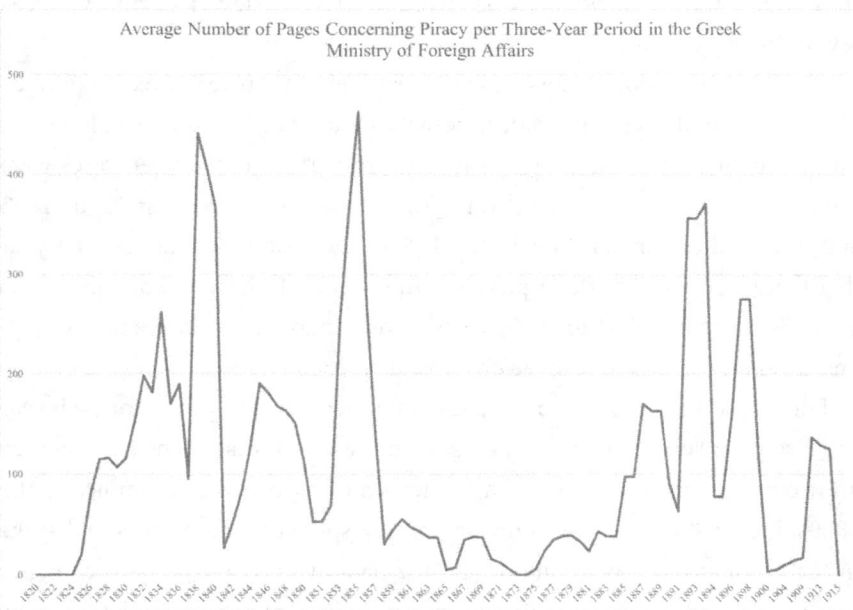

Figure 1.2 Average number of pages per three-year period concerning piracy, YE

piracy cases, as well as the importance of and amount of attention paid to piracy by the Ministry of Foreign Affairs.

The Ottoman archives stretch much further back than the Greek archives, as it is the state that both knocked out the Byzantine Empire and lasted into the days of fighter planes and chemical warfare, collapsing as did so many other European empires in the aftermath of the First World War. For this study, I begin tracking occurrences of the term *korsan* (using textual context to remove non-maritime piracy) in 1820, one year before the onset of the Greek War of Independence. Exempting the first decade of the twentieth century, the overwhelming majority of documents referencing piracy in the Ottoman archives for the time period of this study concern the Mediterranean.[78] The last cases of piracy that appear in the Ottoman archives are from the 1910s, the last full decade of the Sublime Porte's existence before collapsing and fragmenting into various colonial mandates and nation-states.

When these documents are grouped by decade, we can more easily see the decreasing trend of piracy in the Mediterranean over the nineteenth and early twentieth centuries. The pivotal point between averaging three cases every two years and one case every two years occurs in the 1850s, apparently as a result of the Crimean War. The conflict resulted in the signing of the Paris Declaration Respecting Maritime Law which placed an international ban on state employment of privateers. While the methodology utilized to gather these documents results in only a handful of returns of Ottoman documents referencing "*korsan*" across all seas per decade, the number of results in the nineteenth century is comparable to most decades outside of a considerable spike from roughly 1195 Hijri (1780 Gregorian) to 1236 H (1820 G). Those four decades contained over half of the Ottoman documents with a reference to the Turkish word for pirate or privateer and coincided with a period of military and social reform to be discussed early in Chapter 2. The spike in the early twentieth century mostly occurred in the Red Sea and is a continuation of trends that I discuss in Chapter 5.

When looking at the number of Mediterranean pirate raids in both states combined, we see a small bump in the last two decades of the nineteenth century. This bump is much more minor than the page count relating to piracy in the Greek Ministry of Foreign Affairs suggests. This methodology of counting events rather than pages proves more consistent given changing

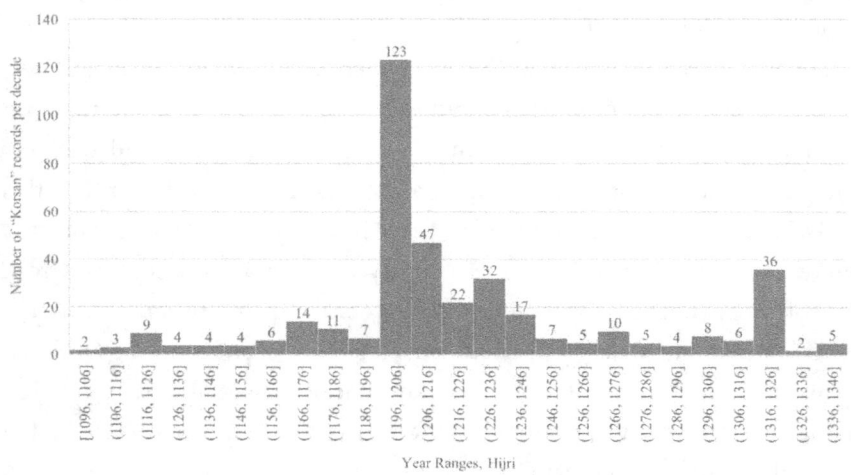

Figure 1.3 Frequency of *"Korsan"* in BOA, 1096(1685) to 1343(1924), All Seas

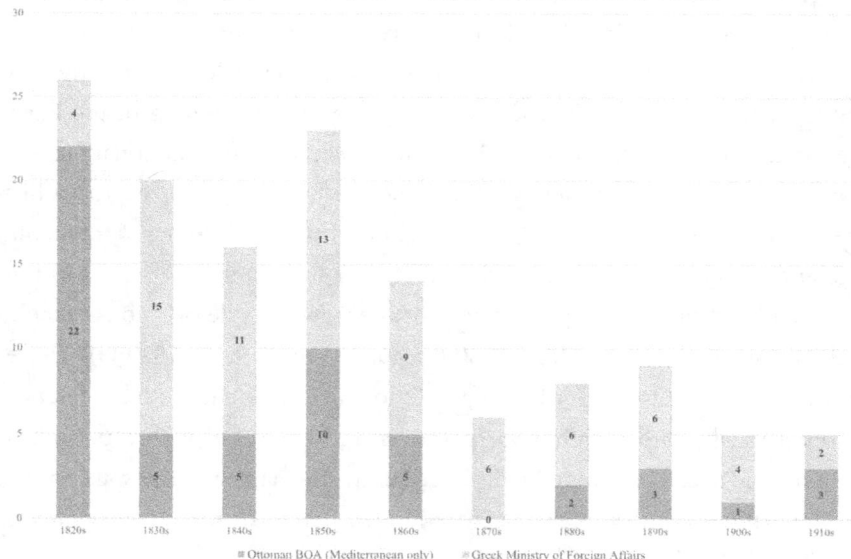

Figure 1.4 Number of documents concerning Mediterranean piracy, BOA and YE

bureaucratic practices over the century and will provide the basis of discussions of the piracy data in this book.

Book Layout

This book examines Mediterranean piracy's severity, nature, and use in state-building projects in chronological segments marked by periods of conflict and reform. The introduction discusses different categories of non-state maritime violence, the geography of Mediterranean piracy, and the end of traditional corsair societies. It then offers a statistical overview of nineteenth-century reports of piracy in the Greek Ministry of Foreign Affairs and Ottoman Prime Ministry archives.

The second chapter begins the chronological narrative that will carry through the rest of the book. It looks at the 1820s and 1830s together as a great period of Ottoman upheaval and civil war, beginning with the Greek War of Independence in 1821 and carrying forward with Mehmed Ali of Egypt's uprising against the Ottoman Empire which lasted until 1840. While the Ottomans cast all rebels as bandits and pirates, even the revolutionary Greek government lost control of many sailors, labeled them as pirates, and sought foreign assistance in eliminating them. I use Crete as a case study, as it was an Ottoman island that became a major base for Greek revolutionaries that turned to piracy. They raided friend and foe alike to support themselves, becoming a major point of contention between rotating Greek revolutionary governments and European allies and eventually leading to the allied massacre of these pirate-revolutionaries. While Greece gained sovereignty by 1832, Crete instead became a territory of Egypt and its new struggle against the Ottoman Empire. In addition to the standard Greek, Ottoman, and British sources used for the revolutionary period, I also use relevant Egyptian and Algerian sources.

Chapter 3 examines the period of political reforms that followed this period of strife: the beginning of the *Tanzimat* reforms in the Ottoman Empire, the 1839 Edict of the Rose Garden, and the introduction of a constitution in Greece. This period of liberal reforms in the region correlated with an increased rate of piracy, matching that of the 1830s, which lasted until the end of the Crimean War in 1856. While Greece ceased commissioning corsairs after gaining independence, they utilized non-state maritime violence to their advantage by enacting policies for their navy to allow fleeing pirates to escape into Ottoman waters and harry their rivals. Greek regional governments protected pirates who had raided the Ottoman Empire and crossed over into their jurisdiction, describing them as rebels who continued the work of the revolution three decades prior. The nature of piracy, captivity, and state-pirate relations had changed in the post-Barbary Mediterranean.

Chapter 4 looks at a period of legislative and maritime-policing reform and economic stagnation beginning with the aftermath of the Crimean War. The war ended with the drafting of the Treaty of Paris and the Paris Declaration Respecting Maritime Law which legislated a ban on privateering among its signatories. The expansion of the Ottoman Navy, patrols by the British fleet, and the end of state-sanctioned maritime raiding led to a negligible reduction in cases of piracy in Greece and the Ottoman Empire. Newly independent Italy imitated unsuccessful Ottoman and Greek policies to use its military to suppress brigandage and piracy without improving the rural economy, and likewise failed to prevent such outlawry. With ransom markets long gone, pirates grew more violent as they no longer had a profitable way to dispose of their captives. It was not until the Aegean regional economies took off in the 1870s that fewer individuals committed piracy and instead picked up the plow to participate in the cash-crop craze. The fifth chapter discusses reports of piracy dropping by half which and their correlation with the phylloxera epidemic that wiped out Western European viticulture and the resulting currant boom's growth of the Greek economy. The Ottoman Aegean experienced economic growth during this period, despite the bankruptcy of the central government. Land reform and resettlement programs allowed economically disadvantaged populations to partake in the agricultural activity driving the regional economy, lessening the need to turn to outlawry.

Chapter 6 concludes with how different states viewed piracy during the 1897 war. Classic cases of piracy had diminished by this period, and when viewed from both Greek and Ottoman sources, we see what the Ottomans called a pirate ship, the Greeks viewed as a regular naval unit under orders to break a ceasefire to harass the Ottomans. This tactic was consistent with their efforts on land to rely on irregular forces and even release brigands from prisons to destabilize Ottoman control and weaken the Sublime Porte's position at the negotiating table. While the Ottomans had an unmitigated victory on land, their fleet had decayed over decades of neglect as funds had fled westward to pay the public debt. This was emblematic of the Ottoman ability to enforce order through a regular army coming to an end as their Balkan foes returned to using the tactics of irregular warfare.

A brief conclusion considers why an entire century of piratical activity in the Eastern Mediterranean fell from historical memory. Chrono-thematic narratives oversimplify historical trends by excising data that does not match expectations; corsairs dominated discussions of early modern piracy, so piracy was supposed to end with them. Pirates continued raiding into the early twentieth century, but their place in state-building changed as modern states reevaluated the role of irregulars and filibusters.

2

Piracy during the Ottoman Civil Wars

The story of the Greek War of Independence usually focuses on the battles and campaigns that took place on land, and typically ends in 1832 with the arrival of Otto of Bavaria as the first king of independent Greece. Local Greeks, other *zimmi* (Ottoman non-Muslims), diaspora Greeks, philhellenes, and the Albanian warlord Ali Pasha colluded and took arms against the sultan, each for their own purpose: for a restored Byzantine Empire, for a republican government in place of the sultan's *divan*, to realize a romanticized vision of ancient Greece, for Christians to throw off Islamic rule, or for more power within the existing Ottoman hierarchy. It is a story in which bandits led the charge against the sultan's forces sent to suppress the insurrection. John Koliopoulos introduced the concept of "military enterprisers," explaining that the bandit lords who participated in the revolution were more interested in benefiting themselves than in creating a democratic, liberal nation-state.[1] He also explains how the state that accorded bandits who took leadership roles during the revolution like Theodoros Kolokotronis near mythological status for their efforts did an about-face when the war was over and the new government came to view these power-hungry military men as more of a menace than as national heroes.

The traditional narrative limits the broader importance of the uprising on regional geopolitics. It begins looking north to the Balkans, where the Greco-Russian Demetrios Ypsilantis led a failed uprising in Wallachia and quickly centers upon the Peloponnese where the rebellion managed to eventually succeed. The international diaspora and philhellenic support from Western Europe, Russia, and even the United States receive attention in the classic narrative, but the only glance south is to see Egypt as an invading army under the Ottoman banner. The Greek uprising against the Sublime Porte not only established the independence of a new small kingdom, perhaps presaging the empire's eventual piecemeal partitioning, but in the following decade also provided inspiration to both internal and external actors looking to seize power from a weakened sultan.

This chapter focuses on the naval campaigns in the Aegean and adopts a transnational approach in order to highlight the interconnected nature of the Eastern Mediterranean, where the histories of the Aegean archipelago, Egypt, North Africa, the Levant, and Anatolia were deeply entangled. It centers on Crete, an island that was part of both the Greek and Egyptian uprisings against the Sublime Porte, to complicate the narrative of religious conflict by showing Westerners fighting Christian pirates on Crete, Algerian corsairs offering humanitarian aid to Crete, and Mehmed Ali of Egypt governing the island with ambiguous religious rhetoric.

In the area around Syntagma Square, the political center of Athens, countries from around the world compete for real estate for their embassies. While not the biggest, the closest embassy to the square belongs to Egypt. Most Greeks think little of this fact. Greece is in the present day a member of the European Union, so why would the embassy of a seemingly insignificant African country occupy such prime diplomatic real estate? Historically, both Egypt and Greece shared a desire for autonomy or independence from the Ottoman Empire. Political expedience led them to be on opposing sides during the 1820s insurrection, but soon thereafter both waged open war against the Sublime Porte as a common foe and became exemplary post-Ottoman states.

The uprising against the Ottoman Empire in the Archipelago Province during the 1820s has been viewed in a number of ways. Independent Greece cast the events as a glorious national revolution, liberating the Greek nation from the shackles of Ottoman oppression. Western powers saw the uprisings as a chance to free a Christian population from its Muslim overlords. The Sublime Porte saw the rebellion initially as a bandit war, where gangs led by *klefts* threatened imperial rule, and the Porte responded accordingly by deploying irregular forces and militia to crush it. Ottoman reports frequently described acts of insurgency as bandit or pirate attacks, as they did in 1821, the first year of the war, when "Greek pirate vessels" raided İstanköy (Kos) and injured a black Ottoman soldier whose comrades in arms then massacred sixty islanders.[2]

The Sublime Porte viewed rebellious *zimmi* as bandits to be put down by the sword but offered pardon to those who peaceably returned to Ottoman governance. Already in 1821, the Ottoman rear-admiral had already lost control over the discipline of his marines who plundered Ottoman Christian communities in the Dardanelles region which had not risen up in rebellion. Ottoman military and political leadership denounced these raiders as bandits and irregulars who did greater harm to the mission of pacifying the rebellion.[3] The Sublime Porte described both treasonous Greek rebels and unruly Ottoman forces with rhetoric of banditry and piracy.

Greek rebel naval forces described themselves in the same terms as the gangs of bandit-irregulars on land, as *kapetani* (captains) leading privateers instead of bandits.[4] The revolutionary government had very little control over these forces which were often more interested in booty and prizes than in the struggle for national liberation. They frequently clashed more with other Greek *kapetani* than with Ottoman forces. For example, George Koundouriotis of Hydra and Botasses of Spetses were instrumental in fighting against the supporters of Kolokotronis in what amounted to a civil war in 1824.[5] In the best of cases, rebel sailors blurred the legal distinction between pirate and privateer and sailed as far as Beirut, where in 1826 they pillaged the Levantine city and unsuccessfully tried to encourage local Christians to join the rebellion.[6] By 1827, the condition of the rebellion grew dire, so many rebel mariners abandoned their commissions and instead openly turned to wanton plunder. The Greek revolutionary committee decried this wave of piracy and requested assistance from the allied fleet under Lord Codrington to pursue the rebels-turned-pirates and restore order. While the pirates in Ottoman sources were often just political rebels, those who were also labeled "pirate" by Greek rebels were truly without allies—enemies of all.

In the decades leading up the Greek War of Independence, the Ottoman Empire was attempting to transition its military away from relying on irregulars. While Selim III's New Order reforms were aimed at modernizing the army and navy from the 1790s onward, the 1820s and 1830s under Mahmud II were the first decades that saw the first effective steps to implement those reforms.[7] The first move was the elimination of the old janissary corps and the establishment of the new, conscript-based force called the Victorious Soldiers of Muhammad (*Asâkir-i Mansûre-i Muhammediye Ordusu*), which entered the fray late and was initially unable to deal with the rebellion.[8] Naval reforms became necessary after the defeat of the Porte's North African vassal states and their corsair forces. During the Greek War of Independence, the forces that the Ottomans fielded on both land and sea were mostly irregulars.

The 1820s were a period of modernization in the region. Egypt had standardized its *fellahin* army and the Ottomans purged their janissaries in favor of a modern Western-style army.[9] Greece created a standing army initially manned primarily by Bavarians, to the chagrin of the *kleft* lords. At every step there was resistance, and these standing armies only entered the war toward its end, if at all. Irregular forces battled during what they perceived to be possibly their final days. Once military standardization was completed, opportunities for vertical mobility as a military entrepreneur diminished.[10] The leaders of irregular units had to either prove themselves as critical to the state's security or challenge the writ of the state itself.[11]

Another aspect of modernization during this period was in maritime transit technologies; steamships were up and coming, and one of the first used in combat was the *Karteria* built for combat in the Greek War of Independence. To bolster its army of rebels and philhellenes, the revolutionary Greek government took out a series of loans in 1824–5 from Britain totaling over one million pounds. The intent of this money was to hire Lord Thomas Cochrane, a Scottish naval mercenary with fresh record of success leading the navies of Brazil and Chile in their independence wars. Greece ordered an elite flotilla for him to head consisting of two frigates and six steamships from British shipyards. A series of delays, mismanagement, and embezzlement led to only one steamer and one frigate, the *Karteria* headed by the philhellene Captain Hastings and the frigate *Hellas* headed by Lord Cochrane, arriving on time to participate in the war. One other steamer arrived only for the end of the war, the other four were scrapped, and the second frigate was sold to the United States to pay for unexpected overages in costs for the first. The *Hellas* and *Karteria* served as flagships for the revolutionary fleet but did little on their own to stand against the Ottoman navy or control piracy as it spiraled out of control during the revolution.[12]

The main advantage steamers offered was mastery over nature by allowing travel irrespective of winds or currents. Several disadvantages came along with reliance on coal to fuel travel. Coal was a sparse resource in the Mediterranean and importing large quantities of it proved expensive. Burning fuel also led to visible plumes of smoke that hindered any attempt at stealth. These drawbacks led early steamers to rely heavily on sail technology for general travel and only engage their steam engine when the winds did not align. One last drawback of steamers, both powered by paddle like the *Karteria* and by propeller as later became the standard, was the draught jutted deep into the water, making travel through shallow littoral difficult.[13] As concerns shifted from conventional warfare to patrolling the seas for pirates, the cost and disadvantages of steam technology dissuaded both Greece and the Ottoman Empire from adding steamers to their fleet for another two decades, as will be discussed in Chapter 4.

This chapter looks at the 1820s and 1830s as decades of upheaval and civil war, beginning with the Greek War of Independence in 1821, then continuing with the war from the North African perspective, ending with Mehmed Ali uprising against the Ottoman Empire. I use Crete as a case study, as it was an Ottoman island that became a major base for Greek revolutionaries who turned to piracy. They raided friend and foe alike to support themselves, becoming a major point of contention between various Greek revolutionary governments and their European allies and eventually leading to the allied assault on these pirate-revolutionaries. While Greece gained independence by 1832, Crete remained under Muslim suzerainty, first as a territory of Egypt and then as an Ottoman province once again.

Gramvousa: Rebels, Sailors, Pirates, Prey

On an islet off the northwestern tip of Crete a castle stands atop a cliff, resisting the beating of ocean waves and the wear of time. The shallow lagoon of Balos, filled with clams, connects this island to the parched peninsula jutting out from Crete. At low tide, men and animals can cross on foot and harvest clams for food. When the tide rises, small ships can pass over this strip where ships of deeper keel would run aground.

Gramvousa, as both the fortress and island are known, was constructed by the Venetians between 1569 and 1584. It was meant to guard ships passing through the Gulf of Kissamos headed to and from Venice. As the peninsula leading to Gramvousa was inhospitable, the only feasible way to supply the fortress was by sea. After Ottoman conquest of the island in 1669, the Venetians retained control of Gramvousa, Souda, and Spinalonga, wherefrom they commissioned anti-Ottoman corsairing expeditions crewed primarily by local Cretans that raided their co-islanders who were now in the Abode of Islam.[14] When the Venetian garrison commander betrayed Gramvousa to the Ottomans in 1691, the conquerors let the fortress go derelict.

As nothing but a skeleton crew patrolled the crumbling fortifications, Gramvousa was vulnerable to attack. When Greek insurrection broke out in 1821, the Ottoman military was occupied with suppressing the rebellion. While Ottoman forces were distracted, Cretan and Greek rebels seized the fort and used it as a base for conducting raids. Ottoman troops were able to secure most of Crete, but the island-fortress once again remained outside of the Sublime Porte's grasp. In 1826, the arrival of the North African fleet cut off the rebels on the island from the revolutionaries in the Morea.

Deprived of supplies and information, the rebels at Gramvousa became focused on survival. They had their ships, they had protective walls, and they had a shallow littoral environment around them over which they could pass with ease but larger ships of war could not. These maritime men of violence turned to piracy in order to survive and would gain the ire of Greece's Western allies, ultimately bringing the two into open conflict.

By 1827, piracy was on the rise throughout the Greek world, including Gramvousa. Ibrahim Pasha, the son of Mehmed Ali, led the Egyptian expedition to aid the Ottoman efforts to quash the Greek rebellion. His successful march through the Peloponnese forced Greek military forces to scatter and the Greek revolutionary government retained control over only a very small part of the peninsula. Cut off from any logistical support, Greek rebels throughout the region simply sought survival and personal plunder. Syros, Mykonos, Samos, and Gramvousa were key areas which turned to piracy and where pirates could fence their goods.[15] The Greek government, led at the time by Petrobey Mavromichalis, was accused by the Great Powers of allowing piracy to flourish.[16] The British Admiral Codrington wrote to the Mavromichalis government to threaten action against Greek corsairs who disregarded their commissions to attack only Ottoman forces and instead roved as far as Malta and Sicily where they seized neutral and allied merchant vessels as prizes which were then deemed legitimate in sham tribunals.

Greek Corsairs under the signature of Mr. Glaraki, the Secretary to the Provisional Government, instead of acting against the Ottoman forces has interrupted and plundered our Vessel pursuing regular and lawful commerce, even on the Coasts of Malta and of Sicily. Our Vessels so seized and so plundered, have been declared lawful prizes by a Tribunal not guided by law of equity, and nominated by the same Provisional Government whose members share a twentieth part of the booty; whilst Pirates, and the owners of the Pirate Vessels, are suffered to continue their depredations unpunished.[17]

Internal Greek correspondence in late 1827 used terms like "shame," "abominable," "cursed," "infamy," and "unholy and inhuman" to describe piracy, showing the government's general opposition to the chaos pirates created.[18] Nevertheless, the Great Powers expressed concern over attacking the pirate-rebels at Gramvousa due to their nominal affiliation with the Greek state.[19] Without direct approval from Mavromichalis, the Greek-revolutionary pirate nests were untouchable.

The revolutionary government was unable to contain the outbreak of piracy in 1827, as they were hanging on by a thread until the Battle of Navarino in October of that year provided an opportunity for the allied squadrons from Britain, France, and Russia to utterly destroy the Ottoman and North African fleet. The elimination of Ottoman Navy changed the dynamic at sea. There was less need for privateers commissioned to hunt Ottoman ships that became sparse, and the momentum of the war swung in favor of the Greeks. International support intensified to help wrap up the revolution and stabilize Greece. And lastly, the allied squadrons were able to shift their attention from fighting the Ottomans to suppressing piracy. The following year would bring a change of guard within the Greek government. No longer would it be led by rebels who had fought the Ottomans from the very start of the revolution.

In 1828, Ioannis Kapodistrias came to Greece as its new governor. Kapodistrias was far more concerned with Greece fitting into a Western system of diplomacy than trying to simply co-opt every agent of violence in his territory. Having gained substantial diplomatic experience in Tsar Alexander's court at Saint Petersburg as the Russian Minister of Foreign Affairs, he expected his troops to be regular and regulated. Pirates and *klefts* had no place in his vision for Greece. Once in office, Kapodistrias gave Admiral Codrington and the allied fleet the go-ahead they needed to crush the pirate-rebels at

Gramvousa. There and elsewhere the Greek and allied fleets were able to pursue and prosecute pirates with extreme prejudice. Kapodistrias is typically credited with directing Andreas Miaoulis to eliminate piracy in the region, but Despina Themeli-Katifori warns us that the narrative does not end so neatly.

> Most of those who wrote about Kapodistrias's efforts to organize the Greek state also mention his attempted persecution of piracy. However, they all perceived the subject in a superficial way. They limited themselves to the narration of Andreas Miaoulis' expedition against the piracy centers of North Sporades, as well as the attack of Gramvousa by the French and the English. These undertakings, indeed spectacular and effective, managed up to an extent to discourage the pirates, who were convinced that the period of anomaly had ended. However, these actions did not complete, nor were they possible to end, the attempts to secure the Greek seas from the pirates that hurt the traffic and transit in the Eastern Mediterranean. These [pirates], even though they knew they clashed with the organized state, could not possibly transform overnight into law-abiding and peace-loving citizens.[20]

Kapodistrias's attempts to eliminate the pirate nest in Gramvousa were initially successful in curtailing much of the pirate raids occurring in Greek waters. He was less successful in his attempts to keep employment levels high for sailors and in instituting land reforms to provide land to settle former corsairs based out of Mani, Messinia, and Lakonia, the stronghold of the Mavromichalis and Kapetanakis clans. By 1829, Petrobey Mavromichalis attempted to regain political power by fomenting this discontent by labeling Kapodistrias as authoritarian and encouraging the population of the southern Peloponnese to once again take up piracy and act against the Kapodistrias-led government.[21]

The Last Call of the Corsairs: North African Intervention

By the nineteenth century, the elite military force of the Ottomans, the janissaries, had become uncontrollable. During the early centuries of Ottoman expansion, janissaries were conscripted from the empire's *zimmi* population. They were recruited through the *devşirme* as children, converted to Islam, and trained to be the elites in either the military or bureaucracy, depending on their skills. The system was predicated on the periodic acquisition of new recruits, but once the janissaries organized and demanded that their position become hereditary, corruption became rampant. From the early eighteenth century to their bloody abolition in the nineteenth century, they were more like a mafia than a military organization. Sultan Selim III had planned to create a modern, professional military (*nizam-ı cedid*) to replace them in the late eighteenth century, but this move only increased their discontent, leading to a series of janissary uprisings over 1806–8 that toppled three governments and deposed then executed two sultans.[22] Where he failed, Sultan Mahmud II succeeded. Viewing the old janissary forces as the largest threat to the empire, even with the Greek rebellion ongoing, the sultan planned an operation that has come to be known as "the auspicious incident." On June 15, 1826, Mahmud II incited a janissary revolt and ordered the new *nizami* military to attack the janissaries and burn down their barracks. Thousands of janissaries were slaughtered and those who survived were imprisoned or exiled. An Ottoman declaration from 1828 reviled the destroyed janissary corps as bandits, crypto-Christians, and conspirators.[23]

Weakened by the violent change of guard, and with it clear that the officials in the Archipelago Province were unable to suppress the rebels on their own, Sultan Mahmud II called upon his other provinces for military aid. The most powerful of the forces mobilized to suppress the rebellion were from Egypt and North Africa. Mehmed Ali of Egypt had his own *nizami* forces, and Tunis, Tripoli, and Algiers brought with them their corsair fleets. These provinces were all closely communicating with one other, sharing intelligence, and generally taking their orders from Cairo rather than İstanbul.

The Greek rebellion was one of the last instances where corsairs were called to action on a large scale by a state. Ibrahim Pasha led Egyptian forces to the Morea to suppress the Greek rebellion, but his fleet was not only Egyptian. Closely aligned with him were the corsair-regencies of Tunis, Tripoli, and Algiers. Each of these cities was an autonomous territory of the Ottoman Empire. Since the early modern period, they were notorious for not just governing themselves, but also for acting independently from the Sublime Porte and conducting their own diplomatic relations from foreign powers. They paid tribute to the Ottoman Empire and answered its calls to arms, but they decided irrespective to the sultan's will with whom they would be at peace. Whereas Egypt had developed its military largely along Napoleon's model, involving paid conscript soldiers that were not reliant on plunder, the other North African provinces were still reliant on booty to pay their troops.[24] Internal Algerian correspondences from the 1820s are useful to illuminate the last call of the corsairs—to suppress the Greek rebellion.

The insurrection created a wide-scale disruption of daily life. Constant warfare made it unsafe to continue working, especially when that work could not be done within a safe haven surrounded by city walls. As workers declined to head out to the fields and the grain mills, agricultural production plummeted. Famine ensued.

On the island of Crete, the *kadı* of Chania petitioned the pasha of Algiers for relief from famine, as the Ottoman garrison on Crete was unwilling to share food with the local populace. Algiers was an autonomous element within the empire that was worthy of petition when official channels were failing.

> All the inhabitants of the well-guarded city of Chania; all are your slaves, all are miserable, helpless and unhappy. They have all gathered in the courtroom of noble and resplendent justice, and they resolved to send this missive to beg compassion. The request made by the inhabitants of this city tends to obtain prompt assistance in grains of all kinds, of which they are well acquainted with the name, but of which they are utterly deprived. For more than forty days, the mills have been closed and the inhabitants, your slaves, are in distress and calamity: they are in the face of death. We sent almost ten letters in various countries to solicit food, we spread the news of our distress in all places, but until today we did not get anything. It is also in vain that we asked rations to the governor of the citadel who commands for the Padishah.
>
> So we turn to the borders of Algiers the victorious, and we ask for prompt help in wheat and barley. Our country does not have and yours is abundantly provided with this generosity. We address all the notables, all the custodians of authority and we give them notice of our position.[25]

Chania was a city with large numbers of both Muslims and Christians. The Muslim leader of the district was responsible for all residents, regardless of their faith. In his plea, he did not distinguish that the relief should target residents of only one religion, nor does he explicitly blame or call for aid from agents based on religion. In the chaos of rebellion, his eyes appeared unclouded by rhetoric of holy war. Instead, he seems simply interested in ending the suffering of his people. In many ways, this was exceptional given the brutal levels of sectarian violence during the revolution.

As the rebellion in the Peloponnese gained traction and grew more violent, Muslims in the region began to flee for their lives. In 1821, the first year of the uprising, the capture of Tripolitsa resulted in the execution of all Muslim and Jewish residents, even though the revolutionary forces had promised them a safe evacuation. The message was clear. The Greek rebels were uninterested in allowing Muslims to continue living in the region under Christian rule. As the Greek rebels controlled the isthmus at Corinth, there was no land route for the Muslim refugees to escape on foot. This meant that they could only evacuate the region by sea. The Ottoman Navy was primarily manned by Egyptian and North African ships, so many of the refugees were ferried south across the Mediterranean. The Algerian agent in Tunis, Moustafa ben Gabes, actively updated the Algerian Naval Minister Ibrahim on the resettlement of refugees and progress of the war.

> I will inform your lordship that various people from Morea, who have settled in our town, have received from their country letters which announce that Koptan Bey is at Navarino with thirty-two ships of our master the Sultan. The ships of Tunis are with him. They wait for Lord Ibrahim Pasha to arrive from Kolmata [Kalamata], and when he reaches Navarino they will leave for Mani. As for the honorable and illustrious, formidable and magnanimous leader, the lord Capitan-Pasha, he is at El Medelli [Mytilene] with the surplus of the victorious fleet.[26]

In the early years, as Ibrahim Pasha was reconquering the Peloponnese, there was reason for the Muslim refugees to be optimistic about returning home. The revolution seemed to be nearing an end as Egyptian forces pacified the region. As already seen in the case of Chania, local Ottoman officials were using rhetoric which suggested that they were interested in reestablishing peace and normal relations for both their Muslim and Christian subjects. The Peloponnesian Muslims ultimately found themselves permanently excluded from independent Greece. For a moment, however, there was a light at the end of the tunnel as Ottoman forces continued to score military victories, and local leadership began to plan for reconstructing in the postwar.[27]

Where the *kadı* of Chania wrote to the pasha of Algiers in secular language, the Algerian agent in Tunis, Mahmoud ben Amin Essekka, wrote to Hussein *Dey* openly using the rhetoric of *gaza*, or holy war. The language of religious conflict permeates every document produced by Algiers during the Greek War of Independence. At times, this rhetoric was backed up by concrete actions that directly contradicted the goal of reestablishing order at the war's end. "They announce that Ibrahim Pasha has arrived at Navarino, and has brought about five thousand Greek prisoners, men or women, large or small. Lord Ibrahim Pasha received from the Sublime Porte a sword and a caftan. He was appointed in person to be General-in-Chief at sea."[28] The enslavement of these five thousand Greeks has become a major factor in Greek complaints about Muslim atrocities. The Ottoman Law of Release and prisoner-of-war systems were not applicable to rebels, corsairs, and slaves trafficked into the Ottoman Empire. When the Greek rebellion broke out, the sultan authorized his troops to enslave for compensation anything from single enemy combatants to whole regions. Eventually the slave markets became so saturated that rebel heads, ears, and other trophies were sent to İstanbul in lieu of living captives. This led to such levels of international opprobrium that the Ottoman Empire never again enslaved its own people during an internal revolt.[29] This egregious example of human trafficking is worthy of complaint, but it is worth remembering that Egypt and the North African provinces maintained complex relations with all sides involved.

While Mahmoud ben Amin Essekka cursed Christianity, Algeria continued to do business with neutral Christian trade partners like Britain. "The English ship which had left Algiers for İzmir, chartered by merchants of Algiers, was stopped by the Greeks, who removed all that he carried in terms of money and goods, so that it arrived empty to İzmir.[30] May the most-high God exterminate them!"[31] British and French merchants continued in their important role in domestic Ottoman shipping. Western philhellenism during the Greek rebellion was not reason enough for Algerians to disrupt their own trade. This particular example is interesting, because it reverses the traditional ethnic roles of the early modern period. Traditionally, there was a dispute about Christian corsairs using the rhetoric of holy war to target Ottoman shipping, even when the ships were manned by Greeks or Venetians.[32] In this case, there were Greek rebels plundering Ottoman ships manned by Westerners. The same balance between commercial contact and confessional conflict from the previous era was still present in the early nineteenth century.

The Battle of Navarino and the total destruction of the Ottoman and Egyptian fleets changed the course of the war. The Egyptian and North African fleets were reduced to flotsam. Ottoman forces lost the benefits that naval dominance affords: surveillance; resupplying food, munitions, and manpower; and denying the enemy the same. Mehmed Ali ignored orders from the Sublime Porte to have Egyptian land forces set Morea ablaze in retaliation, and instead recalled them and Ibrahim Pasha to Egypt.[33] From an Algerian perspective, this loss was doubly disastrous.[34] The French, British, and Russians were cooperating and were committed to creating an autonomous or independent Greece. But more so, the corsair fleet, the wooden wall that protected the Barbary Coast, had fallen. The imperial powers of Europe were now able to go after the North African regencies more aggressively. Three months before the Battle of Navarino, Mahmoud ben Amin Esseka's report shows that Algiers was already wary of war with France.

> We received from Alexandria a letter from Captain Moustafa-Rais, dated 24th of Hidja. He came by way of Malta and encloses a letter to Lord Ibrahim-Aga. He announces in this letter that they were preparing to leave Alexandria, but that the news of the war with the French being reached in this city, the Lord Mehmed-Ali-Pasha opposed their departure and said, "I will not let you go until I receive a letter from Algiers."[35]

France had already attacked Algiers in 1815 in an attempt to end white slavery. The assault in and of itself led to no permanent changes, as Algiers resumed taking captives once it rebuilt its fleet. This led France to consider three options when dealing with North Africa: accept matters as they were, wait for a local "Barbary revolution" by North Africans to bring themselves into the fold of "civilization," or lastly, to pursue *"la mission civilatrice"*—the imposition of Western norms upon the area by way of conquest.[36] With the loss at Navarino, Algerian intelligence reported that the French were preparing for an African invasion.

> I will inform your lordship that French dogs are preparing to go to Algiers in the spring. They prepare twelve bombards, each with two bomb mortars, one at the bow and one at the stern. Four are ready, and they work for others.

They say they want to divide their attack between Algiers, Bone and Oran [other cities in Algeria to the west and east of Algiers].[37]

There were several factors influencing France's decision to send its fleet to blockade and eventually invade Algiers. Philhellenism was widespread among French republicans, but the Bourbon monarchy was interested in maintaining its alliance with the Sublime Porte. There were debates about white slavery, previously alluded to. The French expectation that they would find thousands of European captives in North Africa was wildly overblown. When French forces arrived, there were only around 200 captives, mostly Greek, Italian, and Spanish, in the hands of slave traders. All of them were men, which also confounded the French expectation they would find harems filled with fair European maidens. Lastly, the establishment of a colony in North Africa would allow for easier access to resources to satisfy the French demand for cash crops.[38] These factors shaped the attitude for French public opinion.

The incident that compelled France to finally intervene had more to do with courtly behavior and outrage. During the French revolution, the government borrowed heavily from two Jewish merchants in Algeria who were in the business of redeeming captives. The restored Bourbon monarchy refused to honor the debts racked up by the revolutionary French Empire. Tensions with its creditors grew and exploded in the flyswatter incident of 1827. The French consul Pierre Deval had met with the Algerian *Dey* Hussein to discuss their financial and political situation. Negotiations devolved into exchanges of insults whereupon the *dey* produced a flyswatter and struck the French consul several times. The French monarch Charles X was outraged and responded by sending a squadron to blockade Algeria's port until receipt of an official apology.[39] This blockade remained in place until France's decision to colonize Algiers in 1830. The invasion only took six days and, though it met resistance from all Algerians regardless of religion or ethnicity, the French forces were too strong. The decade of the Greek revolution, then, ended with the demise of the North African corsair-states. From this point on, France would rule Algeria until 1962.

The Death of Democracy and the Birth of Modern Greece

When Greece had won the war at sea and gained independence guaranteed by England, France, and Russia, the conflict against the Ottomans ended and the conflict between Greeks began. Petrobey Mavromichalis refused to follow Kapodistrias's leadership, particularly when the governor began to undermine the very constitution under which he had been elected. This led the new leader of Greece to charge the old one with treason.[40] Meanwhile, at sea, the two remaining admirals of the Greek revolutionary fleet clashed in a struggle for dominance.[41] Kapodistrias, once a seasoned foreign minister of the Russian Empire, was unable to govern the nascent Hellenic Republic.

On October 9, 1831, relatives of Petrobey Mavromichalis approached Kapodistrias while he was at church and assassinated him, stabbing him in the stomach and shooting him in the head.[42] With few exceptions, Greek historians of piracy argue that maritime predation came to an end with Kapodistrias's death. Kostis Konstantinides goes one year further, arguing that piracy ended in 1832, with the arrival of King Otto and his Bavarian forces.[43] The consensus among historians, then, is that Aegean piracy ended with the creation of the independent Greek Kingdom.

An exception to this orthodoxy is George Kolovos. He suggests that piracy persisted deeper into the nineteenth century. Like all other historians discussing Mediterranean piracy thus far, he abandoned the level of detail used earlier when he shifted his discussion to piracy after the revolution, giving vague allusions and no concrete citation or example:

> Kapodistrias, however, knew that in order to eliminate piracy, the root causes, i.e. the economic and social problems that caused and maintained it, had to be eliminated. For this reason, he tried to integrate into the armed forces or employ in the cultivation of the land unemployed seamen and irregular soldiers, and refugees. But the economic difficulties of the state prevented the exploitation of all these unemployed, which caused their dissatisfaction with the governor. Piracy began to slowly reappear. So long as the re-establishment of the unemployed was delayed, the complete elimination of piracy was difficult.
>
> After Kapodistrias's murder, piracy cases multiplied, and with such audacity that they did not hesitate to capture a naval warship. Sources mention the case of a warship that was converted to a pirate ship. It took several years and the concerted actions of subsequent governments to fight the phenomenon. However, whenever the central administration weakened due to the government, constitutional and state changes that took place until the middle of the second half of the nineteenth century, pirates' activity increased.[44]

Although his narrative of the postrevolutionary period is sparse, Kolovos gives a good summary of factors that affected levels of piracy in Greece over the nineteenth century. A strong economy and licit employment combined with a stable government which worked toward eliminating piracy kept would-be marauders from taking to the account. My research finds the strength of the central government less important, as the next two chapters show that limits on the Greek monarch's power put in place by the 1844 establishment and 1864 reforms of the Greek constitution did not initiate a lasting rise or decline on the rate of piracy in Greece. Kolovos is the only researcher to suggest that piracy continued with any regularity after the revolution, but a handful of others have discussed individual cases of piracy occurring later in the century. The epilogue of this book deals with these cases that were previously treated as oddities.

Kapodistrias's assassination and the subsequent civil unrest led European powers to view Greece as unready for democracy. In keeping with the strong preference of the conservative leaders of restoration Europe for absolute monarchies, they abolished the republic and, after a lengthy search, selected in 1832 Otto of Bavaria to be the first king of Greece. Weakened by infighting that was tantamount to a civil war and just over a decade of conflict, the Greek political leadership had no choice but to accept the imposition of an absolute monarch. The switch to autocracy, however, did not end the struggle at sea. The only year of Otto's reign for which the Greek Ministry of Foreign Affairs did not record any incidences of piracy in the Aegean was 1858. The Bavarian monarch may have had absolute power—at least until 1844—but he did not have absolute control.

The following example gives us an insight into the nature of piracy during Otto's reign. In 1835, the Hellenic royal ship *Samos* was patrolling the northern border in the Sporades. It pulled into an island harbor to take refuge, but four freshly commandeered pirate ships crewed by seventy men were also docked there. The crew of the *Samos*, upon realizing this, demanded that the pirates surrender; instead, when they confronted the marauders, it was they who were easily overpowered. Thus, the *Samos* was captured and became the fifth ship in this pirate armada, which soon took to sea and commandeered a sixth ship. They then targeted an Ottoman warship as their seventh victim, but were unsuccessful, as the military crew repelled them. While fleeing the battle, the *Samos* became stuck between two rocks, and so the pirates took off all its supplies and scuttled the ship. Days later, Greek warships came to repair and reclaim the Samos.⁴⁵

From this incident, we learn a few things. First, this is the largest pirate raid during the postrevolutionary period reflected in the archives used in this study. The crew size of these pirate ships included a full contingent of sailors but only a modest raiding cohort to attack and board enemy ships. This was a departure from one common pirate tactic of the early modern era: to have enemies surrender without resistance by overwhelming their victim with a swarm of marauders, thus hoping to actually avoid combat and incurring losses.⁴⁶ This episode also suggests that pirates were still operating in small fleets. It was not just one vessel conducting the raid but several, and the large number of pirates across the flotilla allowed them to capture more ships and to add them to their fleet. This event mirrored the typical growth of pirate enterprises in the Mediterranean, starting with five to ten men seizing a swift merchant ship, capturing more crew members, vessels, and arms, and eventually capturing and upgrading to a frigate.⁴⁷ This episode contrasts with records from later in the nineteenth century that show most pirate raids being launched from a single vessel. Lastly, these pirates were both particularly bold and interested in adding warships to their fleet, despite the increased risk compared to capturing merchant ships. Typically, pirates would use any type of ship they could get, even if it did not have weaponry on board, such as permanent artillery. They could easily fire swing guns over the sidewalls of a merchant ship. Also noteworthy about this episode is that the pirates attacked both Greek and Ottoman warships. The former seems to have been taken more by surprise than direct assault, while the latter was attacked, albeit unsuccessfully, after an open pursuit at sea. Attacking warships was always risky and pirates usually avoided attacking them to minimize risk to themselves. Indeed, the failed attempt to take the Ottoman warship in this case led to the pirates losing the Greek warship they had captured. For whatever reason, these pirates thought the rewards of capturing a warship outweighed the risks of attacking it.

Although Greece gained independence, it was not quite the maritime nation we think of today. During all of Otto's reign, the Kingdom of Greece controlled only Attica, the Morea, and a few nearby islands. The remainder of the Archipelago Province remained in Ottoman hands. Crete, the largest island, was granted by the sultan to Egypt as a reward for Ibrahim Pasha's efforts in suppressing the Greek rebellion. Little did the sultan know that Mehmed Ali was planning a rebellion of his own.

Egypt's Rise from Cretan Eyes

Mehmed Ali of Egypt had not answered the sultan's call to crush the Greek rebellion out of good will. He expected to be rewarded for his efforts. His main goal was to add Syria and the Levant to his administration, and the resources that those would bring him. Instead, Mahmud II offered him Crete and the Hijaz.[48] To Mehmed Ali, this was not the lofty honor he was hoping for. He already controlled Crete from his efforts against the Greeks, and it was a much smaller, resource-poor territory. Worse still, the territory was still prone to rebellion.

To help in controlling the island, Mehmed Ali set up a bilingual state newspaper for the island, *Vaka-yı Giridiyye* or "Events of Crete."[49] This newspaper ran weekly throughout the 1830s and published on both domestic Cretan affairs and international events. From its pages we can follow the course of the Egyptian uprising against the Ottoman Empire from a unique perspective. For example, in issue 71 on September 6, 1832, we see the rhetoric used to build a common identity between Egyptians and Cretans. "Four enemy warships are coming, but the divine powers believe that the sea belongs to Egypt ... To get God on our side and celebrate the Regent [Mehmed Ali] with joy, there will be three days of cannon fire from the fortresses of Chania, Souda, Gramvousa, and Kasteli Kissamou."[50] Egyptian leadership chose to utilize vague religious rhetoric that did not openly preference either Islam or Christianity in their administration of the island. The sea which surrounded was cast as belonging to Egypt with divine approval. At the same time, the second sentence serves to remind Cretans of the Egyptian military presence on the island, domesticate it by retaining place names, and celebrate it by use of celebratory cannon-fire. The fortress at Gramvousa returned to state-use under Egyptian rule. It became an island-fortress where people were sent to exile.[51] In some ways, the island remained a place for outlaws. Only instead of the walls protecting pirates by keeping the state out, they protected the island by keeping brigands in.

Ultimately, Egypt's uprising against the Sublime Porte ended in 1840 in defeat. The Great Powers rallied behind preserving Ottoman territorial integrity to preserve the balance of power in Europe. While Mehmed Ali and Ibrahim Pasha could outmaneuver the Ottoman Army, they were unable to defeat a united European front at the same time. Mehmed Ali ceded his territorial control over Crete and the Hijaz to the sultan and renounced his ambitions over Syria in exchange for peace and officially recognized hereditary rule over Egypt and Sudan.

From Crete, a conflict typically cast as Greek Christians loosening the yoke of Ottoman-Muslim oppression appears quite different. During the rebellion, Greek pirates at Gramvousa fought against the Ottomans, but raided both Western and Ottoman trade ships until they were finally exterminated by Western warships. In Chania, relief from famine for both the Christian and Muslim residents came from Algiers, whose *dey* sent aid even while emphasizing sectarian differences and sending corsairs to quash the rebellion in the Morea. Egyptian governance of the island again tried to soothe the sectarian divide by employing sufficiently ambiguous rhetoric where both the Christian and Muslim residents of Crete could rally under the banner of Mehmed Ali. Although this conflict was the closing chapter of corsairing in the Mediterranean, a practice traditionally told through the lens of a primordial religious struggle, the sharp religious divide seemed already dulled in the early nineteenth century. As piracy continued in the region without the state-supported corsairing or privateering structures, the notion of religious divide driving piracy would only grow more tenuous.

The elimination of corsairing and continuation of piracy in the 1830s set new standards for maritime raiding in the nineteenth century. After the fall of Algiers, the default meaning of the term *korsan* in Ottoman documents adjusted to new realities and shifted from meaning corsair or privateer to meaning pirate. Organized privateering expeditions had fallen out of use by the 1830s and were formally outlawed in 1856. The petty piracy that had always plagued the Mediterranean persisted past the proscription on privateering. The next chapter will examine the nature of Mediterranean piracy after the era of letters of marque, prize tribunals, and legalized ransom came to an end and show how Greece continued to exploit the blurred lines between pirate and rebel even after the revolution.

3

A New Age of Piracy

The 1840s and 1850s were a period of political reforms that were prevalent in the Eastern Mediterranean and Europe at large. In Greece during the 1830s, the state was still adjusting to the new realities that it faced. During the same span in the Ottoman Empire, the Porte struggled in the civil war with Egypt that broke out after the Greek rebellion. Once the dust from the conflict settled, all involved looked to bring about peace and stability. The Eastern Mediterranean witnessed a nearly two-decade respite after the two preceding decades of wars and uprisings.

Greece and the Ottoman Empire entered new eras around 1840. The Ottoman Empire finally entered an age of peace accompanied by reforms extending fundamental civil rights to its religious minority populations.[1] Greece began to shake off some of its growing pains as the introduction of a constitution in 1844 placed limits on the king's power. The reforms did little, however, to change the rates of pirate attacks from those in the preceding decade: in Greek waters the number dropped from fifteen to five, while in the empire the rate of pirate attacks in diplomatic archives remained the same in both decades at five per decade. The 1840s and 1850s saw much less piracy than had occurred during the war years of the 1820s but a comparable amount to the pre-reform decade of the 1830s.[2] Both Greece and the Ottoman Empire shifted away from commissioning privateers, but Greece continued to use non-state maritime violence to its advantage, or more accurately their neighbor's disadvantage, by chasing pirates into Ottoman waters and refusing to prosecute pirates who had raided Ottoman lands and taken refuge in Greece.

This chapter addresses some of the fundamental questions about the nature of piracy in this new era. Piracy continued in the Eastern Mediterranean region, but was its fundamental character the same? What was the new Greek state's stance on piracy? Were the pirates of this period primitive rebels?[3] What was the makeup of a typical pirate crew? Was ransom a major source of profits? This chapter concludes with a discussion of a case in which the states differed dramatically in their views of an individual who was suspected of being a pirate. Was he an outlaw attempting to deceive them by invoking the classic legal defense that he was an innocent man who had been captured by pirates and forced into service, or was he really just an unfortunate soul who was being truthful in his claim? Like so many other aspects of the mid-century, piracy retained some continuities with past practices but also was generally in a state of transition. Most importantly, as this chapter shows, piracy continued past the coronation of Otto and the colonization of Algiers, contrary to the historiographical consensus.

Breaking with the Past

Greece had gained independence from the Ottoman Empire, but as with most fledgling states, independence also brought vulnerability. Just as American independence meant that the United States had to redefine its relations with foreign states, including the North African Regencies, as it was no longer protected by British treaties, so too did Greece have to find its way in the realm of international diplomacy.

Among the first to seek to exploit Greece's novice politicians was merchant-marine Captain Gestin of the French brig *Marie Joë* in 1840. In the midst of the Greek revolution in 1827, Gestin's vessel was attacked and pillaged by Greek pirates off the coast of Cyprus. Gestin's representative, M. Lagrue, wrote that despite repeated requests, the Greek government had taken no steps toward advancing the investigation. With choice words for what he thought of Greek state efforts concerning piracy, he formally requested that reparations be paid to his client.[4]

The case that the Greek government should bear responsibility for this incident stood on shaky ground. Cyprus was well outside of the territory of what became the independent Greek Kingdom. Greek privateers had indeed sailed to the shores of Cyprus to stir up trouble and gain allies during the revolution, but they only had official support from the revolutionary committee in the first years of the uprising. By 1825, the revolutionary government in Morea lost control of the maritime marauders pillaging faraway Cyprus. Like their cousins in Gramvousa, the privateers had turned pirate and began raiding all passing ships, even those of allies to the Greek cause.[5] The *Marie Joë* incident occurred in 1827 during the presidency of Kapodistrias, under whose leadership Greece strove to suppress piracy, even when pirates were attacking in support of the revolution. As such, Greece could not be faulted for enabling the pirates to conduct the raid in question. Greek diplomats responded by turning down the request for reparations, but they saw the bigger game at play.[6] Accepting responsibility would have laid a Greek claim for sovereignty over Cyprus, a claim which Greece had no way to act upon or benefit from. Were reparations to be granted on such shaky grounds, or even at all, Greek leadership feared there would be no limit to the number of cases that would be brought against the state born in bloody revolution.

Patrolling a porous maritime border is difficult for any state, especially a fledgling, bankrupt one like Greece. British, French, and Austrian cruisers were already present in the Eastern Mediterranean to secure their trade routes and protect their ships from hostile raids. As the first two were among Greece's protecting powers, it is only natural that the Greek Navy would cooperate closely with them. Greece also worked alongside their neighbor and former ruler, the Ottoman Empire, to secure the borders from banditry and piracy.[7] In one case in April 1851, the Hellenic corvettes *Amalia* and *Methoni* worked alongside two French brigs and one Austrian and two Turkish war steamers to hunt "the arch-pirate Negris, terror of the Aegean." It was not until September when the joint squadron captured him at Samos and threw him in an Ottoman prison.[8] During times of peace at least, the Greek and Ottoman navies worked together to hunt down marauders who posed a threat to their common security.

A few years later, in 1854 at the onset of the Crimean War, Greece still had to convince European allies of its vigilance in hunting pirates.[9] The outbreak of the Crimean conflict created a disruption in maritime security. The Ottoman Empire had to focus its resources on fighting against the Russians. Both irredentists and pirates saw an opportunity to profit from the chaos. Seeing weakened Ottoman defenses, Greece unofficially sided with Russia and sent forth irregular troops north into Thessaly and Epiros. Incidences of piracy rose in the region, not altogether challenged by the Greek state which welcomed the further disruption of the Ottoman security apparatus. Once Britain and France joined the fray on the side of the Ottomans, any chance Greek for territorial expansion from the war diminished. Greece, an insular and peninsular state, had no hope of defeating the British Royal Navy. In May of 1854, British and French occupied the Acropolis in Athens.[10] No longer trusting Greece to manage its own affairs, for the remainder of the war they set up a government that was in close cooperation with the two Western powers.

In order to get out of hot water with Britain and France, Greek ambassadors attempted to soothe concerns that Greece would continue to be a destabilizing force in the region by showing that they were stepping up efforts to expel pirates from Greek territorial waters, citing and translating into French internal correspondence from the Ministry of Justice Paulos Kalligas:

> The information of that purchaser which reaches the Minister concerning acts of piracy committed in your area [Negreponte / Euboea], denotes enough that the ordinary vigilance of the judicial authorities is inadequate to repress the scourge which begins to infest the waters of Greece.
>
> Consequently, both the Prosecutors and the Investigating judges must be doubled in vigilance and attention to each case in their respective jurisdiction… At the slightest suspicion they delay the investigation. The alienation of the objects from the piracy which in all probability are clandestinely sold in the same parts of the Kingdom, under their part also the object of the most active surveillance.
>
> For this purpose, in the first instance of an act of piracy, the prosecutors must accurately verify the horrible nature of the objects; they will inventory the incidences for circulation to the investigating judges of the jurisdiction respecting the waters of their coast to be used for attracting the police authorities to their residence.[11]

This letter ends with a commitment to restore normal relations with the Ottoman Empire, an ally of Britain and France. The two Western powers expected that Greece would then cooperate in the enforcement of security along international maritime trade routes. Greek officials laid out a position which at first went unnoticed by its protectors and occupiers, but later grew to be a thorn in their relations: that Greece would purge pirates from its own waters. The problem became that Greece did not explicitly aim to remove piracy from the region overall but simply drove them into other waters. The

Greek plan was summed up by Konstantinos Kanaris, Minister of the Navy, to the Ministry of Foreign Affairs:

> I have the honor to bring to your knowledge the measures which have just been taken by this Ministry against the piracy which has just been manifested on the coasts of the Negroponte and the Northern Sporades, and for the extinction of these flames, which is beginning to infest our territories.
>
> The Royal Golette *Matilda* has received the order to reside in the waters of the Negrepont and patrol constantly, accompanied by the sloop *Delphinie*, along the coasts of this island. She is standing by the Oreos station.
>
> In the Northern Sporades the Royal Cutter *Glaucus* cruises the same, accompanied by the sloop *Panthine*, for surveilling those areas. It is stationed out of Skiathos.
>
> These ships are primarily destined for the extinction of piracy; they shall also lend their appeals to the authorities of those localities and militaries of these localities for the maintenance of public order: Finally, they perform all the duties inherent in the service of the ships of the state, such as the inspection of the papers of the Greek merchant ships encountered *en route*, and so on.[12]

At the time, the allies accepted Greece's plan to increase the security of its maritime border. The resulting cooperation in patrolling and policing the Aegean led to an abundance of documentation concerning regional piracy. Documents from this period of semi-occupation tend to be longer, as officials from different states vied to justify their different understandings of piracy against those of other states. Often, they went into greater depth to determine whether or not the suspects were indeed pirates or not. In one instance to be discussed later in this chapter, a set of documents reveals a fierce debate where the Great Powers accuse Greece of implicitly supporting piracy so long as it occurs in Ottoman territorial waters.

Pirates or Patriots? The 1854 Epiros Revolt

While the Ottoman Empire was focusing all its attention and resources on fighting the Russians, life became more difficult for its subjects whose prosperity was needed to help ease the Porte's financial burdens. In 1854, peasants in the Epiros region took up arms against the state which was leaving them hungry. While this revolt was taking place, reports of pirate raids in the northern Aegean began to flow in. British and French captains and diplomats sent a flurry of correspondences questioning whether these raids had anything to do with the rebellion in the neighboring Ottoman province. In the following missive, the captain of the gollete *Solon* assumed it was pirates, while the captain of the Greek schooner *Mathilde* assumed it was revolutionaries who should be supported or at least not interfered with. Ultimately, the suspects turned out to simply be pirates, not rebels.

> I have already had the honor of telling you about the bands of pirates that left in September and October last summer from Euboea, Skiathos and Skopelo. You thought, you told me, that they were not pirates, but the *reayas* [Turkish: *reaya*. Ottoman tax-paying subjects, especially non-Muslims] that followed the insurrection had fled the Turkish reaction by taking refuge in Greece and eating bread in this country that were trying to return in Macedonia. I am unfortunately able to undeceive you today. Several individuals of one of the bands which I have mentioned to you have been arrested at Samothrace and Thasos, and I have on board one of those brigands whose confessions, of which I agree so much with the information taken by me on various points I recognize a certain value.[13]

The first reports involved an armed ship entering Greek territorial waters and plundering the mainland and the islands north of Euboea. The British royal steamer *Triton* captained by Lieutenant Lloyd encountered this ship and determined them to be pirates. After apprehending them, Lieutenant Lloyd turned the suspects over to the local Greek authorities. Once in Greek custody, the local officials declared that the suspects were patriots from Macedonia and not pirates. Rather than transfer them to Volos to meet justice, the pirates were released. The following correspondence from the British Minister Thomas Wyse to the Greek minister of foreign affairs.

> I beg to call your attention in writing, as I have already done verbally, to a communication received from Euboea respecting the liberation as alleged, by the Authorities of Kerochori, of certain prisoners lately seized and delivered into the hands of the gens d'armerie by Lieutenant Lloyd of H.M.S. *Triton*.
>
> Lieutenant Lloyd met a suspicious looking boat filled with armed men, in the direction of Pontico. On hailing them they gave no answer, and on sending a boat to bring them to the steamer, they received it by pointing

their guns and pistols from the bushes where they had taken shelter, nor was it until Lieutenant Lloyd had sent another boat well armed, and had obtained aid from the peasantry on H. Wild's estate, that after much resistance on the part of the pirates and a sharp firing on both sides, he was enabled to seize a portion of the pirates.

Lieutenant Lloyd, who, under the circumstances might have detained them himself, delivered his prisoners into the hands of the Greek Gens d'armes. The Gens d'armes transmitted them to the Authorities of Kerochori for confinement and trial, as Robbers and Pirates, but it is since **stated that the Authorities have pronounced them to belong to the Patriots who have reentered from Thessaly and have allowed them to go freely wherever they chose** [emphasis my own].

I am persuaded from the zeal which the present Ministers have already shown in repressing crime, that immediate inquiry will be made into this statement, and if found to be borne out by facts, that measures will be taken to punish as it deserves so serious a dereliction of public ... [Document suddenly ends, following page missing][14]

Thus began a period when British and French officials increasingly scrutinized Greece's commitment to uprooting piracy. While the episode was being discussed, Greece's minister of foreign affairs, M. Argyropoulos, was replaced by Alexandros Mavrokordatos.

Mavrokordatos immediately tried to assuage the concerns of the protecting powers by reaffirming Greece's commitment to securing its waters. He claimed that Greek reports concerning the suppression of piracy were deemed to be "most satisfactory," and he declared that

> this happy result is due to the measures taken by the Commanders of the Royal Governments' French and English War ships. The Government appreciates the true value of the services of the Royal naval forces. We give our gratitude and thanks to commanders Rouen of the steamer *Narval* and Wyse of the Frigate *Leander* who contributed to reestablishing public security in our lands.[15]

The new foreign minister's wording and confidence did not put allied officials at ease, as it seemed to suggest that Greece sought only to relocate pirates from Greek waters to neighboring seas. The implications of this policy of relocation rather than persecution will be further explored in the next section. International trade, particularly that of the Britain, France, and their Ottoman ally, remained threatened. Mavrokordatos was unable to convince the British and French ambassadors to have the same confidence in the Greek legal system that he possessed. Thomas Wyse, the British ambassador, offered a detailed critique of the failures of Greece's provincial governments to prosecute suspected pirates, even when there was strong evidence against them. The full text is provided in the appendix, but a brief selection shows Wyse's disappointment with the Greek justice system: "They were, after a short and inefficient examination by the Commissary of Police, recognized as 'Patriots' and not as 'Pirates ... ' It is to be observed that the assessors of Agriovotani and Corbatzi neither read nor write."[16]

The framework in which the provincial Greek administration understood these events was similar to Eric Hobsbawm's picture of bandits as "primitive rebels." These were men of violence, acting out in a social context which the administration more than the pirates themselves viewed as unjust. Greek officials viewed these men as the *klefts* and revolutionaries of the previous generation: every act of violence, every move to break down society was one step closer to emancipation from Ottoman rule. They ignored, of course, that these pirates were also raiding Greek territory and allied ships. To the officials of Kerochori, Agriovotani, and Corbatzi, the question was not so much if these men were pirates *or* patriots, but if they were pirates *and* patriots. Within a framework of primitive rebellion, an act of piracy was an act of patriotism.

Greece Exporting Piracy?

The above documents involving suspected rebels from Epiros who turned out to be merely pirates show the commitment Greece had to securing its own waters, and Western skepticism at Greece effectively doing so. The Greek minister of foreign affairs, Mavrokordatos, wrote that piracy did not exist in the region when British and French warships held clear evidence to the contrary. The foreign ambassadors then suspected Greece of tribalism—favoring ethnic brothers over the law.

Diplomats from the Great Powers were interested in purging pirates, the enemies of all, from all the waters in which they traded. Piracy impacted shipping, both directly, by literally robbing proceeds, and indirectly, by creating a practical necessity in which merchant ships would need to pay higher insurance premiums to traverse pirate-infested waters.[17]

By late 1854, Greece had repeatedly stated its position on how to deal with piracy. In December of that year, Western patience snapped as the Greek strategy proved ineffective at deterring piratical raids upon allied shipping. When Mavrokordatos informed the French delegation of a pirate raid upon a French warship, he did little to address what measures might be taken to prevent such raids.

> A galley, mounted by forty men, marched at intervals from time to time, signaling its passage by the acts of piracy, and even of brigandage committed by its crew and the naval vessel, *Espeax Marte*, by six men armed, traverses in the same guilty vestiges the waters of which they left. The Royal Goletta *Mathilde* was ordered to depart and cruise to prevent pirates from attempting to raid the waters and isles of Greece.[18]

Greece was already scrutinized by the British on the issue of piracy. It had done little to convince its Western allies that it took their concerns about maritime security seriously. The French ambassador, Baron Forth-Rouen, was furious at the Greek government for being disinterested in actually quashing piracy. He started by blaming Greek authorities for refusing to share intelligence with French forces who were hunting pirates and ended with a direct accusation. "It is painfully astonishing that in the Pro Memoria note, the commander of the *Mathilde* was ordered not to purge the pirates, but simply to prevent them from entering into the waters of Greece."[19]

To the French ambassador, Greece seemed interested in reducing piracy only in its own waters while keeping it active in neighboring Ottoman domains. The Greek fleet was told to turn away pirate ships, not capture or destroy them. Seeing the directness of the accusation and fearing repercussions, Mavrokordatos both justified Greek actions and promised vague procedural reforms.

> The memoria which I have had the honor of addressing you on this subject had no other purpose than to inform us of their presence on dimensions which it is not permissible for our warships to explore past a certain distance. As to the orders given to the Commander of the *Mathilde*, ... [They

have been ordered] to commit to document more precise and severe orders relating to the hunt for pirates.[20]

Mavrokordatos listed why Greek warships could not legally pursue pirates outside of Greek territorial waters, but he dodged the question of why they would not prosecute those pirates caught within those borders. The commitment to levy more severe punishments upon pirates remained loose and would not necessarily ease French concerns over Greek security. The promise for more precise orders addressed the concerns that the British had earlier in the year when Greek provincial government did not find the captured pirates to be pirates at all. Legal reform could force provincial government to have a more precise definition of piracy that could not be skirted away from so easily. Of course, these promises were those of a politician aiming at placating a particular audience and were not guaranteed to be bound by a legislative authority.

On several occasions afterwards during the nineteenth century, Greece would implicitly support piracy just outside its borders. This raises the question: why did Greece want to explicitly avoid purging pirates? Some of the answer lies in the feasibility of getting the job done. Committing to a total war on piracy would place a huge burden on resources. With what resources Greece on hand, it was impractical, if not impossible, to have warships patrolling all the coasts of Greece. Addressing Mavrokordatos, Hellenic Naval Minister Konstantinos Kanaris wrote

> as the maritime force which the Government has at its disposal is insupportable, and cannot, therefore, extend its surveillance over the whole extent of our country, we impatiently await our ships retained in the port of Gravisa ... We shall take it upon ourselves to put the newly arrived vessels into operation; and we hope, by their assistance, to completely purge the waters of Greece of all traces of piracy.[21]

If the pirates could be driven elsewhere in a more cost-effective manner, they would become someone else's problem. For Greece's geographic situation, this almost always meant that pirates would be driven to the Ottoman Empire, though sometimes they would head west to the British-held Ionian Islands. Would Greece risk the security of its own waters to ensure that Ottoman waters were less secure? This question will be raised multiple times in this book. During times of peace, Greece generally coordinated security operations in the borderlands with its neighbors. During times of conflict, however, Greece allowed pirates to slip past its borders to weaken their Ottoman foe.

Pirate Kinship Networks

One common question about piracy is who were the pirates? Much like bandit gangs, pirate bands were largely formed from kinship networks. Several primary sources show us pirate crews consisting of nuclear families, extended kinship networks, members of a single ethnic group, and members of diverse ethnic groups. There was a plurality of pirate-crew makeups extant during the nineteenth century. Pirates often affiliated with locals to gain intelligence, access to markets, and places to hide away. This section will provide examples of each of these social networks at play among pirate crews.

When attempting to identify pirates, historians often only have a name to go by. When several individuals have the same surname that probably indicates a close kinship connection. Ethnicity cannot be determined with the same level of confidence. The same person could be recorded as Nikolaos, Niccolo, or Nicholas, depending on the preference of the administrator creating the record. Each of these names suggests a different ethnicity, in this case Greek, Italian, and English or French. Also, individuals could have surnames that do not match the way that they identify themselves. Thus, any ethnic designation from name alone is at best guesswork. In addition, determining a pirate to be Greek does not answer which state they were subjects of. Greeks were likely to be from Greece, the Ottoman Empire, the Ionian Islands, as well as the smaller possibility of them being subjects of other states.

The United States of the Ionian Islands, ranging off the western Balkan coast from the Morea to southern Albania, was historically Venetian lands that, as a result of the French Revolution and Napoleonic conquests, changed hands between French, Russian, Ottoman, and ultimately British dominion. The two most common native languages on the islands were Greek and Italian, and in the mid-century a movement for union with Greece began in 1832, strengthened during the 1848 European revolutions, and ultimately succeeded in 1864. British authorities understood the locals using colonial frameworks of European Aboriginals, Black Irish, and the noble savage.[22]

Concerns over ethnic origin can be seen in the following text: "All these Pirates are Greeks, and from them we know of one named Pietro Leucaditi from Santa Maura [Leucadia/Lefkada]. They exposed with their oath that they have communicated with pirates who cannot be known if they come from Greece or from Turkey."[23] Both the personal and surname of Pietro Leucaditi could be Greek or Italian, depending on if the name was modified by the penman. The "Greek" pirates he communicated with could likewise be either from the Greek Kingdom or *Rum* (Ottoman-Greeks) from the Ottoman Empire.[24] Meanwhile, the Ionian lawman seems to discount the potential of the suspects being Ionian citizens, yet another possible subjecthood common to ethnic Greeks.

One of the most common relations visible among pirates was familial. Oftentimes, two or more crew members had the same surname, suggesting either a filial or a fraternal relation. While anthropological work on Mediterranean families emphasizes the important of extended kin networks (Turkish: *soy*; Greek: σόι), nuclear families remained a critical part of that framework.[25] The following example shows the proceeds from piracy being split among a nuclear family.

> To follow up on my letter of October 29th, you will receive an excerpt from a report by the *Heron*'s Commanding Officer, I am writing to inform you that the Royal Prosecutor of Syra, having interrogated the three individuals whom Captain Lebegue has taken to Henousa, to guide himself in the search for the two pirates who took refuge in this island, one of the interrogated individuals declared who the famous Nicotzara, I find at this moment in Euboea, with five of his companions. This pirate leader has his father, his mother, and several brothers in Chalcis, who are all designated as recalling the proceeds of his robberies.
>
> I presume that the Royal Prosecutor of Syra will transmit this information to the Hellenic Government, and in any case I beg Your Excellency to agree with the colleagues that he be procured without delay for the arrest of the pirate Nicotzara.[26]

The kinship networks seen among pirates correlate to those found on land among bandits. Outlaws may have operated outside of the law, but they did not operate outside of society. Thomas Gallant's conclusion about bandit kinship applies equally to the case of pirates:

if one part of Hobsbawm's argument is that "scratch a bandit and you will find a peasant," then the corollary should be "scratch the bandit next to him and you will find his brother." The social universe of the bandit was replete with constellations of kinship connections. Greek bandits were not lone wolves but collections of kinsmen, and banditry was a family affair.[27]

There are several examples of crews that at first glance seem to be predominately from one ethnic group. This would indicate a departure from the diverse makeup of pirate crews in previous century.[28] When piracy occurs around the Aegean, it tends to be Greek names in the records. When piracy occurs off the coasts of Italy, it tends to be recorded Italian. When the Ionian Islands report piracy, it is often with names that appear as a hybrid of Greek and Italian, though the suspects in question may be another ethnicity entirely, like South Slavic or Albanian. When the Ottomans discuss piracy in foreign correspondence in French, the names tend to be Frankified versions of names that are predominately Greek with hints of Turkish features: Themistocli Dourmeli, Manuel Beynoglidi, Alexandre Aridriadi, Démétre Trakéroglidi, Constantin Holologa.[29] The language of correspondence has a major impact in the appearance of names and can hide the ethnic identity of those who appear in the records.

What can we learn from the following list of suspects in Greece accused of forming a pirate crew?[30] Among the twenty-eight crew members, there are two individuals with the same surname Spyrou and patronym Ioannou, suggesting that they are brothers. The rest of the crew have no family names in common and are less likely to be closely related. The names seem to be mostly Greek, but there are some instances where foreign names could appear Hellenized. Could Rafalias be Raphael? Tzetos Jet? Names like Zachary Michael are ambiguous. Michael Kafetzis (Turkish: *kahveci*, meaning coffee seller) has an ambiguous Christian personal name and a Turkish occupational surname. The accused could all be Greek, or they could be drawn from different ethnicities. Ultimately, determining one way or another by imposing current understandings of ethnicity does not allow for a deeper understanding of these individuals. They may have operated in a multi-ethnic world, but they did not necessarily view it that way. Religious identity remained a more visible and important marker of identity. That could be visible through name, dress, and action.

Ιωάννης Μανώλης Μαυρής	Ioannis Manolis Mavris
Νικόλαος Καζόλης	Nikolaos Kazolis
Μανώλης Μοσχονάς	Manolis Moschonas
Ιωάννης Τζέτος	Ioannis Tzetos
Χριστόδουλος Σαπουνάς	Christodoulos Sapounas
Γεωργή παππά Στρατής Σκοπελίτης	Georgi pappa Stratis Skopelitis
Κώτζος Λιάκου	Kotzos Liakou
Μανώλης Γ. Μποναφής	Manolis G. Bonaface
Γεώργιος Κώστας	Georgios Kostas
Σαντούλας Αντωνίου	Santoulas Antoniou
Χαράλαμπος Κοφτερός	Charalampos Kofteros
Αλέξιος Διακοκκόλας	Alexios Diakokkolas
Μιχαήλ Κατσούλης	Michael Katsoulis
Ιωάννης Βουλής	Ioannis Voulis
Νικόλαος Κατζιώτης	Nikolaos Katziotis
Δημήτριος παππά Ελισσαίου	Dimitrios pappa Elissaiou
Κάρας Δημήτρη Ν. Μαργιός	Karas Dimitri N. Margios
Ιωάννης Δ. Χαλέπης	Ioannis D. Chalepis
Χριστόδουλος Ιωάννου Σπύρου	Christodoulos Ioannou Spyrou
Κωνσταντίνος Ιωάννου Σπύρου	Konstantinos Ioannou Spyrou
Κωνσταντίνος παππαδίτζας	Konstantinos pappaditzas
Μανώλης Παλαμάρης	Manolis Palamaris
Μιχαήλ Διαμαντής Καφετζής	Michael Diamantis Kafetzis
Μιχαήλ Ραφαλιάς	Michael Rafalias
Γεώργιος Π. Στρατής	Georgios P. Stratis
Ζαχαρίας Μιχαήλ	Zacharias Michael
Γεώργιος Δεληγεώργης	Georgios Deligeorgis
Αναστάσιος Κοντραφούρης	Anastasios Kontrafouris

Identity is complicated and multifaceted. In 1848, *Rum* pirates were pillaging Moroccan pilgrims passing through Egyptian waters for the Hajj. Britain assisted with the Ottoman-Egyptian suppression of these pirates by sending over a warship from the Ionian Islands. The captain that was sent to fight these *Rum* pirates appears in the Ottoman documents as Corciyo Kaliga, or Giorgios Kalligas.[31] Simultaneously, we have ethnically Greek pirates from the Ottoman Empire attacking Muslim pilgrims to the Ottoman Empire. And tasked with combatting the pirates and protecting the Moroccan pilgrims was an ethnic Greek captain in the British fleet, likely from the Ionian Islands.[32]

The raids existence initially seems to suggest a sharp line of religious conflict in the Ottoman Empire. This wisp of sectarianism is immediately complicated by the nature of the captain who restored order to the region and defeated the pirates. This incident is perhaps better viewed from a lens of personal profit and imperial control rather than religious conflict. Pilgrims have always been easy prey to ne'er-do-wells along their routes of passage.[33] These travelers were from a faraway land, not neighbors with whom the pirates would daily interact. Likewise, Kalligas was simply a captain from the nearest corner of the British Empire able to send aid.

Pirates relied on forming personal connections with numerous individuals. They did not exist alone at sea, forever separate from society. They needed shelter, both for themselves and their ships. They had to have trading partners with whom to fence their goods. They required informants who could signal to them when they were safe and when they were threatened by a nearby patrolling warship. The shepherd Darba Constandi who aided the Epirote pirates mentioned earlier in this chapter provided many of these services.

> In October it was understood with the names Dimitri Dalaban, Manuelo and Giovani were former insurgents. They fled Sernik to Kero-Chori, and went to Skiathos and Skopelo where they recruited three new companions of the insurrection, Giorgi, Anthony of Hydra, and Hiero Constanti of Hypsara. Thus to the number of seven they were stricken on the delago island they found the shepherd Darba Constandi who gave them food. When you came to this island with your schooner, the same shepherd advised them to conceal their boat and join each other in the mountains. They thus escaped your surveillance, and when you were far off, they were able to raise their boat and establish their cruise in the surrounding islands in the time that bad weather held them up for a few days.
>
> In this interval they plundered a Chiote schooner from Salonica, and before they went to Macedonia they committed new acts of piracy, rewarding the Constandi shepherd by giving him a share of their first booty. He received two meals of flour, chestnuts, apples, a blanket, a double-breasted jacket, and a gun. This shepherd must be arrested and punished for his relations with the brigands. Admitting that he had the strength to give them provisions, nothing can excuse him for having saved his wretches by warning them of your arrival, or of having shared the proceeds of their theft.
>
> If I had not found you, I would have thought it my duty to arrest Darba Constandi myself; But I am persuaded that you will think, as I do, that the

act of complicity with which he has been guilty will not go unpunished; And all that remains for me is to render the Admiral commanding the French forces responsible for the information I am communicating to you by this letter.[34]

As a reward for his aid, the pirates bestowed upon him a share of their booty. Even in this period when organized corsairing societies are no more, there were people who proved themselves willing accomplices to piracy. Shepherds are notorious for living outside the realm of the state and affiliating with criminals who do the same.[35] There were two main factors in Constandi's cooperation with the pirates. One was making a profit from fencing his share of the goods, even if it was only agricultural products and other supplies. The other was the cost of not cooperating. Were he to earn their ire, his flock would make an easy, tasty meal for the pirates, to mention nothing of his own personal safety. Partnering with the marauders would provide useful allies able to provide protection to the shepherd should he find himself in confrontation with authorities who frequently attempted to tax or settle nomadic and pastoral peoples.[36] For those living on the margins of society, siding with pirates and bandits over the state often posed less risk.

Captives or Corsairs?

Traditional networks for ransoming captives faded away alongside the societies that profited from the practice. When a pirate was captured, one common defense was to claim that he had been captured and forcibly pressed into the service of pirates. The 1854 case of Dimitris Koutzoukos is described in a pro memoria sent from the Hellenic Royal House to the French ambassador Baron Alexandre Forth-Rouen. His case a significant because it either suggests the continued existence into the 1850s seamen being pressed into the service of pirates or taken for ransom, or that the captured pirate continued to attempt to deceive authorities by playing a victim of such crimes.[37]

> In March, Demetre Coutzoucos, a resident of Syra, a peaceful and well-known citizen, was taken by pirates on his way to Skyros to fish. After a

thousand instances the pirates finally known to release one of the three mates of the captured ship in order to bring to the family of Coutzoucos some help; But they retained the latter and the two sailors in order to make them useful for the maneuver.[38]

The Corsairs were arrested a little later by a French war-ship along with the unfortunate Coutzoucos and his companions. They were transported to the island of Rhodes, where they were indistinctly booked by the Ottoman Authorities.

The Commander of the French Vessel informed of Coutzoucos' representatives of his innocence and of the injustice he had experienced in confusing him with the pirates, said to have been written to the Admiral who had invited the Consul of France to Syra and has submitted information. M. Guerin having collected at the port office of that island the best information on Coutzoucos's account, had to transmit them to the Admiral.

Nevertheless, the poor prisoner still gets imprisoned at Rhodes, where he writes to his family that, confounded with the corsairs, he undergoes the same treatment as these criminals.

The mother of Coutzoucos and those of the families of the two sailors imprisoned with him come to arrive in Athens to implore the assistance of the Government to favor their liberation.

The French Minister is kindly requested to recall this affair to the Admiral and to hasten these acts of justice by his intervention in favor of Coutzoucos and the two sailors unjustly confounded with the pirates.[39]

The Royal House's description of the incident offers some understanding of ransom during the 1850s. As already mentioned, there was no longer an existing system of ransom. This is confirmed when we see that pirates needed to release one of their captives to inform the families and community of the others who had been taken captive. No longer was there a standardized network of intermediaries that would handle ransom exchanges. If a pirate were to receive ransom payments for his captives, they would need to handle the exchange themselves. For both parties, this greatly increased the risk of the encounter. Either side could set up the other. The families of the victims could notify the authorities and have them lay in ambush to capture the outlaws, or the pirates could overwhelm the families, take the money, and kill, capture, or otherwise incapacitate the ransom-payers.[40] A great deal of trust was necessary for such a system based on direct contact to pay ransom to work. Mistrust was much easier to come by, which is one of the key distinctions between early modern and modern piracy. In the past, ransoming captives was one of the main sources of profit from piracy. Without ready markets for captives, the entire ransom economy fell apart.

As far as Koutzoukos and the other sailors being considered pirates, even from this narrative clearly favoring his release, we see that his contemporaries were suspicious. The Ottoman garrison at Rhodes and the French Navy both saw fit to imprison Koutzoukos along with the rest of those captured on the pirate ship.[41] Only the Greek Kingdom showed interest in arguing that Koutzoukos should be released. The Greek port official of Ermoupoli, writing in July to the Ministry of the Navy, took Koutzoukos's story as true.[42] The defense of his position of innocence rested on his mother's plea that he was a man of good character.

This incident provides evidence that pirates still seemed to be interested in taking captives up to the 1850s, likely for ransom or more generally as a bargaining chip or a hostage for leverage. Later chapters will show that this practice faded away as the century moved along, pirate crew sizes shrunk, the economy steadily improved, and ready access to markets for ransom and slavery diminished. As ransom practices and crew sizes changed, the other characteristics of piracy remained relatively static throughout piracy's decline over the century. Pirates continued to draw upon and interact with similar segments of the general populace. The state, Greece in particular, continued to exploit them during periods of rebellion in the Ottoman Empire by driving them into the neighboring seas. The landmark for the legislative shift against piracy came at the end of the Crimean War. In the 1856 Treaty of Paris, international law turned against the main form of state-supported piracy—privateering.

4

Paris, Patrols, and Persistent Piracy

The Crimean War ended in 1856 with the Treaty of Paris. As part of the more comprehensive program to keep the peace, Great Britain, France, Prussia, Russia, Austria-Hungary, Greece, the Ottoman Empire, and forty-eight other nations signed the Paris Declaration Respecting Maritime Law, which sought to unify international maritime law. The measures agreed to were as follows:

1. Privateering is, and remains, abolished;
2. The neutral flag protects enemy's goods, with the exception of contraband of war;
3. Neutral goods, with the exception of contraband of war, are not liable to capture under enemy's flag;
4. Blockades, in order to be binding, must be effective, that is to say, maintained by a force sufficient really to prevent access to the coast of the enemy.[1]

The opening statement of this document sounded the death-knell for legitimate maritime-raiding.[2] A grand coalition, including the world's maritime colonial powers, agreed to ban the practice of licensed plunder. Attacking a ship became only legal in the context of war, and any merchandise from neutral states was not a legitimate prize. In addition, the requirement of blockades to be effective would stop squadrons from declaring a false blockade to plunder passing ships at random.[3] Trade routes were to be made impassable, not simply preyed upon. Thus, much of the incentive for seeking letters of marque was lost.

These regulations more clearly defined what actions were acceptable for regular naval officers to take. They also clashed with some longstanding maritime traditions that captains considered legitimate. This chapter, in part, looks at the actions of one such captain—Augustus Charles Hobart-Hampden, who for over a decade cruised the Eastern Mediterranean under the British fleet which used piracy's threat to international trade and British imperial interests as reason for permanent military presence, and later as part of the Ottoman fleet. In his years as a captain, he skirted the bounds of maritime law as laid out by the Treaty of Paris, first by acting arguably as a privateer in ordering his men to go undercover as pirates, and later by playing with the definition of piracy so as to label a hostile, neutral ship that broke his incomplete blockade as an act of piracy. Recognizing privateering as illegal removed the line that maritime military entrepreneurs had skirted between piracy and privateering. No longer could marauders pillage ships at sea while claiming legitimacy from a state. Likewise, traditional naval vessels could no longer safely cross the line and act as irregulars without fear of stirring diplomatic trouble.

Naval reforms accompanied the changes to international maritime law during this period. The Ottoman Empire under the reign of Sultan Abdülaziz expanded and modernized its naval forces. The British Royal Navy also further concerned itself with securing the peace in Ottoman waters. Both of these policy changes brought about an increased capacity to enforce maritime laws and suppress piracy. On the other hand, the 1860s were a time wracked by the instability caused by the expulsion of King Otto from Greece, a rebellion on Crete, and the *Risorgimento* in neighboring Italy. These regional political convulsions created security challenges that local powers responded to by increasing their maritime security capabilities. This chapter argues that increased naval military presence alone did little to dissuade the coastal populace of the Eastern Mediterranean from seeking their fortunes via plunder.

Shifting legal circumstances alone did not reduce the frequency of piracy occurring in the Eastern Mediterranean. While the Greek and Ottoman economies remained relatively stagnant throughout the 1850s and 1860s, reports of piracy appeared at the same rates as before the Crimean War. It was not until those economies took off in the 1870s that fewer individuals decided to take to the account, committing piracy, and instead picked up the plow to participate in the cash-crop craze.[4] The next chapter will discuss the currant boom's growth of the Greek economy and its correlation to a halving of reports of piracy by decade.[5]

Figure 4.1 Comparison of documents pertaining to piracy in BOA and YE over fourteen-year periods

Period	Ottoman Empire, All Seas	Ottoman Mediterranean	Greece
1841–55	11	9	14
1856–69	9	9	11
1870–84	10	1	9

When looking at the occurrence of piracy reported in the archives of the Ottoman Prime Ministry and the Greek Ministry of Foreign Affairs, a few trends become apparent. The first is that in the four decades following the implementation of the Ottoman *Tanzimat* reforms which began in 1839 with the Edict of the Rose Garden, the rate of piracy in the Ottoman Empire as a whole remained level. Neither the *Tanzimat* nor the Treaty of Paris triggered a significant reduction in piracy in the Ottoman Empire. When filtering the data by region, it becomes apparent that prior to 1870 nearly all of Ottoman reports of piracy during the mid-nineteenth-century record episodes that took place in the Mediterranean, whereas after that year nearly none did. It is likely that the opening of the Suez Canal and the redirection of trade routes was a major cause of the shifting locations of piracy. Likewise, as will be discussed in the next chapter, unequal economic growth allowed the Mediterranean region to reap the bounties of being the only region capable of producing currants and raisins. While Anatolia was able to meaningfully engage with these market opportunities, other regions of the empire languished in financial chaos. Over the same forty-three-year period, Greece experienced a slow, gradual decline in piracy. However, reports of piracy in the Greek archives continued to occur at higher rates than with their Ottoman neighbors.

Increasing Violence in Piracy

Piracy in the modern era was more violent than its early modern incarnation. In previous centuries, privateering societies had established ransom networks offered an avenue for privateers and corsairs to safely barter off their captives. Lawless pirates frequently accessed these markets, either openly or by pretending to be corsairs.[6] Many captives met a violent end, but the more lucrative destination of most captives was ransom or slave markets rather than the grave or the briny depths. The erasure of both these intermediaries for ransom and slave markets removed a viable means for pirates to profit from human trafficking. Combined with the risk of captives passing on information to naval patrols or testifying at trial, the benefit of guaranteeing the security of captives vanished. The only viable option for pirates was to ensure their captives' eternal silence. It became more expedient to slay rather than enslave victims of a raid.

The case of Giovanni Strati captures the changing shape of piracy in the middle of the nineteenth century. As the established networks of human trafficking and redemption disappeared, pirates such as Strati had less to be gained by preserving the lives and property of his victims.

Giovanni Strati was a pirate from Kefalonia. His crew was largely composed of foreigners with connection to the region, and they sailed under the Ionian flag. He mostly operated around Chios, and he had his ship's papers signed at both Salonica and Syros.[7] Thus, he could show to either Ottoman or Greek authorities that his ship was a legitimate merchantman. While the waters he sailed in belonged to Greece, crossing from the Ionian to Aegean meant that Greek, Ottoman, British, and Ionian authorities all became involved and interested in his capture.

Strati caught public attention when he robbed two ferry boats. After securing his prize, he scuttled the captured vessels rather than keeping them for ransom or to increase the size of his fleet. This signals a few things. First, he was only interested or able to run a small operation. He did not see continued or enlarged profit by adding more ships to make a small armada. Perhaps this was from fear of over-saturating the seas with pirates, or perhaps he was simply uncomfortable with setting up an expanded chain of command where he was not there to control his crew.[8] A small illegal enterprise was more easily concealable as legitimate through false papers and a change in colors. Second, he was not confident in being able to secure ransom. When piracy was supported by society at large, networks were set up that could help the victims recover their family and property from their captors for a fee.[9] In this time period, when piracy was reduced to such a low level, there was no way for a pirate to safely negotiate with those interested in the return of goods and persons. If Strati were to engage in such negotiations, there was nothing to prevent the navy from showing up to capture or kill him. Third, this loss of an avenue for the exchange of persons and property made piracy inherently more violent. Traditionally, pirates had relied primarily on fear as a threat to make their prey surrender without resistance. A victim of piracy would expect financial loss, and possibly a loss of freedom, but there was little for pirates to gain by executing their captives or scuttling their ships when these represented potential profits. The value of these lives and ships was greatly reduced without the possibility of profits from ransoming. Thus, this form of piracy without a safe haven on land was inherently more violent and destructive.

Increased levels of violence appear in other instances as well. The pirate Koutsoura, whom the Ottoman authorities apprehended in 1860 after years of pillaging the Dodecanese, was widely believed to have murdered all his captives.[10] Strati and Koutsoura stood as real examples of the murderous and destructive pirates Alexandre Dumas thought only fiction in *The Count of Monte Cristo*. Piracy was no longer primarily a threat to one's livelihood; it became a threat to one's life.

The reverse trend was true on land; as the nineteenth century progressed, land-based banditry was on the rise, and in almost all instances brigands were able to peacefully ransom their hostages. Wealthy travelers often held kidnapping insurance.[11] The expectation of this insurance and its accompanying network for negotiation and exchange were akin to the maritime ransom networks of the early modern Mediterranean. Ready networks for exchange of captives allowed human trafficking to flourish, but it also allowed an avenue for the redemption of at least some captives. All captives, whether eventually redeemed or forced to languish in captivity, were victims of extreme psychological and corporeal violence.

Captain Hobart's Failed Covert Anti-Piracy Operation

The Treaty of Paris was a legal response to an experienced reality: state-sponsored piracy was officially designated as a thing of the past. So, when

British naval forces disguised themselves as pirates in 1862 (see below), this blurred a line that could be interpreted as privateering—an activity only recently made criminal. Captain Hobart, the man responsible for organizing this clandestine operation, frantically sought to prevent the Ottomans from making any such connection to privateering by putting them on the defensive with complaints of his own. An accusation from the Royal Navy was a worry that no pasha would wish for.

Augustus Charles Hobart-Hampden, first stationed on the HMS *Foxhound* in the Mediterranean in the early years of the 1860s, was a captain of the British Royal Navy. Prior to becoming an officer, he was part of Britain's global abolitionist efforts to hunt slaver ships in the south Atlantic.[12] British lawmakers considered any ship to be partaking in the global slave trade, regardless of jurisdiction, to be a pirate ship to be hunted down and brought to justice. Despite being employed in a noble cause, his own sympathies did not focus on the moral rectitude of human trafficking and slavery but rather on adventure. Between his stints in the Mediterranean and during the American Civil War, he aided the Confederacy by running supplies past the Union blockade. Had he felt strongly on the issue of ending the slave trade, he would not have aided one of its last strongholds. His moral compass was centered around profit and adventure, not philanthropy.

It is worth examining Hobart in more detail because he will feature prominently in this chapter: first in 1862 when he devised a brash plan to covertly hunt pirates and lashes out when that plan ends in catastrophe, and again in 1867 when he used his own experience of running blockades to gain Ottoman naval commission to stop Greek blockade runners from supplying the rebellion in Crete.[13]

On May 16, 1862, Edward, the Prince of Wales and heir to the British throne, arrived in Rhodes as part of his grand tour through the Mediterranean. British officials in the region scrambled to prepare an itinerary with which to honor his royal highness. The British Consul, Robert Campbell, arranged to bring the prince incognito, under the alias of Baron Renfrew, into the city of Rhodes for a visit to some ancient Phoenician ruins on a nearby island.[14] Campbell forwarded a report that day to the Foreign Office in London stating that three days earlier a pirate trabaccolo had left from Cape Crio (now Cape Deveboynu) and pursued a bombard from Chios around the islands of Symi and Seskli.[15] The report continued that during the afternoon in which the report was delivered, a trabaccolo flying the Ionian flag attacked a Samiote vessel close to an uninhabited island near Symi. The pirate vessel was described as having a dark-colored hull capable of carrying 25–30 tons, sails of various shades and cuts that were swapped out often, a crew of nine men outfitted in Western clothing, and as being registered as a merchant ship. The report ends with rumors of a second, smaller trabaccolo roving the seas around Halki and Kastellorizo and notifying London that Commander Augustus C. Hobart was deployed in pursuit of the pirates. A later report described the suspected pirate ship as follows:

> This vessel has hanging outside her, harpoons, and other fishing gear, has always on board a quantity of sugar, coffee, salt &, the whole, of course, for the purpose of deception, and hoists sometimes the Greek, sometimes the Ottoman, but more generally the Ionian flag. She is accompanied by two small boats called Paranzelle, in the fore part of which, close to the bows of each, is a cabin where the arms and ammunition are kept concealed. Her master has large eyes, wants one of his front teeth, is slightly marked with the small pox [sic], has long light coloured moustaches shaved off under the nose. Her crew consists of 17 men of which only six are put down in the Bill of Health.[16]

The British fleet stationed in the area was concerned about the danger of pirate activity with royalty in the area, but the commanders sensed an opportunity to impress their future king. To truly create a good impression, they needed to go above and beyond what normally would have been expected of them.

One day after the prince's visit, Captain Augustus Hobart of the HMS *Foxhound* planned to eliminate the pirate threat. To avoid the possibility of local informants notifying the pirate ship of his fleet's movement, a small crew would purchase a trabaccolo and attempt to go undercover as pirates in an ill-conceived plan to pursue their quarry. Lieutenant Doughty was responsible for leading the operation and was assigned a crew of eight men. He was to cruise around Knidos, one of the suspected pirate haunts, while Hobart would lead the *Foxhound* to patrol Symi and Lieutenant Montager was to patrol around Marmaris, northeast of Rhodes. During this time period, there were pirates operating outside of Kastellorizo, who remained at large.

On May 20, the Ottoman Governor-General was patrolling the Anatolian coast with his steam warship when he came across a vessel that seemed to match the description of the one marauding the region: a trabaccolo with a host of men dressed in European fashion. Immediately he set upon and captured it and its crew. The men, who appeared to be pirates, were bound, tossed into the hold, and tortured for two hours without any attempt at interrogation. The captives' protests that they were indeed Englishmen on an anti-piracy expedition themselves fell upon deaf ears. The Ottoman officers suspected that their naval uniforms, insignia, and other property had been stolen. After several hours, the pasha came to accept that perhaps the suspects were indeed Englishmen. The Ottomans confiscated the British weaponry and gave leave to the crew to return to the *Foxhound*.

The following morning, Lieutenant Doughty hobbled back to Hobart and told him what had transpired. This put Hobart in a pickle. On one hand, he had created a potential diplomatic disaster by recklessly ordering a covert operation in Ottoman territory, an act that could be construed as an irregular military action, in this case privateering, in violation of a number of treaties. On the other hand, he had enough British pride and pomp to make any foreigner fear an offended Englishman. He chose to avoid giving any explanation of his actions by expressing outrage over the Ottoman actions against his crew. All he had to do was level accusations about "barbarous Turks" attacking "civilized Englishmen." Hobart demanded that the Ottoman Governor-General punish the men responsible for attacking his crew, overlooking the issue that those men were acting correctly in attacking what, to all appearances, were pirates and not British naval forces. Whether Hobart's chastisement of the Ottomans was rooted in arrogant bravado or carefully calculating how to cover his own faulty decisions cannot be determinately settled. In his report, he seems conscious of the fact that this incident could have created a flash point between Britain and the Ottomans were it not resolved quickly. Whether he realized that when he demanded retribution against the Ottomans who tortured his undercover sailors remains unknown.

Hobart's covert sting operation seems to have been an exception to Britain's anti-piracy operations. Typically, frigates boasted the union jack to advertise their dominance over the waves by virtue of countless vessels and overwhelming firepower. Conducting covert operations came with unnecessary risks that could cause greater criminal cooperation and hardship among the local populace.[17] British naval command was displeased with Hobart's efforts and did not renew his post after his first tour of duty in the Mediterranean. Hobart took a hiatus from the Royal Navy to enrich himself by running the Union blockade of the South during the American Civil War. The next mention of him being in the Mediterranean is in 1867 when Grand Vizier Fuad Pasha hired him to replace Admiral Sir Adolphus Slade as the naval advisor to the Ottoman government at the rank of vice admiral.

Abdülaziz's Naval Expenditures and Otto's Expulsion

In 1861 Sultan Abdülmecid passed away and his brother Abdülaziz rose to take his place. Abdülaziz viewed the navy as a critical feature of Ottoman defense and implemented reforms to both modernize the Ottoman Navy and expand it to be among the world's largest. The Ottoman Navy had not grown on such a scale since the times of Süleyman the Magnificent.[18] Size, however, was not everything.

Sultan Abdülaziz had an amateur interest in naval affairs but did not personally have or adequately surround himself with advisers experienced enough to oversee the efficiency of his spending on naval matters. Englishmen like Augustus Hobart were brought in to help guide Ottoman naval efforts. During much of his tenure as a high-ranking naval adviser beginning in 1867, his reforms for officer training were simply for the recruits to translate British ship handling manuals without ever heading out to seas and putting any navigational principles into practice. Just as the sultan's hires proved ineffective so too did his purchases. Abdülaziz was willing to purchase ships with all the latest technologies of the era, whether or not they were practical or even useful.[19] The result was a hodgepodge of various cutting-edge ships that were selected by how innovative and exciting the ships' salesmen made them out to be rather than chosen with concern for cost or how well they would complement the goals of the Ottoman Navy.[20]

Abdülaziz's spendthrift upgrade of Ottoman naval forces drained the treasury. In 1874, the Sublime Porte declared bankruptcy. The coming financial crisis would freeze the Ottoman Navy in the state it was at the end of Abdülaziz's reign in 1876.[21] The enthusiastic spending on a military meant to preserve Ottoman sovereignty did just the opposite. In 1881, Ottoman finances were placed under the strict control of European powers running the Ottoman Public Debt Administration.

Greece did not expand its navy between 1853 and 1873, but it did upgrade some of its ships to account for advances in steam-engine technology. By 1873 the fleet contained two ironclads and several steam-powered ships of war.[22] Compared to the sultan's lavish spending on his fleet, the Hellenic Navy's expenditures during this time were modest.

By 1861, the Bavarian monarchy in Greece was in hot water. The *Megali Idea* was stalled by the Great Powers agreeing to protect the integrity of Ottoman territory to preserve the balance of power and curtail Russian expansionist ambitions.[23] Greeks frustrated by these setbacks to irredentism turned to violence. In 1861, radical nationalist university students unsuccessfully plotted to assassinate Queen Amalia, who had yet to produce an heir, and in early 1862 elements of the military revolted in Nafplion. The Bavarian dynasty managed to control these revolts, and in an attempt to better understand the public frustration, King Otto embarked on a tour of the Peloponnese in October of 1862. While he was out of the palace, several army garrisons revolted throughout Greece and the Hellenic Royal Navy mutinied.[24] When Otto tried to return to the palace, a naval blockade in Piraeus prevented him from doing so. When Greece's Protecting Powers confirmed that they would not come to the king's rescue, Otto was forced to flee the country on a British warship. The lack of a clear heir, one of the reasons for his overthrow, also meant that for a period Greece would be without a head of state. Six months would pass before King George of Denmark would be selected to replace Otto's Bavarian dynasty.

The beginning of King Otto's reign of Greece was marked by an increase of piratical activity, and so was the end of his rule.[25] The revolts that resulted in the expulsion of the king led to a temporary weakening of the Greek state's security apparatus. The chronicles of the Hellenic Navy describe this as a period when peripheral regions experienced a surge of banditry and piracy.[26] The Ministry of Foreign Affairs archive does not reflect such a surge with instances of international piracy.[27] This tells us that the surge of violent robbery was primarily domestic in nature, in terms of both perpetrators and victims. During the chaos of the dynastic transition, Greeks were robbing Greeks.

The Blockade-Runner *Arkadi* and Greek Violations of International Maritime Law

Greece's strategy for irredentist expansion was rooted in a contradiction. On an official level, Greece could not openly engage in warfare with a much larger and more powerful Ottoman Empire and expect any level of success, so it maintained an official policy of neutrality and cooperation. On an unofficial level, Greece fostered popular organizations that aimed to incite Ottoman Greeks to revolt in favor of union with the Hellenic Kingdom. The tension between these two positions during the 1866–9 Cretan revolt threatened either to end Greece's official neutrality or to alter the interpretation international maritime law concerning blockades.

In August 1866, rebellion once again broke out on Crete. After a brief period of relative success, the rebels' luck eventually started to run out. On September 13, the Ottoman Navy enacted a blockade of the island in order to slow down the flow of supplies from Greece to the rebels. Trade ships were only allowed to dock at the five ports of Herakleion, Spinalonga, Rethymno, Chania, and Souda, and the Ottoman Navy reserved the right to inspect any ships found in the vicinity of Crete.[28] Greek ships routinely disregarded the Ottoman blockade and smuggled arms and irregulars to the island.

On October 21, the rebels' situation became dire. A group of Cretan insurgents had retreated to the Arkadi monastery along with civilian women and children, numbering around 400 in total. Western war-correspondents had embedded themselves within the Ottoman forces to report on developments. As the Ottomans surrounded the refuge and closed in on their foes, the rebels decided that rather than surrender to the Ottomans, they would have everyone gather around the gunpowder stores and commit an explosive mass suicide. The journalists' cables would ensure that it was an explosion heard around the world.

On July first of the following year, the *London Times* reported an incident of the Greek ship *Arkadi*, named after the infamous incident that would bring Western attention to the Cretan uprisings, claiming to be neutral attempting to run past the Ottoman blockade of Crete. The Ottomans claimed the right to examine neutral ships for illegal goods, particularly weapons and ammunition, that were being smuggled into Crete to arm the insurgents. Greece was officially neutral, as the conflict was an internal Ottoman affair, and the Greeks claimed the right as neutrals to bypass the blockade.

When the Ottoman Navy stopped the *Arkadi* for inspection at the nearby island of Antikythera, it hoisted the Greek flag, opened up its hidden gun doors, and opened fire on the Ottoman steamer. Ottoman authorities argued that this action constituted an act of piracy and held the Greek government responsible. Greece's relationship with its protecting powers, France, Great Britain, and Russia, limited the Ottomans' ability to retaliate against Greece's flagrant violations of international maritime law. Indeed, *The Times* reflects this when it writes that the Great Powers would prevent the Islamic empire from declaring war upon a Christian state for legal satisfaction. Were the Ottomans to inflict damage upon Greek national ships that could potentially trigger war with the protecting powers.

> The Greeks and Turks concur in their statements of the facts of the case; it is only in characterizing these facts and in the reasoning deduced from them that they differ. The Greeks state their case thus:—The *Arkadi*, having landed a cargo of volunteers, arms, and ammunition within the line of an effective blockade, and having on board men in the service of the Cretan insurgents and petty officers of the Greek Royal Navy, was pursued by an Ottoman man-of-war, which fired to bring her to. Two Ottoman frigates were in sight. The Ottoman captain endeavoured to enforce the right of search, but the *Arkadi* ran out to sea and resisted. A running fight was carried on until the Greek blockade-runner found shelter in a Greek port. The Greeks say that the blockade-runner was so well armed, and fired into the Ottoman man-of-war with so good an aim, that the Turks had 11 men killed, among whom there were two officers. The blockade-runner had only one man killed and two wounded. The Greeks consider that the Turks were guilty of a gross infraction of neutrality, because they pursued the *Arkadi* into Greek waters, and remained for some hours off the entrance of the port of Cerigotto, where she sought the shelter of neutrality.[29]

Greek naval chronicles confirm that the *Arkadi* was one of several ships smuggling munitions and irregulars to Crete.[30] It is important to note that the Greek defense of their actions was not to proclaim that the *Arkadi* was a legal merchant ship innocent of any wrongdoing but rather to redirect blame toward Ottoman pursuit of the ship and to raise issues of areas of legal jurisdiction. Cerigotto is an alternate name for Antikythera, a minuscule island off the northwestern shore of Crete which only supports a population in the double digits. The *Arkadi* managed to find sanctuary there, as it was on the Greek side of the maritime frontier between the Ottoman Empire and Greece. Greek diplomats had led the Ottomans to believe that it was illegal for an Ottoman ship to pursue a blockade-runner within four miles of any non-Ottoman island. The Ottoman navy waited offshore for a supposed trial, and the Greek navy deployed the steamer *Ellas* to secure the *Arkadi* and escort it back to the Greek port of Piraeus. By the time the Greek warship arrived, the *Arkadi* and her crew had already slipped past their Ottoman pursuers to the island of Syros.[31] After the Treaty of Paris, a blockade was only considered legal if it was effective. Since the violating party managed to get away, Greece could claim to have done nothing wrong as the blockade its ship escaped would be rendered illegitimate. In many ways, the brevity and simplicity of language in the Declaration of Paris left it open to such interpretation as all its core tenets could be worked around legally.[32]

> The Turkish Government, taking a different view of the case, declares that the blockade of Crete has been all along conducted in strict conformity with the principles of international law as it has been laid down by Christian nations, and that it has taken for its guide in all doubtful points the conduct of the United States of America during the blockades that arose out of the insurrection of the Southern States. The Turks say that they treated the *Arkadi* as having all the rights of a neutral engaged in blockade running. While she was landing a cargo for the insurgent States of Crete (it seems the Cretans have three provisional Governments), they endeavoured to exercise the right of search in order to ascertain whether her proceedings were legal or illegal. The blockade-runner, trusting to her wonderful speed and powerful armament, hoisted the Greek flag, opened her concealed ports, rand out her rifled guns, and directed heavy fire on the Ottoman steamer, which was a small vessel. The Turks argue that by this conduct the *Arkadi* has forfeited her rights as a neutral blockade-runner, and ought to be regarded as a pirate. The Turkish Admiral sent an officer on shore at Cerigotto to deliver a protest, but as he could find nobody to whom he could deliver it, he posted it up on the wall of the townhouse. The Ottoman Government asserts that the Greek Government is bound to treat the *Arkadi* as a pirate, and appeals to the three Great Powers, the protectors of Greece, who prevent the Sultan from declaring war on a Christian State for legal satisfaction.[33]

Up until this point the journalist had offered a summary of events from both Greek and Ottoman perspectives. Rather than simply reporting the facts, the author had an argument all along, stating that backing the Greek position would shift the balance of international law to favor states neutral to a conflict. His analysis was clearly rooted in a religion-based civilizational worldview.

> Cretan blockade-running threatens to modify the law of nations for the benefit of neutrals. The naval engagement which occurred between a Greek merchantman and a Turkish man-of-war, in the opinion of the people of Syra, establishes the principle that a blockade-runner is entitled to carry guns and a numerous crew to serve them, and that she can legally resist the right of search by a blockading squadron, even when pursuit is commenced in the blockaded waters, if she can succeed in getting out of these waters. There is no doubt, as they say at Syra, that this enlargement of the rights of neutrals will prove conducive to the extension of Christian commerce and Christian civilization in the Levant. Humanity may, perhaps, require that Mussulman navies should not in future be allowed to exercise the rights of blockade against orthodox insurgents, though this would be a violation of the principle of religious equality in Turkey which is so dear to Russia. Diplomacy and hypocrisy may, however, overcome all difficulties.[34]

What we see reflected here is a clear bias in favor of Christendom. The author would prefer to change the rules that all nations must abide by before allowing an Islamic state to gain an edge over a Christian one in any circumstance. The author of this article was British, not Greek. The Greek violations of the Ottoman blockade in Crete did little to impact the lives of Englishmen, yet the author immediately and unabashedly took the side of the Greeks, even when they openly and brazenly violated a legally established blockade. Britain was a neutral party in this conflict, which again was in theory an entirely domestic Ottoman affair. Yet when international law as agreed upon benefited an Islamic empire over a Christian state, the rules changed. These treaties primarily served as a veneer to legitimate European hegemony, and the moment they impeded that goal, they were quickly tossed aside. Of course, this was a piece of journalism prone to sensationalism and was not an official policy memo. Nonetheless, the *London Times* was the premier paper of its day, and not a fringe publication out of touch with the British populace.

While Britain remained officially neutral yet sympathetic to the Greeks and Cretan rebels, Captain Augustus Hobart returned to the Mediterranean after years of running blockades for the Confederates during the American Civil War. Ever the profiteer and still unable to find a post as captain in the British Navy downsized after the Crimean War, he saw an opportunity to further enrich himself. This time, rather than helping Greeks run the blockade, he pitched to Fuad Pasha, the Ottoman minister of foreign affairs, that he could help strengthen the Ottoman blockade of Crete.[35] Hobart's plan involved bending international law to favor the Ottomans, and Fuad Pasha was pleased to hear of a way to have these laws favor the Ottomans. Hobart was enlisted in the Ottoman fleet, not as a captain, but as a vice admiral.

In his memoir, Hobart recounts how he nearly reproduced the *Arkadi* incident with another Greek ship violating the Ottoman blockade. He approached the blockade-runner *Enossis* and fired a blank, a signal for the suspect ship to show its flag, whereupon the Greek ship fired its guns at the Ottoman Warship. Hobart considered this an act of piracy and pursued the *Enossis* through Greek territorial waters to Syros. He then stayed with the suspect ship until a trial could be held so they would not run off and unload their cargo on Crete.[36] The last part is the only way that Hobart's plan differed from the *Arkadi* incident. Previously, Ottoman warships had only stayed a few hours, and when they broke their post the blockade-runner had managed to escape. The Greek navy attempted to scare off Hobart by sending over a frigate, but upon approaching his vessel they did not fire, supposedly from lack of powder. Hobart remained until Ottoman reinforcements arrived to seize the *Enossis* and distribute its crew throughout the surrounding islands.[37] Remaining vigilant in Greek waters until a trial could be convened led to Hobart's initial success and helped him gain further prestige in the Ottoman ranks.

As the *Arkadi* had escaped its trial, the same ship continued to smuggle guns and fighters to Crete. Nearly two months later, on August 20, the Ottoman Navy was able to bring an end to the nuisance the *Arkadi* caused. The Sublime Porte commissioned a new, speedy ship of its own: the *İzzeddin*. Orders were given to Vice Admiral Hobart to captain it, whereupon she was quickly able to intercept and capture the *Arkadi*. Rather than simply return or scuttle her, the Ottomans redeployed her as an Ottoman warship.[38]

For his aid in improving the efficacy of the blockade and suppressing the Cretan rebellion, Hobart was promoted to rear admiral of the Ottoman fleet. He eagerly adopted the moniker "Hobart Pasha" and enjoyed the luxuries of Ottoman nobility while enthusiastically adopting a radically pro-Turkish narrative.[39] For all his enthusiasm and early success for the Ottomans, he turned out to be one of Sultan Abdülaziz's less effective hires. As mentioned before, he took little interest in an actively reforming the Ottoman Navy.

Ultimately, Greek violations of the Ottoman blockade as a neutral party failed to hold international attention as long or strongly as needed for diplomats to seriously discuss reforming maritime law. The Great Powers were not adequately concerned by Christian Greece being on the wrong side of the law in relation to the Islamic Ottoman Empire to modify international law for all nations.

Italian Unification and Adriatic Piracy

The rise of Italy as a new and powerful state led to shifting trade routes and a new balance of power in the Adriatic provinces of Greece and the Ottoman Empire. Over the early years of the 1860s, Giuseppe Garibaldi's *Risorgimento* made great strides in unifying the fragmented kingdoms of the Italian peninsula. What was once a series of minor kingdoms and colonies of various imperial powers became a contender on the regional stage. A unified Italian state presented new mercantile opportunities. At the same time, Italy had to learn the ropes of dealing with both domestic and international security challenges. Much as the Italian *carabinieri* had to deal with bandits plaguing the Italian countryside, so too did the new state need to deal with piracy, with Italians both conducting and being the victims of piracy.

The nascent Italian state treated brigandage as more than just a security threat. In their attempts to eliminate brigandage, Italian *carabinieri* sought to make a public display of having captured brigands acknowledge the legitimacy of the *Risorgimento* in exchange for small tokens of retaining honor during their execution. Dealing with non-state violence was key to Italian nation building.[40] Like the Ottomans during this period, Italian policy was to violently suppress brigandage but did little to address the economic conditions in rural society that created it.[41]

On August 6, 1863, Italian pirates assaulted the Greek merchant brigantine *Suzanna* captained by Theodoros Orfanos at cape Zafferano just east of Palermo. This started a whirlwind of diplomatic correspondence as both countries had recently had a regime change: unification in Italy and the coronation of King George in Greece. Initial reports claimed that the pirates were aboard two ships carrying forty men. Two months later, the Italian Navy had apprehended fifteen of the pirates led by Raffaelo and Salvadore Versaci. An auditor sequestered their booty and returned to Orfanos his portion.[42] He was not their only victim. In this instance, it was Italian inability to patrol its seas that led to the raid of a neutral, foreign merchant ship. Five years later, Italy's failure to secure its seas would lead to Italian shipping being attacked by foreign raiders.

On August 16, 1868, the Italian legate Chevalier Joseph Bertinatti wrote to the Ottoman minister of foreign affairs, Fuad Pasha. He complained about the Italian ship *Angelo dell' Abbondanza* (Angel of Abundance) being attacked in the Ionian Sea outside of Cotrone (present-day Crotone) by three Turkish pirates one month earlier in July and requested that the Ottomans do whatever is necessary to ensure such acts of piracy are not again committed. Meanwhile, the Italians sent the royal corvette *Varese* to patrol the Ionian Sea.[43] The Ottoman archives contain no copy of a response to Bertinatti. They only contain a translation of the letter into Ottoman.

This is an interesting case as it is one of the few instances from this era where a foreign power accused Ottoman/Turkish pirates of leaving imperial waters to raid in foreign ones. Of course, the Ottoman Empire at this time still held onto much of its southern Balkan territories, so the Ionian Sea was as much Ottoman as it was Italian or Greek. This particular raid happened off the shore of southern Italy. This was deep enough into Italian territory to be outside of any waters which the raiders might have thought were contested neutral or in another country entirely. Naturally, plundering fifteen tons of goods from a ship is a crime regardless of jurisdiction, so the culprits would have been unconcerned with whether this would become a diplomatic snafu or not. Unfortunately, lack of additional correspondence suggests that these marauders were not found by the authorities, so we cannot confirm the initial reports that the pirates were indeed "Turks," be that word meaning Ottoman subjects, ethnic Turks, or Muslims of other ethnicities like Albanians or Bosnians.[44] Were those reports correct by any of those definitions, this incident would seem to prove the exception to the observable trend regarding culprits of piracy in the post-Barbary Mediterranean.

Upon completion of the Suez Canal in 1869, merchants from Italy and the Mediterranean began sailing further east into the Red Sea to compete in local markets. The sudden demands of new merchants for goods led to high levels of competition for available commodities. Both Italian and local merchants quickly turned to smuggling and piracy to bypass trade regulations and gain further access to goods and markets. In 1885 a strong local firearms trade developed to arm these merchants-turned-pirates.[45] After the opening of the Suez Canal, most of the piracy in the Red Sea targeted European shipping. This dynamic led the Ottomans to scale back their own resources in suppressing piracy.[46] It became the responsibility of Europeans to protect their own merchants. Over the following decades, Italy would expand its military presence in the region alongside its growing economic interests.

Conclusion

This chapter has shown that shifting domestic and international law alone did little to reduce the number of pirate raids in the Eastern Mediterranean. The Treaty of Paris outlawed privateering, and Sultan Abdülaziz greatly modernized and expanded Ottoman naval forces. In the debates about how to deal with piracy, including those taking place in the twenty-first century, there is often a political divide in terms of strategy. On the one hand, you have hawkish politicians and military officials advocating for increased legal pressure and military action as the path to eliminating pirates. On the other hand, there is a more humanist and economical approach that aims to eliminate piracy and other criminal activity by creating better legal options, either through availability of peaceful professions or through enrolling these individuals in the state's security forces.

The period examined in this chapter shows the results of legislating against maritime crime and increasing enforcement without any noticeable change in economic condition. In short, people continued to turn to piracy at the same rate as before. New maritime laws were not evenly applied. The British advocated changing international maritime laws before allowing those laws to favor the sultan's blockade of Crete over the brazen violation of that blockade by Greece, a Christian nation. During the 1860s, the Eastern Mediterranean only experienced increased legislation and enforcement but not an increase in prosperity that could ripple through society and offer opportunities for economic success through all strata of society.[47] While legislating against piracy alone would not solve the problem of piracy, it did create a culture where piratical activities were frowned upon, in particular by the state. Obviously, states had always opposed pirates, labeling them as the enemies of civilized society; yet it used to be *par de course* to co-opt these crews as corsairs and privateers. This practice had already been fading, but the Treaty of Paris formalized the move away from employing privateers in state naval forces. While piracy was no longer legally acceptable, it was still economically viable to turn to this crime. Pirates could no longer straddle the law in hopes of employment as privateers, but they could choose to operate wholly outside of it.

5

Currants, Capital, and Declining Piracy

The Eastern Mediterranean became deeply integrated into the world economy during the 1870s. The Suez Canal had been carved into the Egyptian landscape in 1869, and thus became a gateway allowing interoceanic steamers to navigate between the Mediterranean Sea and the Indian Ocean.[1] Some of the piracy that plagued the Mediterranean began to spill over into the narrow corridor of the Red Sea.[2] A global ecological phenomenon caused by the phylloxera epidemic led to devastation in Western Europe and an agricultural boom in the Eastern Mediterranean. Increased trade led to new economic opportunities, and these led to a significant decrease in regional piracy as people took to the land instead of taking to the account as pirates.

Phylloxera decimated Western European vineyards, but the plague never reached the Aegean.[3] As a result, for roughly the last third of the nineteenth century Greece was the sole European exporter of currants, grapes, and wine. The Greek economy benefited enormously from this position. As economic conditions improved, it became more popular and profitable to take to the land and begin farming cash crops.[4] This created an easy opportunity to generate wealth within a legal framework. Many people that would have otherwise turned to piracy instead turned to the vineyards or related tertiary industries with raisins as their new *raison d'être*.

This type of agriculture-centric economic growth would primarily benefit the land-owning class. As both Greece and the Ottoman Empire were largely semi-peripheral agrarian societies, this still encompassed large swathes of the population. Over the nineteenth century, Greece and the Ottoman Empire came up with strategies to reclaim land lost to climate change resulting from the Little Ice Age of the early modern era that destroyed irrigation works and turned much of the region into malarial swampland.⁵ In 1871, the landowning class in Greece greatly expanded as a result of land reforms. Tenant-farmers and temporary workers would have also profited from this increased commercial activity, even if they did not own their own farm.

Over his several tenures as prime minister, Harilaos Trikoupis sought to rapidly industrialize Greece in what would now be considered a Keynesian attempt to grow the economy out of debt. This created jobs for the urban working class, and so rural dwellers left the countryside for Athens in droves.⁶ The working class could also head out to the fields to take part in the currant economy as temporary labor.

This chapter first shows the reduction in piratical activity in the Mediterranean beginning in the 1870s. It then argues that this reduction was primarily a result of improvement in the regional economy under a political context when Greece and the Ottoman Empire were cooperating with a common goal of ending piracy in the region. In the Ottoman Empire, the peasant economy continued to grow even as the state finances languished and were placed under the control of the Public Debt Administration (PDA). The chapter ends by considering the disparate emigration situations in the two states: how those policies impacted the regional economy, and how those demographic flows figured into the economic opportunities of the working class.

The Decline of Piracy in the Late Nineteenth Century

Only three cases of Mediterranean piracy appear in the Ottoman archives during this period. The first was in 1883 when the Ottomans tracked a British-state pirate-flagged armored steamship named *Cockatrice* (*İnglizi devletinin kokatreis nam korsan bandıralı ... çerhli vapuru*) from Kalas to Malta, suggesting the Ottomans viewed them as privateers.⁷ The second occurred the following year, when the Ottomans described a Greek privateer ship heading from Odessa to Piraeus in similar terms.⁸ Lastly, in 1887, Ottoman naval forces pursued and captured a Greek ship suspected of committing acts of piracy around Samothrace and İmroz (present-day Gökçeada).⁹

While these cases represent a dramatic decrease in Mediterranean piracy, Ottoman domains were not free from the scourge. After the opening of Suez Canal, trade through that region sharply increased, and so did the piracy that leeched off it. Eight instances of piracy in the Red Sea and Persian Gulf are reported in the Ottoman Prime Ministry archives during the period 1870–96.[10] The first decade of the twentieth century saw over twenty cases reported in the Red Sea alone. For comparison, in the period covered in this book until this chapter, 1830–69, only one case of piracy in the Persian Gulf in 1847 and none in the Red Sea appear in the Ottoman Prime Ministry archives.[11] In the 1820s and 1830s, Britain deployed its fleet to crush pirate nests in the Persian Gulf and Arabian Sea. By the late nineteenth century, pirates had learned how to evade the patrols of British steamships. Pirate raids on the gulf's pearling industry continued into the early twentieth century.[12]

The Ottoman archives failed to pick up on two cases of transnational piracy in Ottoman waters during the 1870s. First, in 1877, fourteen Greek pirates were caught raiding the island of Rhodes. Ottoman gendarmes quickly responded to the threat, and after killing the pirate chieftain, the remaining pirates surrendered to local authorities.[13] The second occurred in 1878, when "corsairs" attacked the anchored Ottoman ship *Saint Nicholas* in the Dardanelles, near Berguz (present-day Umurbey).[14] This document comes from a period when the Ottoman and Greek states were actively cooperating in securing their land and sea borders to prevent criminals from gaining asylum by crossing jurisdictions.

Cooperation between the Greek Kingdom and the Ottoman Empire had evolved and intensified ever since Greece became a sovereign state and an international border was drawn to separate the southern tip of the Balkan Peninsula from the rest of the Ottoman Empire. In his study of Greek and Ottoman policing of their shared border, George Gavrilis traces the evolution of the interaction between the two boundary regimes from chaos and little cooperation in the immediate aftermath of the Greek Independence War to the 1850s when joint action, treating the borderland as a mutually policed zone, and sharing of intelligence became frequent.[15] By the 1870s, the two states increased their cooperation but began viewing the border as a line rather than a shared zone.[16] A line could be demarcated on the land, but maritime borders are more slippery. The impetus for both states to snuff out international crime came in 1871.

That year, Greece experienced international embarrassment after brigands killed a group of British and Italian aristocrats. This incident, known as the Marathon murders or the Dilessi murders, caused the entire country to appear wild and unable to police its lands. It became a massive point of contention with Britain.[17] To satisfy its ally and protecting power, Greece implemented a wide-scale suppression of banditry in the following years that succeeded in reducing banditry to tolerable levels.[18] The Ottoman Empire followed suit, eager to avoid similar Western criticism.[19]

The cases of piracy that appear in the Greek archives confirm a high level of cooperation between Greek and Ottoman officials to root out piracy at sea in the same way that Greek forces strove to end banditry on land. On October 15, 1879, Tevfik Pasha, then Ottoman Ambassador to Athens, wrote to his Greek counterpart that the pirate Spiros Vlavianos was found in the environs of Iraklia and Schoinoussa, just south of Naxos.[20] One hundred days later, Theodoros Deliyannis, at the time serving as the Minister of Foreign Affairs, wrote back to Tevfik confirming that the Hellenic authorities had succeeded in the capture of the pirate Spiros near Syra. In the same span, Ottoman forces in the archipelago were able to identify two shepherds who served as his accomplices, Manolis and Yorghis.[21] In order to facilitate the trial of these two for being accessories to Vlavianos's crimes, Greek and Ottoman officials were eager to share intelligence and resources to bring peace to their shared seas.

It should be noted that at this point, both states had experienced longstanding mutual peace. Other than nominally mobilizing against the Ottoman Empire during the Crimean War, an action which resulted in the immediate British occupation of Athens and no actual fighting between the two Mediterranean militaries, the Greek Kingdom and Ottoman Empire had maintained a state of peace since the establishment of Greek independence, going back fifty years. Even as Greek irredentism was entering the state's diplomatic rhetoric by 1879, the Sublime Porte sated the Greek lust for Ottoman lands by ceding Thessaly to Greece in 1881, bloodlessly granting the province in the hopes of continuing peaceful relations.[22] Thus, it should be no surprise that these states would generally be willing to work together to achieve regional harmony and in this historical period increased efforts to suppress international crime.[23]

Phylloxera, Currant Monoculture, and Economic Growth

During the last third of the nineteenth century, the entire Mediterranean economy was temporarily transformed by the introduction of an aphid from North America known as phylloxera. The name translates as "dry leaf" for the effect of killing the roots of vines which serve as their primary source of food. Vineyards in Spain, France, and Italy were devastated by the swarm. For unknown reasons, the insects never spread to Greek and Anatolian vineyards that produced the grape known as both the Zante currant and the Corinth raisin.[24] Spared from the scourge, Aegean farmers found themselves with a monopoly of production over the popular and profitable grape and wine markets. To take advantage of this opportunity, farmers ripped up their grains and replaced them with vines. Seeking to maximize profits during this period, the Greek state drained its swampy lowlands, implemented land reform to place farmers on those new productive lands, and placed a 25 percent export tariff. The Ottoman Empire undertook similar land transformations in Levantine lowlands. The primary difference was the chosen crop for monoculture in Syria and Cilicia was wheat, where production soared from 20 million bushels exported per annum in 1840 to 50 million by 1888.[25] Public health added further incentive for Mediterranean states to drain swamplands; as populations were burgeoning from growth and migration, new settlements were created in malarial plains.[26] The 1858 Ottoman Land Code added new mechanisms for the Ottoman Empire to settle farmers on previously vacant land, but even with these efforts the population still remained lower in Konya and Syria than it had been in the sixteenth century.[27] Terraforming the wetlands, though initially costly, provided arable land and an environment safer from disease.

Viticulture is more labor-intensive than olive production. Owners of currant-plots would need to hire fieldworkers to tend to and harvest the grapes, a job that requires more care and more time than the brief period required to harvest olives or other fruit.[28] The shift to currant monoculture greatly increased the demand for labor. This included both unskilled seasonal labor needed to harvest the grapes and more skilled labor for related tertiary markets, such as barrel production, lumber, and transport to support the growing market.[29]

In 1871, Prime Minister Alexandros Koumoundouros implemented sweeping land reforms in Greece. The Greek state sold national lands to the public in a manner that restricted the ability of wealthy families to envelop lands into their plantations as they had in the 1833 redistributions under King Otto, and instead allowed the number of small- and medium-scale landowners to rise. While these distributions began in 1871, it was not until the end of the decade that the distributions had fully passed through the state bureaucracy and the new plots began to bear fruit. Recently established banking systems, alongside an influx of foreign capital, helped to distribute loans to prospective landowners.[30] At the same time, many peasant farmers were only able to purchase a small plot of land and were unable to remain solvent through substandard harvests. Crop yields in Greece could vary greatly year to year, so over time these small plots would be sold from desperation to large landowners in a return to rural economy reminiscent of *latifundia* estates.[31] Still, overall profits grew substantially and were distributed more horizontally across Greek society than they had been in the past.

The increase in agriculture activity was both top-down and bottom-up. The state was responsible for draining the swamps on state lands, such as Lake Kopais in Boeotia.[32] Ottoman farmers generally retained their petty producer structure, exporting a wide variety of crops rather than switching to cash-crop monoculture.[33] Ottoman smallholders who came into ownership of vacant land due to the 1858 reforms only succeeded in creating piecemeal land transformations, compared to reforms in France where the government would forcibly step in to drain swamps when landowners were unable to.[34] Greek landowners privately owned their lands, so they were active in constructing terraces, draining wetlands, and other long-term investments to increase the arable land in their position.[35] These investments, which were intended to corner the currant market, had a secondary effect of boosting olive oil production. It is common practice in Greece to lay vines between rows of olive trees, as the two do not compete intensively for resources. Greek olive oil production mirrored currant production in the second half of the nineteenth century.[36] The proportional growth of the olive oil export sector still accounted for a smaller portion of the economy than currant exports, which during the 1870s and 1880s accounted for over half the revenue from all Greek exports.[37]

Two thirds of agricultural grants given to landowners between 1883 and 1892 were given for production of raisins, showing their dominance in the

Greek economy.³⁸ This trend toward monoculture paid off in the short and middle term, but it led to disaster once European vineyards recovered and France imposed the Méline tariff to slash imports and protect its recovering wine industry which resumed exporting to the global economy. No longer able to compete with the recovered vineyards in France and Western Europe, Greece's economic outlook plummeted.³⁹ Lack of economic diversification meant that Greece could not handle the collapse of one of its sectors. In 1893, Prime Minister Harilaos Trikoupis addressed the Parliament and began his speech with laconic prose: "Regretfully, we are bankrupt."

Whereas in Greece this era ended with bankruptcy, the Ottoman Empire began this period in the red. Starting in 1851, Reşid Pasha sought to renew the Porte's coffers with loans from European states. Sultan Abdülmecid rebuffed the attempt, fearing the empire would become addicted to the loans, unable to shake off its debt, and susceptible to further foreign interventions.⁴⁰ Once the Crimean War started, its constant escalation forced the Ottomans to borrow funds to cover military expenditures. At first, the terms of the loans held favorable conditions for the Ottomans, as the British and French were interested in having a strong Ottoman bulwark against the Russians in the Crimean War, but over time the interest rates became more predatory. As the initial spate of loans agreed to by the sultan was in the context of military necessities rather than economic growth, the Ottomans did not experience the economic growth required to gain a net profit and pay off the interest. The problem deepened under the reign of Abdülaziz.

As discussed in the previous chapter, Sultan Abdülaziz undertook a number of costly reforms of the Ottoman military, with a particular emphasis on the navy. As these were largely in the form of purchases from foreign dockyards, the Sublime Porte's purse was draining into foreign coffers. In order to pay off the interest on long-term loans, the Ottomans were pulling higher-interest short-term loans. In 1875, the Ottoman Empire was unable to procure all the funds for a major loan payment and entered bankruptcy. The following year, all loan payments had ceased. Sultan Abdülaziz was deposed in May of 1876 and found dead in the palace weeks later. He was briefly succeeded by Sultan Murad V, whose reign only lasted the summer before being deposed and replaced by Sultan Abdülhamid II.

Seeking to recover previous investments made in the Ottoman Empire, European diplomats convinced Abdülhamid to issue the Decree of Muharram which established the PDA in 1881. The PDA was a bureaucracy led by an Anglo-Franco-German troika meant to control Ottoman finances and extract state revenue to pay off the delinquent debt.[41] To accomplish this, they implemented a number of taxes in the Ottoman Empire which were to be paid directly to the PDA. As the returns on Ottoman investments resumed, European companies embarked on new projects in the Ottoman domains, such as the construction of railroads and mines. European investors were able to guarantee profits, as the Ottoman Empire agreed to pay the shortfall between realized and expected profits on many projects.[42] As its role in Ottoman finances grew, so too did its size; by the start of the First World War, the PDA had a larger staff than the Ottoman Ministry of Finance.

As in Greece, the Ottomans had also implemented banking reforms that allowed extensions of rural credit for agriculture. While the Ottoman Empire had enacted land reforms in 1858 and 1867, much of the land remained as state land (*mulk*), and tenants would need to obtain official permits to adjust crop production or build news structures.[43] In addition, there was an economic disincentive, as the tenants did not own the land, so they would not profit from investments for long-term gain. Only wealthy owners of *çiftlik* estates were able to fully benefit from the recent agricultural changes. It is these estates that generated much of the local economic profits while the imperial finances languished.

Reşat Kasaba argues that the expansion of the capitalist world economy to include the Ottoman Empire, particularly the *zimmi* merchants, led to a period of growth in the Ottoman coastal cities that were most connected to global trade networks.[44] He provides a table that expresses the trade, both imports and exports, of İzmir in 1988 British pounds sterling. From 1839 to 1860, Smyrniote exports went from a low of £800,000 in 1846 to a high of £2,888,840 in 1856, averaging around 1.7 million British pounds of exports for recorded years. After 1860, the value of exports very quickly doubled and remained stable at approximately 4.1 million pounds sterling.[45]

Reşat Kasaba's appendix is useful for understanding the changing tides of trade over the nineteenth century. Table A2 shows the price and quantity of exports from the Ottoman Empire to the UK of particular goods, including raisins and opium. Beginning in 1856, opium exports began to skyrocket from around 20,000 pounds sterling the previous year to £361,000 in 1872.[46]

The Crimean War temporarily drove up the price of raisins, and Ottoman merchants responded to market pressure by upping their exports to England. Ottoman raisin exports to the UK increased threefold during beginning in 1870, but prices did not inflate as one would have expected from the phylloxera epidemic. Table A5 shows price and export tonnage from İzmir specifically. When comparing prices of currants versus their revenue (see Figure 5.1), we can see that increased revenue was primarily driven by an increase in production and export quantity, rather than primarily by price. The increase in market price that currants would fetch, while significant, was not exorbitant.

As both states increased exports of commodities, they witnessed innovations in and expansion of merchant shipping. From 1860 until the end of the century, maritime transportation gradually both moved away from sailing and to steam. During this period, the ratio of sailing versus steam ships calling upon İstanbul's harbor went from an 80/20 percent split, respectively, to 5/95 percent. Yet at the same time, there was no gross reduction of sailing ships. This demonstrates the dramatic rise in shipping that took place over these

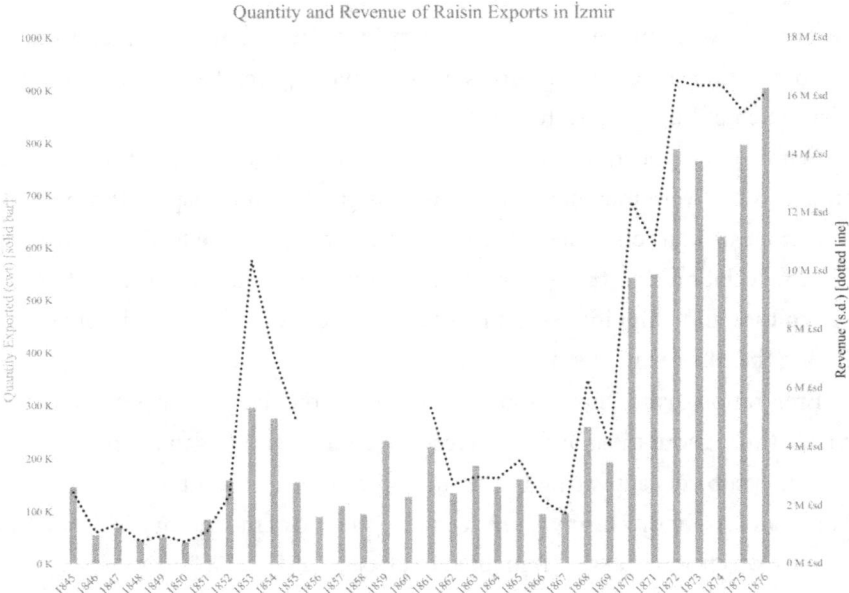

Figure 5.1 Raisin export quantity and calculated value in İzmir based off Table A5 in Kasaba, Reşat. *The Ottoman Empire and the World Economy: The Nineteenth Century.* (SUNY Press, 1988), 126

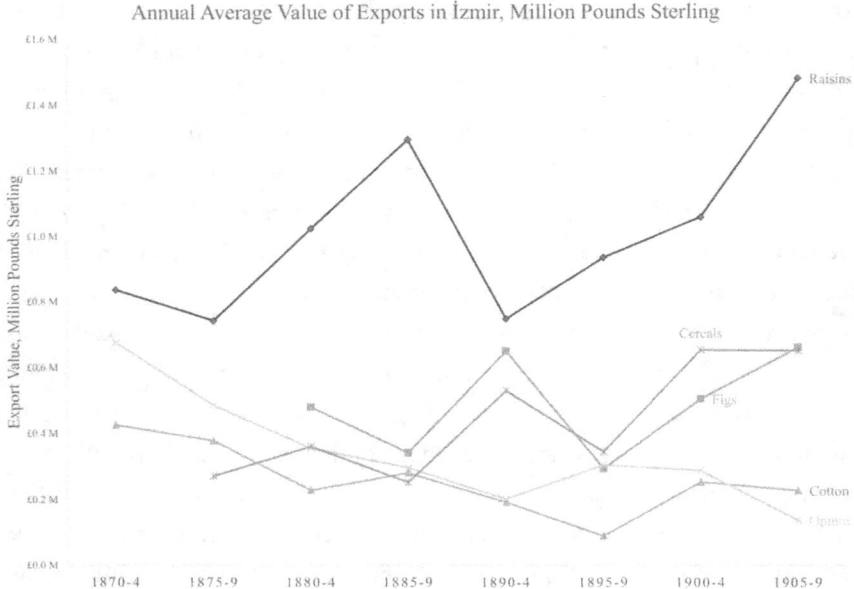

Figure 5.2 Based off data in Roger Owen. *The Middle East in the World Economy, 1800–1914.* (I.B. Tauris, 1993), 111, 201

decades.[47] Exact numbers and timing vary by country, but these figures reflect a more enthusiastic adoption of steam technology in the Ottoman Empire than much of Europe and the West.[48]

When job opportunities were created on land for production of cash crops, so too were merchant-maritime jobs created to transport those goods to European markets. These increases had a synergistic effect of increasing legitimate labor and trade opportunities on both soil and sea. In Greece, agriculture and shipping were the leading sectors of economic development during the nineteenth century.[49]

Emigration from the Ottoman Empire to the New World remained a trickle throughout most of the nineteenth century, with less than one hundred Ottoman subjects appearing in the immigration records of the United States, Brazil, and Argentina in any given year until the end of the century. This was due to a ban on emigration that remained in place until 1896/7.[50] This conservative emigration policy kept around a greater population than the economy would naturally retain, boosting the supply of cheap workers and increasing the competition for non-skilled labor.[51] After Russia conquered Caucasia in 1878, a wave of Muslim refugees entered the Ottoman Empire. The Porte laid out plans to settle them throughout the empire, made more urgent by the fact that some of the jobless refugees occasionally turned to brigandage to support themselves when necessary.[52] A system of internal passports helped the empire control the movement and manage the distribution of poor and unemployed people categorized as vagrants. For those that could not be directed to labor markets, state plans involved distributing charity, pressing them into the army, or imprisoning them.[53] Once the emigration ban was lifted, thousands of Ottoman subjects would leave the sultan's domains each year.

In contrast, Greek subjects would emigrate from their homeland at greater rates. This led to labor shortages which in turn forced landlords to create better economic incentives to lure tenants to work their land.[54] This in turn made economic growth more horizontal, where both proletariat and bourgeoisie stood to profit off economic gains. Thus, an entrepreneur making their living illegally would have a greater incentive to try a lawful line of work. Traditionally, having enough capital to be a proprietor would be the only way to effectively profit off of an agricultural enterprise, while the field workers would be mere subsistence farmers. The economic boom coinciding with low population density form continuous emigration and following Greece's 1871 land-redistribution program created the conditions that would make it reasonable to till a small plot of land and realize profits of substance rather than subsistence.

The increase in economic activity preceded the drop in Aegean piracy by a few years. The delay was possibly due to the human element of taking time to enter a new developing field. It takes time to adjust to new market opportunities, especially when agriculture is involved. A newly planted grapevine takes years to reach maturity and bear fruit. It follows that there would be a delay before entrepreneurs could partake in the currant cash-crop craze and realize a return on their capital.

In the previous chapter, we saw that legal reforms and increased enforcement of maritime law were put into place, but that the rates of piracy did not decrease significantly. It was only with increased economic opportunities that piracy diminished. This has a parallel with twenty-first-century piracy in Indonesia. Sumatran pirates were notorious for raiding the straits of Malacca in the early years of the new millennium. After the 2004 Indian Ocean earthquake and tsunami that devastated the region and took over 200,000 lives, countless foreign-aid dollars flowed in for the reconstruction of society. Remarkably, regional piracy was almost eradicated as would-be pirates found it more profitable to work in the reconstruction of a society that was experiencing greater capital flows than before the disaster. Writing on the matter, Catherine Zara Raymond argues that to keep piracy from resurging "economic development must be encouraged among the coastal areas of Indonesia and Malaysia in order to reduce unemployment, and corruption of local officials also needs to be addressed. However, antipiracy measures already in place should not be neglected."[55] Successfully suppressing piracy involves both the carrot and the stick: taking anti-piratical measures to dissuade individuals by creating risk of punishment, and improving the economic opportunities available to the masses to make legal employment viable and enticing.

The same is true of nineteenth-century Mediterranean piracy. In both instances the region had been plagued by piracy, several regional and global efforts were made to combat the problem without fully successful results, and in both cases the greatest success followed economic improvement that filtered down to the lower classes. While enforcement capabilities were useful for reducing piracy, it is worth remembering that Sultan Abdülaziz's infatuation with modern warships was a large part of what brought economic ruin upon the Sublime Porte. The growth of the agrarian economy as well as tertiary industries and expansions of the banking sector in both Greece and the Ottoman Empire allowed for an increase in the Aegean economy. This made it more profitable to partake in licit trade surrounding the currant boom than to take to marauding the seas.

6

Piracy during the 1897 Greco-Ottoman War

Greece's economic boom resulting from currant monoculture led to a disastrous economic collapse once European vineyards recovered and rival raisins hit the market. The Trikoupis government fell and was replaced by a hawkish, conservative administration that sought to rally Greeks' hopes by waging an irredentist war of expansion against the Ottoman Empire. While the war was raging, reports emerged of Greek pirates raiding Ottoman waters. Were those ships sanctioned by Greek authorities, they, and more importantly the Greek government, would be in violation of the ban on privateering set half a century prior by the Paris Declaration Respecting Maritime Law.

This chapter shows how the Greek and Ottoman states perceived and reacted to wartime piracy during the end of the nineteenth century by focusing on the 1897 Greco-Ottoman war. The incidents of wartime piracy were intrinsically and justifiably linked more to suspicion of enemy involvement in encouraging maritime raiding across the border than piracy occurring during times of peace. After offering a brief background concerning frequency of reported piracy and issues of contention leading up to the war, I assess the condition of both navies and states at the start of the conflict. By 1897, both states had declared bankruptcy. The difference was that the empire had done so in 1875, while Greece did not until 1893. Ottoman austerity, then, as opposed to Greek debt-spending, led to the Greek Navy being better prepared for war. Rather than discussing the naval battles between the respective fleets, this study focuses primarily on two incidents when unidentified Greek ships raided the Ottoman Aegean coastline after the truce had been concluded but before the peace treaty was finalized. Both cases are discussed in documents found in the Ottoman Prime Ministry archives and were referenced in Greek-British diplomatic correspondence and intelligence reports.

During its retreat from Thessaly, the Greek Army opened up prisons to allow brigands to hamper Ottoman attempts to administer the occupied territories. I argue that the appearance of Greek pirate ships in Ottoman waters after a decade of their absence suggests that this was consistent with Greek efforts to challenge Ottoman security capabilities during the ceasefire by generating criminal activity. The use of maritime and terrestrial irregulars helped Greece weaken the Ottoman security apparatus, but by subjecting Aegean and Macedonian Greeks to violence at the hands of raiders from the Greek Kingdom, the policy weakened Greece's ability to implement its long-term strategy of inspiring Ottoman-Greeks to rebel. The chapter ends by contextualizing piracy's position in relation to the irregular warfare on land that became common in late nineteenth-century Macedonia.

Background to the War

In the last third of the nineteenth century, the expanding global economy reached a level of volume that necessitated an increased level of maritime security, enforcement of which led to a decline in piracy.[1] The frequency of reports about piracy recorded by the Greek Ministry of Foreign Affairs declined from several cases each year before 1870 to six cases per decade, or just over one every two years. The number of documents pertaining to Mediterranean piracy in the Ottoman Prime Ministry archives drop to zero throughout the 1870s, with only two cases appearing in the 1880s, and the three cases that will be discussed in this chapter all occurring in 1897, during and in the immediate wake of war between Greece and the Ottoman Empire. Wars and demobilizations are known to cause spikes in piracy, either during their duration by employing and encouraging pirates to raid the enemy state or in their aftermath by creating unemployed sailors with military skills.[2] It does not appear that is the case here. The Greek Navy remained mobilized while peace negotiation took place, so there would be no sudden surge in unemployed sailors.

Prior to the outbreak of war between Greece and Turkey in 1897, the last documented incident of Greek piracy in Ottoman waters was recorded ten years earlier, in 1887 off the coast of Samothrace.[3] Counting non-Greek piracy in Ottoman seas, the last case to appear in the Ottoman Prime ministry archives was an English pirate ship in 1890 outside of Fao.[4] The Ottoman archives show three incidences of Greek piracy upon their shores in 1897, one during the war and two during the period of armistice and peace negotiations.

The Greek irredentist gaze had fixated upon Crete ever since the Greek War of Independence. Many Cretans had risen up then, and many more continued to rise up in subsequent rebellions against the Ottomans. After Egypt handed back Crete to the Sublime Porte in 1841, Crete came to be ruled by a series of corrupt rulers who ignored imperial edicts aimed at improving life for Ottoman Christians. Cretans split into three factions that either wanted to remain part of the empire with the liberal *Tanzimat* reforms actually enforced, to become an autonomous province of the empire, or to break off and unify with Greece.[5] This led to a series of rebellions in 1866–9, 1875–8, and 1895–8. As a result of the Russo-Turkish War, the 1878 Treaty of Berlin established autonomy and self-governance on the island which nominally remained part of the sultan's domains. This was known as the Halepa pact. The Christian populace gained many rights, including use of Greek as an official language, the right to bear arms and join the gendarmerie, the right to control some of their own finances, and amnesty for those who took up arms in rebellion. The agreement pacified the Cretans until the terms were again violated in 1889 and the autonomy granted under the Halepa pact was rescinded. Crete was returned to direct Ottoman rule, this time under Cevat Şakir Pasha.[6] In 1895, Şakir Pasha formally suspended the civil liberties of Cretan Christians. This fomented discontent and within a year caused another full-scale rebellion on Crete.[7]

In the same year, the conservative Theodoros Deliyannis became prime minister of Greece. After his generation-long rivalry and several years rotating power with his liberal rival Harilaos Trikoupis, the Greek economy that had skyrocketed because of the currant trade became bankrupt in 1893 as European vineyards recovered and American viticulture took off. With things beginning to look dim economically, Deliyannis decided to win Greece a nationalist victory. Hosting the first Olympic Games satiated the national pride of Greeks, but only one year later the pride of reviving the Olympics faded and the people once again grew restless. Deliyannis had expansionist aspirations to both his south and north. He sent irregular forces, largely recruited through the irredentist organization National Society, south to assist the Cretan rebellion against the Porte and encourage the island's unification with Greece.[8] After stirring up trouble in Crete and enraging the Sublime Porte, he sent thousands of irregulars north into Macedonia on March 24, followed up by the Greek Army on April 18 in a failed attempt to further the *Megali Idea*.

The Greek invasion of Macedonia was an unmitigated failure. The war lasted only a month and Greece lost every single battle. Rather than gain territory, Greece had lost Thessaly to Ottoman occupation. A refugee crisis started as people fled from enemy forces and attempted to retreat into territories still held by Greece. Greece exacerbated the problem by sending bandits into Ottoman-occupied Thessaly to stick a thorn into Ottoman attempts to enforce order. These bandits proved more of a plague to the resident populace than the administration, so the flow of refugees south into the Hellenic Kingdom continued. On May 20, Deliyannis signed a ceasefire with Sultan Abdülhamid II.[9] King George demanded Deliyannis resign for bringing Greece to ruin. When Deliyannis refused, George replaced him with Dimitrios Rallis as prime minister.

The Condition of the Fleets

The Ottoman Empire still stood among the great imperial powers of the late nineteenth century, and it had an army to match. The one area where the Ottoman military was bluffing in regard to its strength was at sea. The Ottoman Navy had become decrepit since the 1877–8 Russo-Ottoman War. Lacking funds due to stringent payments imposed by the Ottoman Public Debt Administration, one of the major austerity measures the Sublime Porte undertook was to pull funding from expensive military projects. Warships ranked at the top of this list as they were truly titanic undertakings. Whereas Sultan Abdülaziz recognized the importance of naval power and opened up the coffers for the *kapudan paşa* (grand-admiral), Sultan Abdülhamid's hands were tied by severe budgetary constraints.[10] The money needed to build and maintain a modern navy simply was not there. As such, the Ottoman Navy could not properly maintain its vessels. By the time 1897 rolled around, years of lying dormant in the Golden Horn left their guns rusty and the crews green. Only two ironclads, the *Mesudiye* and the *Neçm-i Şevket,* along with the torpedo-boats *Berkefşan* and *Peleng-i Derya,* were fully operational at the war's start.[11] The majority of the Ottoman fleet dated to the 1860s and it had last exercised in formation in 1877.[12] The war with Russia consumed the coal reserves which fueled the Ottoman Navy, and bankruptcy halted further production in the mines. Severe coal shortages restricted the ability of Ottoman steamships to complete routine voyages.[13] The Ottoman Navy had mobilized to try to limit Greek infiltration of Crete, but the warships had rotted over decades of neglect since their last use. The guns had mostly rusted through, and in some even the steam engines struggled to carry the ships. The few functioning ships made their way to the island but could only be used as a symbol of Ottoman naval power: impressive on the outside but defunct to those who knew their inner workings.

Figure 6.1 Abdullah Fréres, photographers. "[The cannon drill on the Imperial Ironclad Frigate Mes'udiye] / Constantinople, Abdullah Frères." Photographic print. Constantinople: [between 1880 and 1893], no known restrictions on publication. From Library of Congress: *Abdul Hamid II Collection.* https://www.loc.gov/pictures/item/2003671378/ (accessed May 1, 2020)

At the onset of Greek hostilities, the Ottoman fleet put on an exercise to practice engaging with an enemy fleet. Foreign naval advisors deemed this exercise a total failure as the aim and reload time of the Ottoman fleet would allow any competent enemy ship to approach close enough to inflict severe damage upon the Ottoman fleet while risking little as the Ottoman cannonade would splash harmlessly into the sea.[14]

Between the Keynesian debt-spending of Harilaos Trikoupis and the militaristic conservatism of Theodoros Deliyannis, Greece had managed to produce and maintain a modern navy. On paper, the Greek Navy was far more prepared for war than the Ottoman Navy. Between 1889 and 1892, Greece built three coastal defense ships capable of going seventeen knots which were named after the islands that provided its revolutionary war fleet: the *Hydra*, *Psara*, and *Spetsai*. All three were either undergoing major modifications or being overhauled in French shipyards from the winter of 1897. When Greece declared war upon the Ottomans, it seems no one had consulted the navy to confirm the condition of the fleet or set up a war plan. High value Ottoman targets such as Salonica which were vulnerable to maritime harassment were largely untouched by the Greek fleet. The main wartime actions of the Greek fleet were to bombard Preveza with its gunboats and cruisers, assault a few low-value targets, and attempt to demolish coastal railways outside Salonica. Once the war began to turn in favor of the Turks, the Greek Navy's primary duty became to transport retreating Greek troops back to the kingdom.[15]

While neither the Greek nor Ottoman fleet was ready to fight an effective naval engagement, the Greek fleet was more capable of patrolling the seas, controlling shipping, and limiting enemy fleet movement. Of course, this was only because the enemy fleet was barely seaworthy. This dominance over the waves also meant that Greece could effectively counteract maritime crime such as smuggling and piracy, should it choose to do so. The majority of the functioning Greek fleet was light gunboats and torpedo boats. These were fast and useful in littoral combat, particularly against piracy. Large warships could not pursue smaller vessels into shallow waters and often lacked the speeds to pursue pirate skiffs even in open seas.

Greek naval superiority led the Ottomans to avoid direct confrontation at sea and to opt to supply their army by land whenever possible. The Ottoman

Navy largely remained outside of the conflict. The Greek Army was getting crushed on land, and the navy was unable to produce a decisive sea-battle against the skittish Ottoman Navy. Despite the naval advantage laying with Greece, on May 14 the Ottomans managed to capture several Greek pirate ships (*Yunan korsan gemileri*) in the Aegean.[16] This was the first instance of Greek piracy the Ottomans had dealt with in a decade, but the details were hidden in the fog of war.

Concern over Irregulars while Drafting the Peace

Near the end of the war the Ottomans had placed 3,000 Albanian irregular troops at the Anatolian coastal town of Çeşme.[17] The Greek military noticed this movement and feared that they would be sent to Chios, a largely Grecophone and Orthodox island still under Ottoman control which lay under Greece's irredentist gaze. Painful memories of the brutal Ottoman punishment of Greek rebellion on that same island three quarters of a century before were burned into the Greek and Western collective consciousnesses.

Part of this fear was justifiable, as Albanian irregular troops were notoriously more chaotic than Turkish regulars. The following British intelligence report addressed to Consul-General Blunt is from the town of Kitros just north of Mt. Olympus, part of the Ottoman territory invaded by Greece.

> Great tranquility reigns in this district. The Greek fleet no longer harries the coasts, and the Ottoman troops preserve their conciliatory attitudes towards the Christian inhabitants.
>
> A battalion of Anatolian Rediffs [reserve troops], the 4th of the 26th regiments, under the command of Bimbashi Selim Bey, quartered partly on my property at Kitros, and partly in the surrounding villages, behaves admirably, and the soldiers lay hands on nothing, not even an egg …
>
> Persons coming from Thessaly state that the Albanian volunteers there have pillaged and sacked many properties, several of which belong to Turkish Notables, and even to the Civil List of the Sultan.
>
> There seems to be some truth in it, for it has been noticed that Albanians, passing through Caterina on their return from the war, had in their possession not only cattle, but valuable objects which they tried to sell in the market.[18]

The report dates to June 1, 1897, just one week after the cessation of open hostilities. We can easily see how the Greeks had distinct expectations between Ottoman regular and irregular soldiers. The same holds true for Ottoman concerns between Greek regulars and irregulars.

When it became clear Greece would lose the war, rather than surrender the land peacefully, the Greek Army sought to despoil what they could and maximize the headache of Ottoman officials seeking to enforce order. Greek authorities in Larissa opened up the prisons and allowed freed brigands to engage in open pillage. Greek officials intended to do the same in Volos, but local townsmen resisted to the point of open rebellion. Ultimately, Greek authorities transferred the prisoners of Volos to Athens rather than unleashing them upon the city.[19]

After the Ottomans regained control of Thrace, they sent their troops further south into Thessaly. As the Greek Army was totally routed, there was no effective military limit to how far the Ottoman forces could push. The only limit was what was politically feasible and reasonable to the Great Powers that guaranteed Greece's independence. The empire tempered its ambition and pushed only for the re-annexation of Thessaly, which had been peacefully ceded to Greece in 1881 in order to appease Greek irredentism. Clearly the initial goal of bestowing Greece a territory to satiate its expansionism did not lead to long-lasting peace, so the Sublime Porte requested the territory back. In addition, when Thessaly was handed over to Greece, Greece also became responsible to pay off that province's portion of the Ottoman debt. Facing its own financial struggles, Greece never fulfilled this condition. It began to look like the Ottoman Empire would grow as a result of Greece's attempted war of expansion.[20]

Greece reacted to this possibility by increasing its effort to despoil Thessaly in order to stick a thorn into the Ottoman occupation. British intelligence reported that the mountains northwest of Trikala were held by insurgents armed by the Greek *Ethniki Etaireia*. These rebels were provided with arms but were without food, so they resorted to pillaging the countryside to sustain themselves. Unfortunately for the locals, this pestilence did not stop with stolen grain. The rebels turned into vicious marauders as they expanded from thievery into captive-taking. For example, at one point they demanded a ransom of 20,000 drachmas from the family of a wealthy Jew they had abducted. The author of the report claims that such despicable activities curbed the rebellious enthusiasm of the Greeks living under the Ottomans. Locals viewed these provocateurs as "not merely patriots or political agitators, but robbers and brigands."[21]

In the summer following Thirty Days War all did not remain calm on the seas. While the May 20 armistice had been declared and diplomats were gathering in İstanbul to discuss the final terms of peace, a scourge that had bypassed settlements on the Ottoman Aegean coastlines for a decade had returned. Already once during the war had they make an appearance and what should have been a peaceful summertime was interrupted by two more pirate raids.

The second raid of the year occurred on the twenty-first of May. Just one day after the ceasefire was signed, a steamboat of the Nemçe Postal company was heading on its delivery route from İstanbul to Karaağaç. It was passing in front of Mt. Athos when Greek pirate ships approached and seized the steamboat. The pirates brought the prize ship to Tirekili. Upon receiving news of this incident, the Nemçe Post sent a telegram to Mehmed Ali, the captain of Karaağaç's port.[22] No official Ottoman reply is included in the archives. Either this was handled at a local level or the incident was ignored by the Sublime Porte which was more focused on wartime and occupation logistics. Either way, the Ottomans did not consider the incident a breach of the ceasefire, or at least one worth resuming combat over. For this to be the case, Ottoman officials must have taken the telegram at face value that even though the ship was manned by Greeks, they were pirates and thus not taking orders from the state.

Concerning regular naval activities at sea, Greece sent over ships to harass the Anatolian littoral immediately after the ceasefire despite British suggestions to avoid making any move that might appear hostile to the Ottomans.[23] It may be the case that the previously mentioned Greek "pirate ships" that the Ottomans documented were the same ships involved in this report. The timing matches up, and the locations are not terribly far from each other. As neither of these reports provided ship names, a definite link cannot be drawn. If these were the same ships, then Greek warships operated in a piratical manner. If not, then Greek pirates acted opportunely, and Greek warships were brazenly risking shattering the newfound peace by anchoring in Ottoman territory.

With both sides on edge over enemy irregulars and desperate navies, the armistice terms were drawn up with particular reference to these fears.

Terms of the Armistice at Sea
1. The Greek fleet shall quit Ottoman waters and those of the littoral occupied.
2. Vessels flying either the Ottoman or a foreign flag shall be free to enter and leave Ottoman ports and ports to the north of the line of demarcation fixed by the Armistice Convention of the May 22, and shall not be subject to visitation.
3. Navigation remains free for the ships of the two belligerent parties, provided that merchant-ships shall not enter the ports of the opposing party.
4. Navigation in the Gulf of Arta remains free for both parties.
5. The Ottoman Government undertakes not to reinforce its armies of operation by sea by the introduction of munitions, instruments of war, or troops.
6. The revictualing of the army shall be effected twice a week through ports under Ottoman rule.
7. The violation of occupied or national territory, by bands of irregulars, whose formations by the State can be proved, shall be regarded as a violation of the armistice.
8. The non-observance of paragraphs or clauses of the said Convention or Appendix shall involve the rupture of the present armistice, and the offending State shall bear the responsibility.[24]

Many of these articles directly address both the completed and feared use of military irregulars. The first article, for example, directly addresses Greece's use of maritime irregulars on the Anatolian coast. That the Ottomans describe these ships as pirate ships in their internal correspondences and yet refer to them here as part of the Greek fleet is important for understanding their view of piracy near the close of the nineteenth century. To them, there remained little distinction between the enemy state's fleet and vessels employed in the service of that fleet. To the Ottomans, a *korsan* was not necessarily totally separated from state connections as the term "pirate" suggests in English, where the entire point of employing rhetoric about privateers is to dodge responsibility for their actions.

Articles two, three, and four at first seem to discourage naval blockade and normalize trade relations, but neither state had a navy powerful enough to enact an effective blockade to begin with. With a smaller fleet, it is more effective to return to the practice of seizing enemy ships, both mercantile and military. These practices fall more under the prize-taking rules of early-modern privateers than the blockade and contraband running conducted by larger modern navies. Thus, these articles target use of irregular maritime troops during the war.

Article five also seems to be a standard clause that would apply to restricting the reinforcement of the regular standing army. The context given by the Greek correspondence shows that this clause was really meant to prevent the feared movement of Albanian irregulars to Chios and other islands. Article six allows the Ottoman Empire to maintain its occupation of Thessaly in a way that would not stoke fears of further invasion deeper into Greece.

Lastly, article seven goes out of its way to condemn the use of irregulars by both sides. This codifies into law the aforementioned perception of irregulars as simply another branch of the regular armed forces for whose actions the state was equally responsible. It also suggests that this perception was not uniquely Ottoman but rather consistent with broader trends in international law. Britain, France, and Russia were the guarantor powers of Greek independence and played a major role in negotiating any treaty Greece was a part of. They would draft resolutions that helped shape a world in the interests of European imperial powers, be those interests about maintaining the balance of power between the imperial powers, extending their colonial and mercantile reach, or seeking stability in international waters.

While the Western imperial powers had a hand in negotiating the terms of peace between Greece and the Ottoman Empire, they did not assume all the agency in those terms. For example, the armistice effectively created a maritime demilitarized zone which mimicked legislation the Ottomans forced the British to agree to a century before. During the mid-eighteenth century, British privateers repeatedly attacked French shipments in the Ottoman Eastern Mediterranean. This disrupted grain shipments from North Africa and led to famine within the empire. The Sublime Porte demanded that the British cease these raids by threatening to implement shariah law at sea. The British kowtowed to the sultan and acquiesced to the establishment of a no-combat zone which effectively stretched what the Ottomans considered their territorial waters from merely hugging the Ottoman coastline to the entirety Eastern Mediterranean Sea.[25] These norms created by Ottoman diplomats continued to be the basis of maritime peace accords into the early twentieth century.[26]

The armistice at sea would be honored for two months before pirates from Greece would violate Ottoman territory for the third time in a year. On August 12, three caiques and two skiffs appeared on the shores of Limnos. Seven marauders (*korsan eşkiyası*) from Greece disembarked at the Kondias marina (Greek: Κοντιάς, Ottoman: قونديه) and began pillaging the nearby village. Captain Süleyman led a contingent of Ottoman reserve troops to capture the raiders and pacify the area. When the Ottoman guards engaged with the pirates, one of the reserve sergeants fell in battle. Most of the pirates managed to return to their ships and speed away. The Ottoman reserves requested backup and embarked in pursuit of the pirates. They chased them as far as Mytilene before losing track of the lighter and faster pirate ships.[27]

Back on Rhodes, the governor of the Archipelago Province wired İstanbul requesting steamships able to travel at speeds of at least fourteen knots. He argued that given that the Archipelago Province consisted of thousands of islands, these speedy warships should be supplied to the imperial army, reserves, and police for securing the sea routes and the prosperity of his province's inhabitants.

The Deleterious Effect of Irregular Raids on *Rum* Sympathies with Greek Irredentism

How effective was the use of maritime military irregulars during this war for Greece? Certainly, their use caught the attention of diplomats, as the treaties of armistice at sea seem to focus on reigning in the deployment of these irregulars. Ultimately, the Greek-Ottoman border ended up shifting slightly in the favor of the Ottomans. From the standpoint of an expansionary war, the entire war effort was a massive failure, but given how poorly the war went for Greece, ending it near where they started it mitigated the damage of defeat. The failures of the Greek military led to a wartime Ottoman occupation of Thessaly supported by legitimate Ottoman concerns about reversing their former concession of the province to a state that spat on a good will effort to bring peace and stability to the region. As a concession to Ottoman concerns of Greece not paying its share of Thessaly's debt, the peace treaty placed a 4 million Turkish lira war indemnity upon Greece and put the kingdom's finances under the control of an international committee.[28]

The people of Mytilene and Limnos experienced Ottoman policies similarly. They shared similar demographics and were administratively placed in the same province. Mytilene and the other islands in the northeastern Aegean experienced a *Pax Ottomanica* during the last seven decades of Ottoman rule. The Ottomans embarked upon public works projects such as schools and fountains. The economy was growing at a strong rate, but it was the wealthy and middle-class *Rum* elite that were able to most benefit from these changes, as most of the poor, both Christian and Muslim, were left behind.[29] These upper-class Ottoman Christians cultivated a Greek ethnic identity with which they could argue for national rights. At the same time as the Ottomans improved the economy and implemented reforms, they also experienced some failed reforms. Attempts to regulate shipbuilding and sponge diving generated discontent among the Greeks who were employed in those fields, and many Ottoman-Greeks who worked in the affected industries uprooted and moved across the Aegean to Greece.[30] Martin Strohmeier takes the position that Aegean Greek dissatisfaction with Ottoman policy not only pushed them away from attempts to form an Ottoman nationalism, *osmanlılık*, but pushed them closer toward adopting a Greek national identity.[31] Maria Mandamadiotou argues that this discontent has been misinterpreted as suggesting that they desired unity with the Greek Kingdom, when instead they sought more rights within an Ottoman imperial framework. She defends this viewpoint by examining newspapers of the Greek community of Mytilene and highlighting their enthusiasm for the 1908 Young Turk revolution and the restoration of the Ottoman constitution.[32]

If we are to trust the British intelligence report at Kitros about local sentiments in the conflict zones, Greece failed to win hearts and minds by deploying irregulars into Ottoman-controlled lands. The instances of banditry and piracy that occurred in the context of both the war and the general outlawry of the nineteenth-century Mediterranean created a general sense of public panic. Baris Cayli argues that acts of banditry, be they social bandits resisting greater powers or opportunist bandits seeking only their own profit, create an environment where the public sows rumors of imagined bandits that exacerbate paranoia based upon real threats to public safety.[33] Armed incursions, whether they were of the brigands on land or pirates at sea did not emblazon the image of a heroic captain unifying a disparate people upon the minds of Ottoman-Greeks. If anything, contact with such scoundrels undid any positive ideas from the kingdom that might have been brought by Greek merchants or travelers. This certainly would also be the case at Limnos, where Greek marauders shattered the tranquility of the northern Aegean islands. The environment of fear expended resources of the Ottoman forces called in to patrol and investigate reports of threatening vessels. From the eyes of the islanders, the Sublime Porte offered protection from the threat of Greek raiders.

Benefits of Deploying Irregular Troops

Irregular troops provide some positive benefits to the state. They were cheaper to outfit and maintain, obscure the strength and identity of that branch of the state's armed forces, and could undermine the enemy state's guarantee of security to its subjects. For these reasons, Greece had a history of using irregular troops such as during its revolution, the Crimean War, and during attempts to instigate rebellion in Crete.[34]

Irregulars are cheap when compared to a standing army. The state only needs to pay them in times of conflict. It does not need to outfit said fighters excepting in some cases providing their weapons, and many times the men of violence who find themselves employed in the shadows of the state provide their own arms. Irregulars are given neither quarters nor training by the state. The state does not provide them with rations, and thus also saves on the expensive maintenance of secure supply lines. All they really expect from the state is a paycheck, either directly or from the proceeds of prizes taken. Of course, given all these deficiencies irregulars cannot be expected to effectively wage war against a standing army. This concern is why said irregulars are generally directed against undefended civilian populations. A band of pirates or brigands can expect to overwhelm a small provincial police force and then plunder unopposed. This targeting of civilians leads to a disdain among the populace for what they see as brutish cutthroats, the enemy of all. This is where the benefit of plausible deniability becomes important. Greece could deny agency in the actions of these men. As we saw in the 1897 armistice at sea, the burden of proof was upon the offended entity to connect the armed irregular incursion of their territory to the other state.

In strategic terms, deploying irregulars conceals the size and strength of your armed forces. It makes it harder for the enemy to gauge exactly how strong or even who their enemy is. If reports come in about a village being attacked behind the front lines, the attacked state needs to be able to pull armed personnel to secure the area. Irregulars can feign attacks on areas to lead a number of enemy combatants on a chase, thus reducing the number of soldiers the enemy state has ready for battle. When irregulars are able to overwhelm an enemy, they could topple the local government and replace it with a miniature puppet-state, as Greek brigands did repeatedly in Thessaly in 1878.[35]

Lastly, irregulars weaken the enemy state's claim on a monopoly on violence. When the state struggles to provide security to its people, a door opens for other parties to claim the ability to offer that tranquility. For example, Egypt's legitimacy was harmed when its government was unable to effectively stop bandits from terrorizing the countryside. This Egyptian failure fueled Britain's claim in the 1880s that its colonial domination over Egypt would prove to be more effective at providing security. When the British too failed to suppress brigandage, they also lost the claim of being able to offer tranquility to Egyptians.[36] When Greek pirates arrived in Limnos, Greece could claim that it did not give direct orders or even that these were domestic, Ottoman pirates and that the sultan was failing to subdue the menace. The Kingdom of Greece suggested that perhaps it might do a better job than the Porte, as the British initially claimed in Egypt. At the time, such a Greek claim would have seemed particularly weak in the international sphere. The Dilessi murders of 1870 proved Greece incapable of stymieing brigandage even just outside its capital. Yet, for all the international condemnation, Britain did not force Greece to change its constitution or implement any particular reform.[37] More recently, in the mid-1890s, the Sublime Porte had drawn international opprobrium by resorting to excessive violence to suppress Armenian revolts in eastern Anatolia. Part of managing the claim of a monopoly on violence was showing that the power to use violence could not only be wielded by the state but also effectively controlled. Greece was unable to effectively assert its own monopoly on violence, so it unleashed irregulars to weaken the claim of its chief competitor.

Reliance on irregulars to fulfill basic state functions often backfired. Achilles Batalas argues that Greece's lack of a monopoly on violence in the mid-century led to "inverse-racketeering," where the state became a client of bandits and irregulars who offered protection from themselves, other bandits, and Ottoman forces. Irregular captains stimulated banditry and brigandage both to weaken the enemy and to argue for their own future employment: that the state needed those same irregulars to hunt down the brigands they had unleashed.[38] In the 1897 war, Greece continued to rely heavily on irregulars, which resulted in more banditry and piracy. In Anatolia, the co-opting of bandit gangs frequently occurred when the Ottoman sultan was unable to successfully crush them with his regular forces. The *derebeys* were similar to figures such as Ali Pasha Tepedelenli who were bandit rulers who possessed enough power that the Ottoman state forces could not easily crush them and so were legitimized and made governors of the regions in which they resided. In theory they were loyal to the sultan, but in practice they thought little of him and would keep the revenues they earned from taxes and mining.[39] This type of weak central control continued until the twentieth century, when the 1908 Young Turk Revolution overhauled the state with the reestablishment of the short-lived 1876 Ottoman constitution and fifteen years later the Turkish Republic replaced what remained of the empire.

Controlling the Narrative

Naturally, the Ottoman administration and local newspapers would also be able to contribute their own versions of the events in the archipelago. The 1890s were a transitory period when instantaneous long-distance communication was possible but not as evenly applied as today. Given the information technology at the time, the only way for a message to travel faster than a person could carry it was by telegraph. Unlike telephones in the twentieth century, telegraph stations were still few and far between. The Ottoman Empire began building a telegraph network in the 1850s to link up communications with their British and French allies during the Crimean War. During the war, they had successfully built a submarine telegraph line across the Black Sea to the front in Crimea, but the line soon failed after the war. In the following decade, Ottoman engineers laid six more submarine lines through the empire, but five immediately malfunctioned. Up through the 1880s, the only way

Ottomans could reliably electronically communicate was through terrestrial telegraph stations. Several were set up along the Aegean coast, wherefrom ships would need to carry communiques to the islands. Outside of wartime, conservative Islamic clerics derided telegraphy as an unreliable technology, not because messages might not successfully be transmitted, but because they might contain corrupting satanic messages. Sultan Abdülhamid II portrayed the telegraph as a tool of pan-Islamism to build local support for the tool so capable of unifying a far-flung empire.[40]

A person or private entity could not expect to have their own telegraph and operator. The few public telegraph stations that existed were operated and easily monitored by the state. Telegraphs were considered to be relatively private lines of communication compared to the telephone, which more people could listen in on. Telephone lines only began expanding in Western Europe during the decade preceding the Greco-Ottoman War. Underwater telephone lines were first laid down in the English Channel in 1891 and by 1898 only 31,600 telephones were installed in France.[41] Given that the Ottoman request for backup was transmitted from Rhodes, we can ascertain that the Ottomans had successfully laid telegraph lines between Rhodes and İstanbul. This suggests that in 1897 the Ottomans had not yet laid down telephone lines between any of the Aegean islands and İstanbul and that minor islands like Limnos did not have their own telegraph stations. The provincial capitals were connected by undersea wire to the capital, but such projects could not be carried out in the thousands of islands in the Ottoman Aegean. While the Sublime Porte had limited instantaneous communication capability to its island holdings, Greece would not have possessed any such means.

Occasional Greek visitors from the kingdom would not dominate a narrative of events that could explain pirates and other irregulars as nationalist heroes. Locals had negatively experienced the events themselves and published about events in their own autonomous press. Outside of the lived experiences, the Ottomans were able to more easily offer their version of events and explain how their forces valiantly fought off the pirates, even risking their lives to martyr themselves for the safety of the locals. The Ottomans had an established, stable presence on the northeast Aegean islands. There were no oppressive governors that led to discontent and rebellion as had happened on Crete. Without any acts of Turkish repression, the Greek Kingdom had no chance of convincing locals to turn against the Turks. The people of Limnos and Mytilene felt no Turkish yoke tightening around their neck.

States domestically deployed propaganda portraying irregulars as noble bandits trying to unite the nation. For example, in the Cretan city of Rethymno, Greece had placed statues glorifying Cretan irregulars who participated in the Macedonia conflict. The epigraph on the statue of Evangelos Frangiadakis, a captain of over 500 men during the Cretan uprisings and guerrilla chieftain during the Macedonia conflict and 1897 Greco-Turkish War, reads "Bloody freedom / flies high and judges / and crowns all those more / who are fighting for peace."[42] While Frangiadakis also participated in the local Cretan uprisings, most of his military service was spent among bands of irregulars deployed in Ottoman Macedonia. Crete was the focal point of Ottoman misrule in the post-Greek-revolution Aegean. This created groups of disgruntled men of violence who were willing to fight against the Ottomans, be their end goal independence or *enosis* (unification) with Greece. The Greek Kingdom was able to direct these men as irregulars to Macedonia, where the Orthodox inhabitants did not undergo the same oppression as the Cretans and thus had no interest in rising up against the empire. Monuments glorifying the actions of these irregulars are readily found in Crete and the contemporary territories of the Greek Kingdom. In these lands bands of irregulars were seen as freedom fighters.

In the Ottoman Aegean and Macedonia, where these irregulars were deployed to rather than drawn from, guerrillas like Frangiadakis were not heroes. The bands that Greece armed in Ottoman lands were primarily recruited from local brigands who were offered a salary. As Cretans were sent over, they eventually accounted for one third of armed bands roving the region. Even the local brigand-bands, to say nothing of the laypeople, avoided the Cretan squads which they viewed as more violent and unruly.[43] Cretans and Greeks from the kingdom were outsiders and troublemakers. They upset the largely peaceful social order of the region where Christians and Jews could hold land, trade, and even share holy places with Muslims.[44]

Contextualizing Piracy within the Violence in Macedonia

The pirate ships that unexpectedly appeared in Ottoman waters in 1897 served Greek national interests in a mostly different way than irregular brigands deployed to Macedonia did. The main similarity to irregulars in Macedonia in terms of benefit to Greek irredentist goals was that a piratical presence undermined the Ottoman security apparatus. Ottoman provincial officials requested expensive war steamers from a financially constrained Ottoman Empire to be able to secure the shipping lanes and provide a greater sense of security to their islander subjects. It would not be until 1905 when the Ottoman Navy would be able to finally update its fleet and fulfill such requests.[45] Such struggles are familiar to any state attempting to display power over a vast territory. Providing the illusion of power over a densely populated urban center or over heavily trafficked routes and passages is relatively easy. When the Ottomans parked their rotting fleet off the coast of Crete, they were able to project the image of having hulking warships covered in armor. Hidden were the rusty inner workings and the greenness of the crew. It was trickier to actually provide security for the thousands of islands in the Archipelago Province.

The security challenges posed by these few pirate raids in the Ottoman Aegean were overshadowed by Greek and Bulgarian irregular bands roaming around Macedonia forcing peasants to identify with their branch of the church or suffer very immediate consequences. In 1872 the Bulgarian Exarchate broke off from the Orthodox Church, beginning a process of phyletism where the churches would begin to take on ethno-national characteristics and were used in nation-building claims.[46] As the Orthodox Patriarchate positioned itself against its Bulgar rival, it laid policies that made it more Greek at the expense of other Orthodox followers like Vlachs, Albanians, and Slavs.[47] Ottoman rule in Macedonia was thinly held together by an attempt to spread nationalism through institutions such as education. The Sublime Porte had set up many public schools to provide general education and instill a sense of Ottoman national identity. But they also allowed a great deal of autonomy to private educational institutions. Greece took advantage of the ease of access to alternative education to fund private schools to try to instill Greek nationalism within the Greek elements of the populace. They had a two-fold strategy: one was aimed at the middle class and elites with a more traditional education to better understand Hellenic identity, and the other targeted poorer Greeks. These Greek schools attempted to fill the minds of the relatively uneducated peasantry with hatred of Greece's rivals, at this time Bulgaria in particular. The general idea was to have an educated elite rule over a bloodthirsty mob of peasants that would be on the front lines of Greek expansionism.[48] In a world where a person's religion was a key part of their national identity, these violent bands were linked directly to the state whose nation they wished to expand.

The main distinction from Greek irregulars in Macedonia was that the pirates did not seem to be documenting attempts to establish a particular religious and national identity among the people. The pirates did not establish a presence over any sort of duration in the territories they raided, nor did they appear to try to talk to the locals at all. Instead, pillage seemed to be the main focus. Having filled their coffers, Ottoman documents suggest they were quick to leave. In addition, given the few reports we have, it appears that the pirates did not return to raid the same area twice in this period.

For the Rallis government, the opportunity to undermine the Ottoman claim to be providing security made it worth rolling the dice to see whether Greece would be blamed for these attacks. If the attacks were connected to the Greek state, Greece could have been asked to pay a further indemnity, cede more territory, or make other concessions. For its various violations of the treaty, Greece had to pay the Ottoman Empire an additional 100,000 Turkish liras on top of the 4 million lira war indemnity.[49] It seems the Ottomans greatly suspected that the pirate crews that appeared during and after the war were Greek because that is how they refer to them in their internal correspondences. This suspicion was not directly reflected in the treaty agreements which spoke of irregulars in neutral terms while laying out restriction for specific states in other sections of the treaty.

Greece had two main strategies for irredentist expansion. The first was to instill a sense of Greek identity among the *Rum* by educating them to be Greek and then inspiring them to rise up against the Ottomans and demand union with their Hellenic brethren. Greek pirates pillaging Ottoman-Greeks hurt efforts to emphasize Hellenic brotherhood. The second strategy was much simpler: military conquest. Greece had tried and failed in this regard during the 1897 war but would ultimately succeed in the 1912–13 Balkan Wars.[50] The nation-building project in Macedonia proved to be fruitless as victory was won through a four-way alliance against the Ottomans.[51] Victory was won by forcing Turkish troops to defend too much at once. In this way, both bands of Macedonian irregulars and pirates roving Ottoman waters served Greek interests in the same way: forcing Ottoman forces to run around and expend limited resources, weakening their security apparatus. Ultimately, the decision to utilize pirates and other irregulars was more of an issue of military strategy as doing this created chaos in Ottoman lands rather than inspire the will for *enosis* among the *Rum*. The 1897 war ended in defeat for Greece, and the use of irregulars on land and at sea weakened the desire of Ottoman Greeks to embrace the same Greek state that had allowed brigands and pirates to freely raid the countryside during the Greek Army's occupation.

Epilogue: Why Was This All Forgotten?

This work has shown that piracy never completely went away in the Mediterranean during the nineteenth century. Since piracy carried on a century past its supposed end date in the Mediterranean, why then did it fade from historical memory? Was it an intentional project of forgetting a chaotic past in order to place Greece, Turkey, and the other post-Ottoman states among the "civilized" nations of the earth? Or was it simply that the cases of piracy after 1830 remained relatively minor, less able to enthrall the imagination than romanticized versions of the pirate fleets of Hayreddin Barbarossa or even the Greek-revolutionary pirates at Gramvousa had managed to do centuries later? Perhaps the omission has to do with the entire study of piracy, a field which is easily corrupted by the allure of pleasing those eager to hear romantic stories of libertine, seafaring rogues. A handful of sailors stealing mundane items like foodstuffs, a blanket, a jacket, and a gun is a less-interesting story than plundering ships filled with Spanish bullion or cutthroats serving as the soldiers in a holy war in the islands of the Mediterranean.[1]

Janice Thomson argues that modern states' expansion of authority and control over demarcated territory is what led to the regulation and ultimate ban on non-state violence from pirates, privateers, mercenaries, and filibusters. Laws and regulations can always change and allow for the decentralization of violence, but Thomson contends that the public mind thinks of these practices as unconscionable alongside the modern, republican nation-state.[2] Modern empires and nation-states abandoned claims of divine mandates to rule for popular mandates earned by offering security and prosperity to their peoples, and the acknowledgment of piracy would weaken their claim to legitimacy.

There are reports spanning into the early twentieth century. Tülay Artan provides an example sourced from a traveler account. In the first decade of the twentieth century pirates raided a town in the Datça Peninsula and carried off their prize with little resistance. Half a century prior, locals still feared pirates and avoided placing their shops on the waterfront to distance themselves from potential raids. This suggests that pirate raids had become less frequent by this period. Artan joins Thomson in attributing the end of piracy in the region to the rise of the modern state.[3] The last Mediterranean-based document relevant to this study appears in 1910 when Ottoman authorities sent motorboats to monitor the coasts of the Aydın and Salonica provinces to prevent piracy and smuggling.[4] With a slightly broader geographic scope, the last clear incident of piracy occurred in April 1919 in the town of Fatsa on the Black Sea coast of Anatolia. One month before Greece landed troops in İzmir, marking the outbreak of the Greco-Turkish War, three pirates from a gang of fifteen Ottoman Greeks were captured after demanding ransom from a local household, and failing to receive payment, attacked and wounded a child with their firearms.[5] The few registered cases beyond that are obscured by uncertainties of the Greco-Turkish war and the upheaval of Atatürk's campaign to create the nation-state of Turkey.

From an academic standpoint, many of the contributions the study of piracy has to offer in understanding what turns men to violent thievery has already been covered by studies of banditry. Some explanations are found in economic pressure,[6] a culture of honor and violence,[7] kin-group pressure,[8] state weakness,[9] primitive rebellion,[10] and unemployment stemming from military demobilization, loss of land, and mass urban migration.[11] Nathan Brown has shown the political use of denying banditry's existence from the narrative to legitimize both the colonial and indigenous state's rule over a territory.[12] That piracy has been successfully erased from the narrative during a period when Britain colonized or otherwise inserted itself into the affairs of the states of the Eastern Mediterranean is a poignant reminder of their successful cleansing of the historical memory. All involved parties, be they Greek, Ottoman, or British, were concerned with making their subjects feel like their state could better protect them from outlawry and violence than their competitors. If people feel like outlaws are ever-present, they question if the state functions as intended or if there is a better alternative to govern them. No state wanted to appear weak.

Piracy in the Atlantic was also believed to have largely been squashed after its heyday in the early eighteenth century by the expansion of the British Royal Navy. Scholars of the Atlantic and the Mediterranean were in unison in sequestering off piracy to the early modern era and attributing its defeat to a sudden surge in Western warships.[13] Guy Chet has challenged this narrative in the Atlantic and demonstrated that in that region piracy continued into the nineteenth century. Violent maritime crime declined as peace stabilized the region and the economy improved. For him, piracy ends in the Atlantic Ocean with the passing of the 1856 Paris Declaration Respecting Maritime Law.[14] In the Mediterranean, piracy carried on for another half century.

This book is not the first academic work to cite cases of Mediterranean piracy after 1830. There have been a small number of articles that have referred to pirate raids late in the century but did not contextualize them among broader trends concerning piracy.[15] Vice Admiral K. Paizis-Paradelis of the Hellenic Navy briefly argued, without providing evidence, that pirates pillaged the Anatolian coast in 1850 and that small-scale pirate operations occurred in Greek territorial waters in the middle of the second half of the nineteenth century when the Greek central state was weakened by constitutional and political changes.[16] Although he does not explicitly mention it, he refers to the surge in domestic piracy recorded in the chronicles of the Hellenic Navy during the interregnum period of 1862–3.[17] Paizis-Paradelis's framework would be convincing if properly proven, but his contribution has largely been ignored by the scholarship on Greek and Mediterranean piracy due to the omission of evidence.

Spyridon Argyros wrote the one academic work that focuses on piracy that shows evidence of a single pirate raid in the Aegean that occurred after the dust of revolution had settled. In 1860, Greek pirates were raiding Ottoman Limnos and had already attacked the wealthy village Portianon and tortured the family of the *Rum* Efthimios Kellari. When they approached the village Atsiki, the villagers deceptively greeted the pirates with gifts and alcohol, distracting them while they rang the church bells to summon gendarmes from the local Ottoman garrison. Upon their arrival, the Ottoman troops slew three of the pirates, including their leader, and drove the rest away to the jubilation of the local villagers.[18] Argyros does not contextualize this 1860 raid as part of a broader continuation of piracy after the revolution. Instead, he treats it as a mere curiosity.

This book is the first study of piracy itself that corrects the story of piracy's decline in the region. One common and useful method for telling history is to use a chrono-thematic narrative. By assigning a main theme to a period of time, students of history are often better able to discern a main characteristic for each place and time.[19] The downside of this method is that it can distort or cover up blemishes in that narrative. In this case, corsairing has been a dominant theme in the discussion of the early modern Mediterranean. It was a useful foil to discussing themes of conflict, sovereignty, international relations, religion, maritime commerce, and population movements (renegades going to North Africa and ransom networks). Because most non-state maritime raiding in the early modern Mediterranean could be categorized as *corso*, the relatively few scholars who have the languages necessary to conduct research in the Ottoman archives have neglected studying other forms of piracy after corsairing societies entered the dustbin of history. The era of imperial negotiations with violent groups of the periphery had passed, and the nineteenth century was to mark the era of states' consolidation of power.[20] Pirates did not generate the abundant archival paper trail that semi-legal corsairs did, nor did they fit this grand narrative put forth both by the states themselves and the historians that followed. But they did exist, and even if they did not actively consider themselves to be what Eric Hobsbawm has coined "primitive rebels" consciously resisting expanding state powers, their very existence creating violence at the boundaries of state reach at least unconsciously contested state centralization.

The Ottoman and Greek engagement with pirates conform with recent scholarship that grants historical agency to regional actors which were able to pursue their own agendas independent from and in some cases with greater efficacy than foreign imperial powers. Mostafa Minawi shows the Ottoman capability to compete with Western powers when dealing with third-party actors in establishing influence in Africa proving the Ottoman Empire acted as an "agent" rather than an "object" of imperialist history in the late nineteenth century.[21] During the same period, Greek and Ottoman officials also acted as agents in the Aegean when controlling local maritime marauders either through force or co-option. At the same time, Greek and Ottoman officials did not act alone; they also interfaced with imperial navies that patrolled the waters of the globe.

This work eschews the frameworks of imperial, colonial, and national history in favor of a transnational approach. We can only understand international phenomena such as piracy when we observe from multiple perspectives. When Western warships showed up, did they accomplish their goal of securing the seas for passing trade? Was one state able to consistently control another through asymmetrical power relations? Were Greek or Ottoman officials able to act with full independence when pursuing pirates past maritime borders? The answer to all these questions is no. Traditional national histories focus on one country or ethnic group, or at best simply compare a topic in various countries or groups. Historians once cast large, multiethnic empires of the Ottomans and Habsburgs as "prisoners of nations" and told teleological narratives which legitimated the nation-states of today. It is only recently that historians have begun to write on topics in a way that weaves together different regions of an empire and give agency to local actors who act within an international context in a framework that does not favor the imperial center.[22] This transnational approach has allowed research into topics that a nationalist framework would thoroughly distort, such as figures who expressed national identities other than those that exist today or who lived in borderland zones and were deeply involved in the formation of multiple national identities.[23] The Greek and Ottoman Aegean was a nexus that connected the nations and states of the Eastern Mediterranean to faraway empires. It was a zone of contested identity, where maritime marauders manipulated governments into claiming them as patriots to protect themselves from persecution; likewise, governments manipulated the same marauders to irredentist ends.

During the nineteenth century, Greece relied on military irregulars like pirates and bandits to act as filibusters and advance its claims over Ottoman lands.[24] Irregular warfare continued to be Greece's preferred mode of belligerence throughout the Macedonia struggle, ending only with the Balkan Wars. The few remaining pirates of the Mediterranean were no longer useful to the Greek Kingdom after the regular army had succeeded in doubling Greek territory where irregulars had failed. Within the Ottoman Empire, Enver Pasha did not do away with irregular troops so much as transition them into special forces: the *Teşkilat-ı Mahsusa* (Special Organization). Special agents like Eşref

Kuşçubaşı remained under closer control of military leaders than irregulars while allowing the state to retain some distance from the fallout of whether or not special forces obeyed the rules of war.²⁵ During the First World War, the Ottoman regular military had collapsed spectacularly; most soldiers deserted their posts and went home, creating an abundance of armed, disenchanted military men.²⁶ In the final years of the sultans' reign over Anatolia, a culture of paramilitarism had emerged where both locals and the state formed militia-like gangs that partook in a bloody struggle to shape the future of the region.²⁷ Decades after privateering had been outlawed, states were still experimenting with ways to take military action but shed responsibility.

Archival documentation shows that Mediterranean piracy slowly declines until ceasing with the fall of the Ottoman Empire. Ottoman archives end there for obvious reasons. Greek archives end because they restrict access to documents over a century old. This begs the question. Did violent maritime crime in the region fully end after the fallout of the First World War and ensuing Greco-Turkish War settled, did it continue in some capacity, or did it transform into or become labeled as something else?

Appendix

Thomas Wyse's Critique of the Greek Trial of Pirates

YE 1854/55/1 A, #4964, pp. 116–30. Athens, August 30, 1854. Letter in English from Thomas Wyse, the British Ambassador, to Mr. A. Mavrokordatos, Greek Minister of Foreign Affairs.

I have the honour to acknowledge the receipt of your official Notes of the 9/21 and 12/24 Instant with their enclosures, in answer to mine of 25th July, respecting the encounter of her Majesty's Steamer *Triton*, with a Boat, filled with armed Greeks, off the North East Coast of Euboea, and the complaint made of their escape, with the permission of the local authorities, with a request on my part that an investigation should be instituted without delay, into the statement in question.

In reply you inform me that such an investigation had taken place by order of the Greek Government under the direction of the local Authorities, and that the result had been that the parties had not been held quietly, and you enclose me the depositions in which this conclusion is formed.

After a minute analysis of this evidence (rendered difficult by its voluminous character, and the careless manner in which it seems to have been collected and drawn up), I must confess that it presents to my mind any other impression than that of a conviction of its accuracy or the good faith of the persons to whom it was entrusted.

The first point which strikes me is the omission or denial of the important charge of Lieutenant Lloyd on which the whole case rests, and the little pains taken to ascertain how far either are well grounded.

For about a week previous to the arrival of the *Triton*, a Pirate boat, is stated by Mr. Leeves (copy of whose letter, I have the honour to enclose), to have been seen hovering about the village of Corbatzi, and have been fired on by the coast guard at daylight on the 26th June while cruising off the North East Coast of Euboea. Lieutenant Lloyd of Her Majesty's Steamer *Triton* informs Captain

Marios in his official letter (copy of which I have also the honour to enclose), that he observed a caique to shorten sail and pull in for the land. Chase was immediately given, and a boat was sent to overhawl her. It was found that the crew had deserted her, and retired to the Bush, and upon the Boats boarding her, a number of Greeks well-armed, made threatening gestures by pointing guns, and pistols at the Boat's Crew, where upon this immediately returned to the ship and being reinforced by another boat manned and armed, pulled in shore, and on nearing the land, a sharp fire was opened on them from the Jungle, which was returned with shell and shot from the ship, and small arms from the boats, under cover of which the caique was towed off to the ship.

Knowing several of the Proprietors in the vicinity, from whom he had previously learned that a horde of pirates were constantly infecting the adjacent creeks, Lt. Lloyd went to inform them of his capture of the boat, and that the pirates still remained on their lands, without the means of escape, and it was arranged that they should muster the peasantry and proceed to the point where the pirates had retired, and that he himself should return to the spot by Sea.

Lt. Lloyd adds, that by this means 15 of these lawless fellows were captured, all armed with guns, pistols, and knives, that they were given over to the Greek Police, and marched off to Oreos; He immediately returned to Volo.

Now this statement which is circumstantial and clear, on their first being questioned who they were, and what was their business by Balagiacopoulos, "Special Assesseur" of the Village of Agriovatani, is limited to the assertion that they had been chased by an English Ship, and compelled to land. When afterwards examined, the same Assessor of Agriovatani (who could have known nothing but what he heard from these men), on being asked at his examination whether any of the 15 men had fired on the English, replies promptly ("No, they did not fire"), (όχι δεν επυρωβώλησαν). At Corbatzi the 15 men repeated their story but apparently at greater length. They stated that on their way to Oreos for which place they were bound, they fell in with an English Steamer, which sent out a boat to examine them. They affirmed that they had showed their papers and told them they belonged to Karitasso's band and had come from Macedonia. The boat, on this, returned to the Steamer, but a few instants after, made its appearance a second time, accompanied by another boat, both fully armed, and being pursued by these boats, and fired on by Cannon from the Steamer, they were compelled to land and abandon their boat. On the Assessor of Corbatzi asking them if they had offered any resistance to the English, they replied

> No Brother, if we had wished to offer resistance, and especially to the English, we should not have come here, nor do we know for what motive they fired on us and why they pursued us in such a manner since we showed them our papers and they saw we were honest men, and the more so, as we were in a position to resist them had we wished them not to approach us.

In their examination before the commissioner of Police of Istiaion. C Nicolaides by name they declared, they had been stopped and subsequently set at liberty by the *Triton*.

Though the facts stated by Lieutenant Lloyd were in great measure before them in my letter, and this evidence is not only at variance with the statement of Lieutenant Lloyd but with that of each other no cross examination or confronting of witnesses or any other means usually adopted to elicit truth, were adopted; of the various depositions taken, not one is from any person who had been witness of the encounter nor from any of the 15 men in the caique, but from the assessors or local authorities themselves, who repeat hearsay evidence, or verbal evidence given to themselves, they having a direct interest in quashing evidence or modifying it so as to furnish a case to their own advantage.

The same inaccuracy or looseness is to be detected in their statements respecting the capture and detention of the men in question.

Taking the evidence however even as it stands, it does not appear that they had, as they have stated, had of their own accord presented themselves.

The assessor of Agrobotani goes out with his armed villagers to pursue them he takes them with him to Agriovotani, and then sends them on under care of a national guard (to whom he entrusts a letter for the baron) to Kerochori. On their way they are met by the assessor of Corbatzi Demetrius Louzos by name accompanied by Mr. Wild the Proprietor of Corbatzi, a gendarme and a number of armed villagers, in consequence of the information received from the Lt. Lloyd who had come round to Corbatzi that the Pirates were on shore without any means of escape. Mr. Wild however having gone off to the *Triton* where he received from Lt. Lloyd a detailed account of the affray, and which

Mr. Wild afterwards repeated to Mr. Leeves, he found that the 15 men who had been given in charge to the gendarme and the gendarme to whom they had been entrusted and whom Mr. Wild had directed to wait his return, had all gone on to Kerochori. On the same evening Lt. Lloyd sailed for Volo, with the Caique in tow, and under the full impression they the 15 men had, under the escort of the Greek Gendarmerie or Police, been given over to the proper Greek Authorities, to be dealt with accordingly. On their arrival however the same evening at Kerochori, it would seem that their number had unaccountably diminished from 15 to 9. They were, after a short and inefficient examination by the Commissary of Police, recognized as "Patriots" and not as "Pirates," and received passports from the Police, five for Atalanta, and the other four for Lamia.

It is to be observed that the assessors of Agriovotani and Corbatzi neither read nor write.

There is sufficient in what I have just stated to justify distrust in both, in the proceedings and the animus in which they have been conducted, and to call from the Greek Govt., who can only have on object, the sincere and vigorous accomplishment of the ends of Justice, a fresh inquiry under different guidance, into the whole affair.

Notes

Chapter 1

1 Alexandre Dumas, *Le Comte de Monte-Cristo*, Vol. 2 (Paris: Michel Levy Freres, Libraires Editeurs, 1861), 132–3.

2 Historians of Atlantic piracy have debated the merit of using a class-struggle framework to cast pirates as resisting the ever-expanding reach of state. Peter Linebaugh and Marcus Rediker examine the early modern trans-Atlantic maritime working class through the metaphor of the Hydra of Lerna. Each of the heads was one of the divisions of labor constituting a menacing whole which Atlantic rulers seeking to prop up a new capitalist order attempted to slay. At times the proletariat appeared docile and slavish "hewers of wood and drawers of water" or as rebellious and self-active—the many-headed hydra. Rediker and Linebaugh identify four phases of class struggle in the revolutionary Atlantic. The first took place in the commons from 1600 to 1640 when English capitalism spread and expropriated workers throughout the British Empire and its colonies. The second phase occurred on the plantations from 1640 to 1680, when failed uprisings against English capitalism occurred in both the metropole and the colonies, securing the plantation as a foundation of the new economic order. The next phase took place 1680–1760, surrounding the golden age of Atlantic piracy, on board sailing ships which had features of both the factory and the prison. During this period, market oriented maritime states or *hydrarchies* consolidated and stabilized Atlantic capitalism and the slave trade. Rediker and Linebaugh posit that pirate communities endangered the slave trade with their alternative way of life: multiracial, democratic, and autonomous; thus, they were exterminated. This period was followed by a wave of multiethnic worker and slave uprisings in the Americas. From 1760 to 1835 revolts continued until the United States, Haiti, France, Ireland, and England implemented serious reforms, eventually leading to the abolition of impressment and plantation slavery. See, Peter Linebaugh and Marcus Rediker, *The Many-Headed Hydra: Sailors, Slaves, Commoners, and the Hidden History of the Revolutionary Atlantic* (Beacon Press, 2013), 328–9.

3 The beginnings of this branch of discourse can be found in the works of Edward Said. See, Edward W. Said, *Orientalism* (New York: Vintage, 1979), and Edward W. Said, *Culture and Imperialism* (New York: Alfred A Knopf, Inc, 1993).
4 James E. Wadsworth, *Global Piracy: A Documentary History of Seaborne Banditry* (Bloomsbury Publishing, 2019).
5 See, Michael Talbot, "'Ill-Treated by Friends': Ottoman Responses to British Privateering in the Mid-18th Century" (Presentation, *Sylvia Ioannou Foundation Conference: Corsairs and Pirates in the Eastern Mediterranean, 15th-19th c.*, Athens, Greece October 18, 2014).
6 Michael Talbot, "Separating the Waters from the Sea: The Place of Islands in Ottoman Maritime Territoriality during the Eighteenth Century," *Princeton Papers: Interdisciplinary Journal of Middle Eastern Studies* 18 (2018): 61–86. The "Sublime Porte" or *Bab-ı Ali* refers to the center of Ottoman rule, much like how the White House refers to the center of American government.
7 The disagreement over maritime borders almost led to armed conflict in late 2019 when Turkey and Libya ignored the 1982 United Nations Convention on the Law of the Sea to jointly conduct energy exploration in waters south of Crete, which according to said convention lay within Greece's maritime boundaries. Turkey is a non-signatory and Libya signed but never ratified their participation. Libya's government was split in a civil war at the time of the 2019 agreement. Greece has threatened to fire upon any Turkish energy-exploration vessel that enters the territory without express permission, but as of 2020 no violence has broken out.
8 Louis H. J. Sicking et al., "Islands, Pirates, Privateers and the Ottoman Empire in the Early Modern Mediterranean," in *Seapower, Technology and Trade: Studies in Turkish Maritime History*, ed. Dejanirah Couto, Feza Günergun, and Maria Pia Pedani Fabris (Piri Reis University Publications, 2014), 241.
9 Emrah Safa Gürkan, *Sultanın Korsanları: Osmanlı Akdenizi'nde Gazâ, Yağma ve Esaret, 1500–1700* [*Pirates of the Sultan: Holy War, Looting, and Captivity in the Ottoman Mediterranean*] (İstanbul: Kronik Kitap, 2018), 52.
10 Samuel P. Huntington, *The Clash of Civilizations and the Remaking of World Order* (Penguin Books India, 1996).
11 For example, in Molly Greene's study of how Ottoman Greek merchant navigated the religion-centered conflict in the Mediterranean, she contends that "there is the settled topography of a (mostly) Christian northern shore and a (mostly) Muslim southern rim. Given that ideological and political warfare between Christianity and Islam was a central feature of European and Near Eastern

history for many centuries (and is still with us today), it was inevitable that the Mediterranean border between the two civilizations would be a zone of permanent hostility." Molly Greene, *Catholic Pirates and Greek Merchants: A Maritime History of the Early Modern Mediterranean* (Princeton University Press, 2010), 15–16.

12 Richard Harding's discussion of confessional politics and early modern navies centers primarily on Catholic-Protestant hostilities, offering a reminder that such debates do not only apply to the Mediterranean. Richard Harding, *Modern Naval History: Debates and Prospects* (Bloomsbury Publishing, 2015), 66–75. Privateers and corsairs raided across both political and confessional lines.

13 Güneş Işıksel, "Imperial Limits and Early Modernity: Borderland Clients of the Ottoman Empire and the 'Well-Protected Dominions'," *Journal of the Ottoman and Turkish Studies Association* 7, no. 1 (2020): 50.

14 Joshua M. White, *Piracy and Law in the Ottoman Mediterranean* (Stanford: Stanford University Press, 2017), 33.

15 There are several different appellations for Hellenic peoples. In general, languages based in Europe, to the west of Greece, call Hellenes some variant of Greek, from the ancient *Graiki* tribe that settled in southern Italy. Likewise, Near Eastern languages often call Hellenes some variant of *Yunan*, from the Ionians who settled in western Anatolia. Until modern times, the most common way Greeks and their neighbors identified them was as Romans (Turkish: *Rum*), an identity that was typically also attached to adherence to Orthodox Christianity, the official religion of the Eastern Roman Empire. As this was not primarily an ethnic or linguistic marker, *Rum* identity was often extended to other Orthodox Christian peoples. As national Orthodox Churches formed and broke off from the Patriarchate, *Rum* identity gradually shrunk to those who would still identify as Greek Orthodox, which could still include non-Greeks.

16 The root of *ızbandut* comes from the Turkicization of the Italian word *sbandito*, meaning an exiled or banished person.

17 In ancient Greek usage, *leistes* (bandits, from the root meaning "to seize") and *peirates* (pirates, from the root meaning "to attack") were interchangeable and could describe non-state raiders on either land or sea. Aaron Beek argues that, as has been shown for later periods by Janice Thomson, pirates and bandits should be grouped with mercenaries as military entrepreneurs used in state-building projects labeling raiders as legitimate or illegitimate. Aaron Beek, "Freelance Warfare and Illegitimacy: The Historians' Portrayal of Bandits, Pirates, Mercenaries and Politicians" (PhD diss., University of Minnesota, 2015).

18 The use of *Katharevousa* by the state and its employees as early as the revolutionary period and beyond was a performance of a particular interpretation of what it meant to be Greek: that Greeks have not been "tainted" by history since ancient or Byzantine times. The official use of *Katharevousa* continued until the collapse of the junta in 1974, and its counterpart remained the common spoken tongue of the masses. After almost two centuries of state preference for *Katharevousa*, the common tongue of Greeks would win out as the language of the state. With demotic, loan words from Turkish and other languages would remain in the Greek language, as they had for centuries.

19 See the interrogations of suspected pirates in, Genika Archeia tou Kratous (Greek General State Archives, GAK), K, 47, B, Φ II.

20 Piracy could also prove to be a source of wealth as the communities in which pirates offloaded their goods became more deeply integrated into the global economy through the black market. Selling goods in peripheral markets increased the spread of capitalist penetration outside of the economic core. Thomas W. Gallant argues that military entrepreneurs were "both products of and contributors to the advancement and consolidation of capitalism and modern states." See, Thomas W. Gallant, "Brigandage, Piracy, Capitalism, and State-Formation: Transnational Crime from a Historical World Systems Perspective," in *States and Illegal Practices*, ed. Josiah McC. Heyman (New York: Berg, 1999): 50–1. He proposes that all men of violence were able to cross the boundaries between legality and illegality, performing the same function with different labels: that is, tax-collecting versus robbery. Many scholars have adopted this framework by looking at piracy as an occupation that men, and occasionally women, drifted in and out of, as opposed to being a lifelong career, or worse yet, a form of identity. The scholarship that still refers to pirates as a social group tends to be engaged with romanticized ideas of pirate utopias and proto-democracies. For example, see, Peter Lamborn Wilson, *Pirate Utopias: Moorish Corsairs & European Renegadoes* (Autonomedia, 2003); Linebaugh and Rediker, *The Many-Headed Hydra*. These discourses were inspired by the debate surrounding the social banditry model developed by Eric Hobsbawm, first in a chapter in his book *Primitive Rebels* and then more fully in his seminal study, *Bandits*. See, Eric Hobsbawm, *Primitive Rebels: Studies in Archaic Forms of Social Movement in the 19th and 20th Centuries* (Manchester University Press, 1971); Eric Hobsbawm, *Bandits* (Hachette UK, 2010). Gallant argues that rather than employing Hobsbawm's discreet categories for social banditry, it would be more productive to use a

world systems framework of core, periphery, and semi-periphery, and terms such as labor exploitation, surplus extraction, and capital accumulation. This allows scholars to not only examine pirates in their own right, or only focus on the harm that they inflicted on their victims, but also offer evidence that piracy and banditry could improve economic situations in the countryside by increasing monetization, encouraging marketization, and providing a venue for upward mobility. They also aided in the formation of centralized states either by offering their military services or by providing a target for states which sought to exert their claim to a monopoly on legitimate violence. See, Gallant, "Brigandage, Piracy, Capitalism, and State-Formation," 28, 50–1. It was common for states to use military entrepreneurs in both ways. In the cases of the Spanish coast guard, the later incarnation of Ottoman janissaries (Turkish: *yeniçeri*), and the Greek *klefts*, non-state military entrepreneurs were hired to create order on the frontier. Once the state was able to mobilize a regular army, it turned its new forces on the old irregulars to "neutralize" its old, autocephalous, decentralized forces.

21 See, Mark G. Hanna, *Pirate Nests and the Rise of the British Empire, 1570–1740* (Chapel Hill: UNC Press, 2015), 8.
22 Eyal Ginio, "Piracy and Redemption in the Aegean Sea during the First Half of the Eighteenth Century," *Turcica* 33 (2001): 135–47.
23 See, Daniel Heller-Roazen, *The Enemy of All: Piracy and the Law of Nations* (New York: Zone Books, 2009), 51; and Manuel Tröster, "Roman Hegemony and Non-State Violence: A Fresh Look at Pompey's Campaign against the Pirates," *Greece & Rome* 56, no. 1 (2009): 14–33.
24 See, Alfred P. Rubin, *The Law of Piracy* (Newport, Rhode Island: US Naval War College Press, 1988), 220–57; and Sandy J.C. Liu, "Violence and Piratical/Surreptitious Activities Associated with the Chinese Communities in the Melaka–Singapore Region (1780–1840)," in *Piracy and Surreptitious Activities in the Malay Archipelago and Adjacent Seas, 1600–1840*, ed. Tedd Y. H. Sim (Singapore: Springer, 2014).
25 See chapter 2, "Treacherous Places: Atlantic Riverine Regions and the Law of Treason" in Lauren A. Benton, *A Search for Sovereignty: Law and Geography in European Empires, 1400–1900* (Cambridge: Cambridge University Press, 2010), 40–103.
26 For a general political and territorial history of the Ottoman Empire from foundation to fall, see, Caroline Finkel, *Osman's Dream: The History of the Ottoman Empire* (Hachette UK, 2007).

27 In Ottoman Turkish, the Mediterranean literally translates as White Sea. The Ottoman Turkish either borrows from Arabic (*bahr*—sea) and Persian (*sefid*—white, as well as the genitive construction used) or uses the Turkish form *Akdeniz* (*ak*: white; *deniz*: sea). The choice of terms was used was up to scribal discretion. With the loss of southern tip of the Balkan Peninsula in the middle of the nineteenth century, the Mediterranean *eyalet* was reorganized into a pared down version, the *Vilayet-i Bahr-i Sefid*.

28 Algeria was named as an island province either for having a few islands off the coast that have collapsed into the sea, or as part of the larger Arabic identity of the whole region as being isolated with desert to the south and sea to the north. Arabic uses the same word for island and peninsula, effectively meaning land mostly surrounded by water.

29 Joshua White defines the Ottoman Mediterranean as a unified legal space "dictated by the legal institutional limits of İstanbul's reach within the greater empire… İstanbul did not appoint judges in North Africa as it did for the rest of the Ottoman Mediterranean, and the North Africans followed the opinions of their own jurists above those of the Ottomans' chief jurist in İstanbul, whose opinions were supposed to have the force of law throughout the empire." France and England treated the North African vassals of the Ottoman Empire as independent political entities; the European states disregarded their diplomatic status with the Sublime Porte and conduct both diplomatic and military missions against the pirate regencies. Venice alone would respect its treaties with the Ottoman sultan. See chapters three and four of, White, *Piracy and Law*, 3, 13, 103–80. This book will use the current name for the great city on the Bosphorus. İstanbul only became the official city name in the early years of the Turkish Republic. During the Ottoman era, the city was known as Constantinople in English and Konstantiniyye in Ottoman Turkish, both from the Greek Κωνσταντινούπολις.

30 Piracy tended to resurface in the same areas over thousands of years when geographical conditions that favored it were combined with decentralized states or vibrant trade routes. James Wadsworth argues that the main factor that would allow piracy to be active in an area was the presence of a black market where pirates would be able to fence their ill-gotten goods. Wadsworth, *Global Piracy*, 12.

31 Molly Greene, *A Shared World: Christians and Muslims in the Early Modern Mediterranean* (Princeton University Press, 2000), 13–18.

32 The size and diversity of experiences within Ottoman domains pose a challenge to historians of the empire. Scholars of the late Ottoman Empire who offer a

unified narrative focus upon the modernizing vision of state elites or integration into the world economy. Another common approach is to approach the local experiences as resistance to imperial projects. Cem Emrence suggests examining the Ottoman path to modernity as distinct in different zones of the empire. Rather than take a national or religious framework, Emrence separates the empire into the coasts, interior, and frontier. He demonstrates that the primary path to modernity was integration into the world economy in the coastal provinces, political development and reform in the interior (primarily meaning the capital of İstanbul), and contention in the land frontiers. See, Cem Emrence, *Remapping the Ottoman Middle East: Modernity, Imperial Bureaucracy and Islam* (I.B. Tauris, 2015). Within Emrence's framework, this study focuses on the coastal provinces of the Ottoman Empire and modern Greece. While economic integration and development has a large effect on limiting levels of piracy, it is not the only factor. Maritime marauders only cease to harry the coastline when both licit economic opportunities are available and local, regional, and international authorities dissuade them to profit through plunder. All too often, it was in the interest of a state to allow naval military entrepreneurs to act as filibusters and sow chaos among their rivals.

33 The domestic trade networks of the Ottoman Empire were largely restricted to the three seas the empire included—the Black, Red, and White (Mediterranean) seas. Daniel Panzac identifies four major characteristics of Ottoman maritime trade in the eighteenth century. First, Ottoman domestic trade was roughly double that of international commerce. Major regional industries, such as silk and textile production in Syria for example, were important primarily for satisfying internal, domestic demand. The second major characteristic Panzac reveals is the dominant position held by Muslim charterers in inter-Ottoman trade. Muslim merchants would rent or lease large numbers of European ships for trade throughout the Ottoman Mediterranean. Third, Panzac points to the growing importance of non-Muslims in Ottoman international trade during the eighteenth century. Armenians nearly monopolized the role of banker and money exchanger, and in 1750 controlled the mints in İstanbul. Greeks meanwhile were able to enter maritime trade markets at the expense of European merchants. Panzac attributes the ascendency of non-Muslims in European trade to their roles as brokers in the Levantine trade. The final characteristic Panzac points out is the increasing penetration of European mercantilism into the empire. Simply put, the Ottoman economy was becoming increasingly integrated into the world economy, which was driven by greater demand, and thus higher

prices, for cotton for the booming European textile industry, and increasing New World competition for the traditional Levantine commodities like sugar and coffee. Economic instability led the Sublime Porte to allow the circulation of stable foreign currencies within the empire. The Ottoman long eighteenth century ended in the 1820s and 1830s with the political fragmentation caused by the Greek Revolution, Mehmed Ali's uprising in Egypt, and the colonization of Algiers, all of which led to the reformation of maritime trade relations and a weakening Ottoman role in the world economy. See, Daniel Panzac, "International and Domestic Maritime Trade in the Ottoman Empire during the 18th Century," *International Journal of Middle East Studies* 24, no. 2 (1992): 189–90, 202–3.

34 Readers interested in the effects of the environment and topography upon society can find several studies in the vein of the *Annales* school of thought. Environmental features would lead humans to move and act in certain ways. In this case, merchants would sail along certain passageways that were relatively direct while remaining easily navigable. The predictability of their route also made them vulnerable to maritime predation. Fernand Braudel is one of the earliest scholars of the *Annales* school, and his work specializes in the Mediterranean. He is among the first historians to attempt to integrate the Near East and North Africa as equally important as Europe in the history of the Mediterranean region. For his discussion of the sea, see, Fernand Braudel, *The Mediterranean and the Mediterranean World in the Age of Philip II* (University of California Press, 1995), 103–67.

35 The islets and peninsulas of the Aegean naturally formed a number of "pinch-points" where pirates would haunt passing shipping. Andrew Bevan and James Conolly, *Mediterranean Islands, Fragile Communities and Persistent Landscapes: Antikythera in Long-Term Perspective* (Cambridge University Press, 2013), 193–4.

36 Martin W. Lewis and Kären E. Wigen, *The Myth of Continents: A Critique of Metageography* (University of California Press, 1997).

37 Amedeo Policante, "Barbary Legends on the Mediterranean Frontier: Corsairs, Pirates and the Shifting Bounds of the International Community," in *Corsairs and Pirates in the Eastern Mediterranean, Fifteenth-Nineteenth Centuries*, ed. Gelina Harlaftis (Athens: Sylvia Ioannou Foundation, 2016), 141–50.

38 Lotfi Ben Rejeb, "'The General Belief of the World': Barbary as Genre and Discourse in Mediterranean History," *European Review of History—Revue européenne d'histoire* 19, no. 1 (2012): 15–31.

39 Frank Lambert, *The Barbary Wars: American Independence in the Atlantic World* (Macmillan, 2005), 108.

40 Discussions of Mediterranean piracy tend to focus on the early modern period and end in 1830. Even research that claims to extend into the nineteenth century only does so reluctantly, preferring to stay solidly within the early modern period. For an example of a foundation set of works gathered into one volume adhering to such tendencies, see, Michel Fontenay, *La Méditerranée entre la Croix et le Croissant: Navigation, commerce, course et piraterie (xvie-xixe siècle)* (Paris: Classiques Garnier, 2010). Historians of Mediterranean piracy view this period of Western intervention in North Africa as the end of an era, and Daniel Panzac has even included that designation in the title of his book. See, Daniel Panzac, *The Barbary Corsairs: The End of a Legend, 1800–1820* (Brill, 2005).
41 See, Peregrine Horden and Nicholas Purcell, *The Corrupting Sea: A Study of Mediterranean History* (Wiley-Blackwell, 2000); and, Daniel Hershenzon, *The Captive Sea: Slavery, Communication, and Commerce in Early Modern Spain and the Mediterranean* (University of Pennsylvania Press, 2018).
42 Daniel Hershenzon, "Towards a Connected History of Bondage in the Mediterranean: Recent Trends in the Field," *History Compass* 15, no. 8 (2017).
43 For centuries in Mediterranean Christendom, wealthy men purchased their freedom with their own personal fortunes. Starting in 1581, Pope Gregory XIII set up an institution for the ransoming of Catholic prisoners called the *Opera Pia Redenzione de' Schiavi*. See, Braudel, *The Mediterranean*, 887. In Tunis, certain mercantile communities established a special tax to pay the ransom of captured community members. Catholic monks could enter redemptive holy orders formed with the goal of redeeming captives. The Trinitarians used one third of their alms to ransom Christians from Muslim captors. The Mercedarian order, sometimes referred to as the cult of Our Lady of Ransom, was theoretically willing to exchange one of its members to free a brother of the faith from Saracen slavery. Despite the renown that this cult enjoyed, the only French Mercedarian to actually indenture himself was Sebastien Bruyère, who was held hostage in Algiers from 1643 to 1652. See, Gillian Weiss, *Captives and Corsairs: France and Slavery in the Early Modern Mediterranean* (Stanford: Stanford University Press, 2011), 12, 232. As a pious institution, its main goal was to gain converts in the ever-expanding battle for souls. Much to the chagrin of the church, increased contact with Islam often resulted in Christians turning renegade and converting to Islam. For an example of a Catholic priest going renegade, see Ariel Salzmann, "A Travelogue Manqué? The Accidental Itinerary of a Maltese Priest in the Seventeenth Century Mediterranean," in *A Faithful Sea: The Religious Cultures of the Mediterranean, 1200–1700*, ed. Adnan Ahmed Husain and Katherine Elizabeth Fleming (Oneworld Publications Limited, 2007), 149–72. States such

as France theoretically tolerated individual conversions because of its treaties with the Ottomans, but in practice local consuls strongly discouraged the practice and interfered with apostasy. See, Wilson, *Pirate Utopias*, 13. French and Venetian consuls also took a proactive role in assuring not just the release, but oftentimes the escape of Catholic prisoners held in the Ottoman Empire. See, Mark Mazower, *Salonica, City of Ghosts: Christians, Muslims and Jews 1430–1950* (Vintage, 2007), 104. Protestantism meant northern Europe would not have access to the Catholic Mercedarian and Trinitarian redemptive orders. For the English case, see, Linda Colley, *Captives: Britain, Empire and the World 1600–1850* (Random House, 2003), 54. For the case of Denmark, see, Erik Gøbel, "The Danish 'Algerian Sea Passes', 1747–1838: An Example of Extraterritorial Production of 'Human Security'/Die 'Algerischen Seepässe' Dänemarks, 1747–1838: Ein Beispiel der extraterritorialen Produktion humaner Sicherheit," *Historical Social Research/Historische Sozialforschung* 35, no. 4 (2010).

44 Notable examples include the Jewish population of Ragusa (present-day Dubrovnik, Croatia) and the monks of the Hagia Monastery on Andros. In the Ottoman-allied city-state of Ragusa, the Jewish community regularly paid ransom for Ottoman subjects. "A study of documents from the Ragusan archives which discuss ransom and captivity among the Jews of Ragusa shows us that they made a significant contribution in this field both as individuals and as a community, particularly at a time when the winds of war were blowing in the area and the Jews served as mediators between the Muslim and Christian worlds." See, Moisés Orfali, "Ragusa and Ragusan Jews in the Effort to Ransom Captives," *Mediterranean Historical Review* 17, no. 2 (2002): 27. In return, the state gave Jews preferential treatment in many matters such as consular appointments and state backing against their Christian competitors. Like the rest of the sectarian groups represented in the Mediterranean, Jews also had organizations which would ransom Jewish captives. See, Mazower, *Salonica*, 106; Yaacov Lev, *Charity, Endowments, and Charitable Institutions in Medieval Islam* (University Press of Florida, 2005), 139–40. On the island of Andros, the repeated actions of the monks of the Hagia Monastery show that in the Ottoman Empire sectarian boundaries were not insurmountable walls. Time and again the monks took action to help redeem Ottoman Muslims from a servile fate. In June of 1650 a Venetian galley had lost control of ten of its Ottoman galley slaves. Tasting freedom, the fugitives fled to nearby Andros. Reaching land was not to end their worries as Venetian ships set off in search of these fugitives. The monks of Hagia monastery hid the Muslims from the Venetian search and did what

they could to foster them back to health. When they thought it safe, they took to the sea and dropped off the Muslim escapees in the Ottoman mainland city of Karystos. The waters around the island came to be largely dominated by the Venetians who would have been none too pleased were they to catch their former slaves being transported to safety. The monks were taking a risk akin to that of smugglers transporting contraband or of pirates sailing through hostile waters. These monks repeatedly took these actions in aiding the escape of Muslim galley slaves and bringing them to safety. See, Elias Kolovos, "Insularity and Island Society in the Ottoman Context," *Turcica* 39 (2007): 104 and document 134/135 in Elias Kolovos, Yorgos Vidras, and Aris Kydonakis, *A Database of the Ottoman Documents in the Kaireios Library of the Island of Andros* (http://androsdocs.ims.forth.gr/). The cross-sectarian efforts to redeem captives in Ragusa and Andros serve as a reminder that the early modern world was not viewed entirely through sectarian eyes.

45 Colley, *Captives*, 45.
46 For example, in 1737 France ransomed seventy-five friars from Morocco for a large stash of gunpowder, a sizable sum of cash, and a trade agreement. See, Weiss, *Captives and Corsairs*, 89.
47 Prior to the second siege of Vienna in 1683, the Ottoman Empire had the most formidable military in Europe. Even after Ottoman defeat, even colonial European powers had smaller military forces than that of the Ottoman Empire, or even Morocco. See, Colley, *Captives*, 35.
48 Robert C. Davis, *Christian Slaves, Muslim Masters: White Slavery in the Mediterranean, the Barbary Coast, and Italy, 1500–1800* (New York: Palgrave Macmillan, 2003), 8–9.
49 Ginio, *Piracy and Redemption*, 142.
50 Joshua M. White, "Piracy of the Ottoman Mediterranean: Slave Laundering and Subjecthood," in *The Making of the Modern Mediterranean: Views from the South*, ed. Judith E. Tucker (University of California Press, 2019).
51 Fariba Zarinebaf, *Mediterranean Encounters: Trade and Pluralism in Early Modern Galata* (University of California Press, 2018), 286–9.
52 See, Gelina Harlaftis, "The 'Eastern Invasion': Greeks in Mediterranean Trade and Shipping in the Eighteenth and Early Nineteenth Centuries," in *Trade and Cultural Exchange in the Early Modern Mediterranean: Braudel's Maritime Legacy*, ed. Colin Heywood, Mohamed-Salah Omri, and Maria Fusaro (London and New York: Tauris Academic Studies, 2010), 239; Katerina Galani, "The Napoleonic Wars and the Disruption of Mediterranean Shipping and Trade: British, Greek

and American Merchants in Livorno," *The Historical Review/La Revue Historique* 7 (2011): 179–98; Gelina Harlaftis and Sophia Laiou, "Ottoman State Policy in Mediterranean Trade and Shipping, c. 1780–c.1820: The Rise of the Greek Owned Ottoman Merchant Fleet," in *Networks of Power in Modern Greece: Essays in Honor of John Campbell*, ed. Mark Mazower (New York, 2008): 1–44.

53 Harlaftis, "The Eastern Invasion," 244.
54 Michael Talbot, "Ottoman Seas and British Privateers: Defining Maritime Territoriality in the Eighteenth-Century Levant," in *Well-Connected Domains: Towards an Entangled Ottoman History*, ed. Pascal Firges, Tobias Graf, Christian Roth, and Gülay Tulasoğlu (Brill, 2014).
55 Liam Gauci, *In the Name of the Prince: Maltese Corsairs 1760–1798* (Heritage Malta Publishing, 2016).
56 White, *Piracy and Law*, 5.
57 Greene, *Catholic Pirates*.
58 Emrah Safa Gürkan, "Batı Akdeniz'de osmanlı korsanlığı ve gaza meselesi, [The issue of ottoman piracy and gaza in the western Mediterranean]," *Kebikeç: İnsan Bilimleri İçin Kaynak Araştırmaları Dergisi* 33 (2012): 173–204.
59 In the late eighteenth century, the entire Mediterranean felt the shockwaves of the French revolution and the rise of nationalism. "Velestinli Regas (1757–1798), considered to be one of the godfathers of the Greek national movement, and Rifa'a Rafi' al-Tahtawi, one of the earliest proponents of Arab—specifically Egyptian—identity, spent time in Paris, and they both translated key works of the French Enlightenment into Greek and Arabic respectively." See, Reşat Kasaba, "Dreams of Empire, Dreams of Nations," in *Empire to Nation: Historical Perspectives on the Making of the Modern World*, ed. Joseph W. Esherick, Hasan Kayali, and Eric Van Young (Rowman & Littlefield Publishers, 2006), 212. As Rachida Tlili-Sellaouti shows, the Ottoman Empire and revolutionary France were in dialogue as the French attempted to expand the cultural frontiers of democratic, republican values to include Ottoman Muslims. See, Rachida Tlili-Sellaouti, "La France revolutionnaire et les populations musulmanes de la Turquie d'Europe au moment de l'expedition d'Egypte: une mise a l'epreuve du cosmopolitisme," in *Ottoman Rule and the Balkans, 1760–1850*, ed. Antonis Anastasopoulos and Elias Kolovos (Rethymno, Greece: Department of History and Archaeology of the University of Crete, 2007).
60 See the Foundation Charter (*vakıf*) of the Hafiz Ahmed Agha Library in Rhodes, Greece, 1796. Translated by John Robert Barnes. *Greek Ministry of Culture, Fourth Ephorate of Byzantine Antiquities*, 1998.

61 The island of Malta produced one of the most feared bands of corsairs of the early modern period—the Knights of St. John. Ayşe Devrim Atauz offers a *longue durée* study of Malta and its role throughout history in Mediterranean commerce, piracy, and warfare. The period when the island was controlled by the Knights of St. John stands out, as it was an extra-imperial corsair-state. While not subject to any other state, Malta was dependent on external sources of food, fuel, and other necessary commodities. Thus, the Knights of St. John offered their corsairing services to various European powers in exchange for much need needed political, financial, and material support. In return, Malta served as a sort of naval school for Europeans to get experience roaming the high seas before joining their respective navies. Thus, the main difference between Maltese and North African corsairs, besides on whom they preyed and to whom they prayed, was that the Barbary corsairs provided their services to the Ottoman state, albeit inconsistently, while the knights provided their services to Christian states. Surprisingly, throughout their entire stay on Malta, the knights had only an average of five and a maximum of six galleys. This figure is surprisingly low for an island that wreaked so much havoc on Ottoman, Ragusan, and Venetian shipping. Atauz finds that Malta was of little historical importance in terms of the broader Mediterranean economy, as the presence of the Knights of St. John on the island was inconsequential to the broader regional economy and exaggerated the importance of the island. It was only during their tenure that the island's population increased, with fortification building projects and general support of the pirate industry providing employment for the remainder of the Maltese population, while raiding brought in both consumable and tradable goods. Malta is a perfect example of piracy creating an economic boom. Even though the tenure of the Knights of St. John on the island would constitute what Starkey would call a "long wave" of piracy, the Maltese economy was unsustainable without granted European and stolen Mediterranean resources. See, David J. Starkey, "Pirates and Markets," in *Bandits at Sea: A Pirates Reader*, ed. C. R. Pennel (New York: New York University Press, 2001): 107–24. When the Knights of St. John's properties in France were seized in 1798, the local population happily handed the knights over to Napoleon. Two years later, the British seized Malta, and the island became the empire's major base of operations in the Mediterranean, a role that became even more important after the opening of the Suez Canal in 1869. Malta then operated as a base mid-way between Britain and India, with its importance ebbing and flowing as other Mediterranean islands passed in and out of British imperial control. See, Ayşe Devrim Atauz, "Trade,

Piracy, and Naval Warfare in the Central Mediterranean: The Maritime History and Archaeology of Malta" (PhD diss., Texas A & M University, 2004).

62 This is akin to the phenomenon of Dutch disease, which at its core describes the influx of a resource proving temporarily profitable as labor shifts away from the more sustainable manufacturing or agricultural sectors. Steven Oliver, Ryan Jablonski, Justin V. Hastings, "The Tortuga Disease: The Perverse Effects of Illicit Foreign Capital," *International Studies Quarterly* 61, Issue 2, no. 1 (June 2017): 312–27.

63 White, *Piracy and Law*, 140–80.

64 Lambert, *The Barbary Wars*, 100.

65 Ibid., 123–56.

66 Panzac, *Barbary Corsairs*, 267.

67 See, Asma Moalla, *The Regency of Tunis and the Ottoman Porte, 1777–1814: Army and Government of a North-African Eyâlet at the End of the Eighteenth Century* (Routledge, 2005).

68 Lambert, *The Barbary Wars*, 157–78.

69 Weiss, *Captives and Corsairs*, 151–2.

70 Much of Greece and western Anatolia comprised the *Eyalet-i Cezayir-i Bahr-i Sefid*, Province of the Mediterranean Islands, and Algeria was the *Eyalet-i Cezayir-i Garb*, Province of the Western Islands.

71 In the nineteenth century, humanitarian expeditions were primarily targeted at preventing or ending mass killings rather than making claims over protecting human rights. French intervention in the Greek War of Independence was in line with the nineteenth-century standard of humanitarianism, but their invasion of Algiers was not. Davide Rodogno, *Against Massacre: Humanitarian Interventions in the Ottoman Empire, 1815–1914* (Princeton University Press, 2012).

72 For several instances of how gender and race were portrayed in the Greek War of Independence by contemporary French artists, see chapter eight in, Weiss, *Captives and Corsairs*, 156–69.

73 Ibid., 162.

74 Ibid., 162–7, 257.

75 Janice E. Thomson, *Mercenaries, Pirates, and Sovereigns: State-Building and Extraterritorial Violence in Early Modern Europe* (Princeton University Press, 1996), 144.

76 For examples of memos concerning intellectual piracy and the circulation of pirated newspapers and printed materials that I have expunged from my cases, see Başbakanlık Osmanlı Arşivi (Ottoman Prime Ministry Archive,

BOA) Zabtiye Nezareti Evrakı (ZB) 600/90, and BOA Maarif Nezareti Mektubî Kalemi (MF.MKT) 623/40. I have tagged each case with the location mentioned in the report to be correctly counted or omitted when looking at cases in the Mediterranean versus all seas, and I have omitted cases that are simply reports from elsewhere, such as the famous 1905 mutiny of the Russian battleship Potemkin. BOA Yıldız Perakende Evrakı Elçilik ve Şehbenderlik Maruzâtı (Y.PRK.EŞA) 47/91. Ottoman description of the Potemkin mutiny as "*korsan gibi hareket*" is an early twentieth-century example of *korsan* implying pirate rather than privateer; the mutinous crew was explicitly not following any orders from the state.

77 To accomplish this, I created a program in Python that averages every year's page-count data with the preceding and following year. I have included the raw data in Figure 1.1.

78 The first decade of the twentieth century saw a staggering amount of piratical cases in the Red Sea, particularly Farasan Island (present-day Saudi Arabia) and Massawa (present-day Eritrea). These cases largely involved Italy's expanding interests in the region and Ottoman resistance at both the local and state level. One interesting case features Ottoman naval officers joining local pirates on conducting a raid on Italian shipping. BOA Bab-ı Ali Evrak Odası (BEO) 1753/131422. There are thirty-five documents dealing with this particular issue in the Ottoman archives. The role of pirates and smugglers in the rivalry between imperial powers in the Red Sea and East Africa warrants its own study.

Chapter 2

1 See, John S. Koliopoulos, *Brigands with a Cause: Brigandage and Irredentism in Modern Greece, 1821–1912* (Clarendon Press, 1987).

2 Hakan Erdem, "'Do Not Think of the Greeks as Agricultural Labourers': Ottoman Responses to the Greek War of Independence," in *Citizenship and the Nation-state in Greece and Turkey*, ed. Thalia Dragonas and Faruk Birtek (Routledge, 2004), 72.

3 Ibid., 71–2.

4 Scholars of the Ottoman Balkans have been on the forefront of researching the ways which states have dealt with banditry in their domains, by either confrontation or co-option. John Koliopoulos and Karen Barkey offer what has become the standard account of bandit-state relations in the Greek and

Ottoman fields. See, Koliopoulos, *Brigands with a Cause*; Karen Barkey, *Bandits and Bureaucrats: The Ottoman Route to State Centralization* (Cornell University Press, 1994). Gerassimos Karabelias has attempted to add piracy to Koliopoulos's narrative but did so only at a cursory level more by implication than by depth of evidence. See, Gerassimos Karabelias, "From National Heroes to National Villains: Bandits, Pirates and the Formation of Modern Greece," in *Subalterns and Social Protest: History from below in the Middle East and North Africa*, ed. Stephanie Cronin (Routledge, 2008). While Koliopoulos provides an excellent periodization of Greek banditry, ultimately his book argues that a culture of glorifying bandits as social heroes slowed the Greek march to modernity. Since the publication of *Brigands with a Cause*, postmodern scholars have argued for multiple modernities, breaking from a (Western) Euro-centric grand historical narrative. Karabelias, Koliopoulos, and Batalas all write similarly about the relationship between bandits and the emerging modern Greek state in the nineteenth century. They trace the activities of military entrepreneurs from Ottoman rule prior to the Greek Revolution to the late nineteenth century, when the Greeks disbanded the irregular army and placed more emphasis on their regular army in preparation for war with the other emerging Balkan states. See, Achilles Batalas, "Send a Thief to Catch a Thief: State Building and the Employment of Irregular Military Formations in Mid-Nineteenth-Century Greece," in *Irregular Armed Forces and Their Role in Politics and State Formation* (2003): 149–77; Karabelias, "National Heroes to National Villains"; John S. Koliopoulos, "Brigandage and Irredentism in Nineteenth-Century Greece," *European History Quarterly* 19, no. 2 (1989): 193–228. In Ottoman times before the rebellion, bandit gangs would essentially become the leaders of their territory, able to extract levies from the population and instill fear in them so that they would remain subservient. When they did this without being the legitimate leader of the area, they were known as *klefts*, and if the sultan viewed them as difficult enough to crush, he would merely give them his blessing and place them in charge of the area as protectors known as *armatoloi*. To the peasants, there was no difference between the two; it was merely a name change. It was not a difference of cops and robbers, but of robbers and state-approved robbers. A man could be an *armatolos* one day and a *kleft* the next. During the Greek Revolution, the *armatoloi* saw an opportunity to expand their power, and joined the struggle against their Ottoman overlords.

5   George Finlay, *History of the Greek Revolution*, Vol. 2 (Cambridge University Press, 2014), 331.

6   Theophilus C. Prousis, "Bedlam in Beirut: A British Perspective in 1826," *Chronos: Revue d'Histoire de l'Université de Balamand*, no. 15 (2007): 89–106.
7   Sultan Selim III began a series of deep reforms of the Ottoman state, running it as a statistical empire embracing mass population control similar to its peers in Europe. The reforms of the 1790s were rooted in an internal Ottoman logic, rather than an emulation or imposition of other European empires. Betül Başaran, *Selim III, Social Control and Policing in Istanbul at the End of the Eighteenth Century: Between Crisis and Order* (Brill, 2014).
8   Mahmud II's new regular army differed in several ways from Ottoman armed forces of the past. In addition to ending the janissary corps, he ceased hiring seasonal militias as well. Only born-Muslims were recruited into the Victorious Soldiers of Muhammad, as the sultan suspected part of the corruption of the old janissary corps was due to it being infiltrated by Christians. Frederick F. Anscombe, *State, Faith, and Nation in Ottoman and Post-Ottoman Lands* (Cambridge University Press, 2014), 70–1.
9   Khaled Fahmy, *All the Pasha's Men: Mehmed Ali, His Army and the Making of Modern Egypt* (Cambridge University Press, 1997).
10 The fledgling state of Greece owed its sovereignty in part to military irregulars. The centralizing state tried creating a standardized army, but it relied primarily on co-opting bandits for its security. With a few notable exceptions, banditry remained an internal issue in Greece, and did not trouble Greece's protecting powers. For an instance of Greek banditry troubling Britain later in the century, see, Rodanthi Tzanelli, "Haunted by the 'Enemy' Within: Brigandage, Vlachian/Albanian Greekness, Turkish 'Contamination,' and Narratives of Greek Nationhood in the Dilessi/Marathon Affair (1870)," *Journal of Modern Greek Studies* 20, no. 1 (2002): 47–74. Piracy, on the other hand, inherently posed a threat to international Levantine trade. Incorporating pirates into state security would have undoubtedly led to conflict with British, French, and Russian ships passing through the Aegean. For this reason, Greece was unable to openly support privateers or corsairs, and any support of piracy would need to be unofficial.
11 For a general account on how state rulers went from encouraging non-state violence to eliminating it, see, Thomson, *Mercenaries, Pirates, and Sovereigns*.
12 For an account of the purchases and following misadventures of the Greek revolutionary war fleet, see David Brewer, *The Greek War of Independence: The Struggle for Freedom from Ottoman Oppression* (Overlook Duckworth, 2011), 289–96; and, David Armine Howarth, *The Greek Adventure: Lord Byron and Other Eccentrics in the War of Independence* (HarperCollins, 1976).

13 Steamship technology was deployed with similar considerations in colonial Indonesia contemporary to the Greek War of Independence. For the advantages and disadvantages offered, especially in regard to pursuing piracy, see Campo, JNFM À, "Asymmetry, Disparity and Cyclicity: Charting the Piracy Conflict in Colonial Indonesia," *International Journal of Maritime History* 19, no. 1 (2007): 42–3.

14 White, *Piracy and Law*, 252.

15 Dimitris Dimitropoulos cites Despina Themeli-Katifori, *Η δίωξις της πειρατείας και το θαλάσσιον δικαστήριον: κατά την πρώτην Καποδιστριακή περίοδον* [*The Persecution of Pirates and the Naval Courts during the first Kapodistrian Period*]: *1828–1829*, 1/2 (Athens: National Kapodistrian University – School of Philosophy, 1973), 40–3; and, Apostolos Delis, "A Hub of Piracy in the Aegean: Syros during the Greek War of Independence," 41–54 in the same volume as his own chapter, Dimitris Dimitropoulos, "Pirates during a Revolution: The Many Faces of Piracy and the Reaction of Local Communities," in *Corsairs and Pirates in the Eastern Mediterranean, Fifteenth-Nineteenth Centuries*, ed. Gelina Harlaftis (Athens: Sylvia Ioannou Foundation, 2016), 33.

16 The United States also had a presence in the region during the Greek War of Independence. They were primarily interested in trade, so the Americans were concerned with piracy and sought to protect their own ships but did not actively hunt down pirates. This was largely out of interest in maintaining neutrality in the conflict while negotiating a commercial treaty with the Ottomans. Part was in the interest of maintaining good relations with the Greek revolutionary government, which at times considered these pirates to be revolutionaries, so America could potentially establish a naval base in the Eastern Mediterranean. America was interested in protecting its Mediterranean commercial shipping from piracy, be it Greek or North African, and it had recently lost its base in Minorca after slighting Spain by acknowledging the independence of the fledgling Latin American states. See Konstantinos Hatzopoulos, "The U.S. Navy in the Aegean during the Greek War of Independence, 1821–1829," in *Southeast European Maritime Commerce and Naval Policies from the Mid-Eighteenth Century to 1914*, ed. Apostolos E. Vacalopoulos, Constantinos D. Svolopoulos, and Béla K. Király (Highland Lakes, NJ: Atlantic Research Publications, 1988).

17 The letter continues: "Seeing therefore that little good was to be expected from the Greek armed Vessels, under such circumstances it became the duty of the Admirals commanding the Allied Squadrons to limit as much as possible their power to do mischief." He ends by saying should Kapodistrias assume the

presidency, the allied squadron would treat Greek warships more leniently when they exceed the limitations of their letters of marque. Admiral Codrington to the Greek Provisional Government, February 11, 1828. YE 1828/55/1 #753 pp. 48–9.
18 Dimitropoulos, "Pirates during a Revolution," 30.
19 C. G. Pitcairn Jones, ed., *Piracy in the Levant, 1827–8* (Navy Records Society, 1934).
20 "Οι περισσότεροι εξ εκείνων οι οποίοι συνέγραψαν περί του Καποδιστρίου των προσπαθειών διά τήν οργάνωσιν του Ελληνικού κράτους μνημονεύουν και την επιχειρηθείσαν υπ᾽ αυτού δίωξιν της πειρατείας. Άπαντες όμως ακροθιγώς επελήφθησαν του θέματος. Περιωρίσθησαν να εξιστορήσουν την υπό τον Ανδρέαν Μιαούλην επιχείρησιν κατά των πειρατικών κέντρων των Βορείων Σποράδων και την αναληφθείσαν υπό των Γάλλων και Άγγλων επίθεσιν κατά της Γραμβούσης. Αι επιχειρήσεις αυταί, θεαματικαί πράγματι και αποτελεσματικαί εν τινι μέτρω, κατεπτόησαν τους πειρατάς οι οποίοι επείσθησαν ότι έληξεν η περίοδος της ανωμαλίας. Εν τούτοις διά των ενεργειών αυτών δέν επερατώθησαν, ουδ᾽ ήτο δυνατόν να τερματισθούν αι προσπάθειαι διασφαλίσεως των ελληνικών θαλασσών από τους λυμαινομένους το διαμετακομιστικόν εμπόριον της Ανατολικής Μεσογείου πειρατάς. Ούτοι, όσον και αν αντελήφθησαν ότι ήρχοντο εις αντίθεσιν προς οργανωμένον κράτος, δεν ήτο δυνατόν από της μίας ημέρας εις την άλλην να μεταβληθούν εις νομοταγείς και φιλειρηνικούς πολίτας." See, Themeli-Katifori, *Η δίωξις της πειρατείας,* ια᾽.
21 See, Themeli-Katifori, *Η δίωξις της πειρατείας.*
22 Ali Yaycioglu, *Partners of the Empire: The Crisis of the Ottoman Order in the Age of Revolutions* (Stanford University Press, 2016), 158.
23 Erdem, "Do Not Think," 76–7.
24 Fahmy, *All the Pasha's Men,* 182.
25 A. De Voulx, *Recherches sur la coopération de la Régence d'Alger à la guerre de l'indépendance grecque d'après des documents inédites* (Paris, 1856), #19 February 1, 1827.
26 Ibid., #20. November 9, 1826.
27 "There are about twenty ships in Navarino belonging to the fleet of our master the sultan (may God assist him). One of these vessels is a ship on which the Lord Ibrahim Pasha must embark; the others are frigates and corvettes. Our master the sultan (may God help him!) Has sent about fifteen thousand men from Mahomedan troops. They penetrated and took 'Atna (Athens), at least they seized the city and the Greeks were surrounded in the citadel. We think that today, if it pleases God, they are taken. The Morea and half of the Mani

Mountains are in the hands of the Greeks, but the other half have submitted to the Muslims. Anapol, Kerdas and Drounda remained in the hands of the Greeks. May God destroy them!" Ibid., #24. January 18, 1827.

28 Ibid., #24. January 18, 1827.
29 Will Smiley, *From Slaves to Prisoners of War: The Ottoman Empire, Russia, and International Law* (Oxford University Press, 2018), 166, 176–81.
30 The contemporary Greek name for the city was Smyrna. İzmir is the modern Turkish rendition of the same name.
31 A. De Voulx, *Recherches*, #22. September 28, 1827.
32 Greene, *Catholic Pirates*.
33 Fahmy, *All the Pasha's Men*, 60.
34 For a description of the Battle of Navarino from an Algerian perspective, see Mahmoud ben Amin Essekka writing to Hussein *Dey*, A. De Voulx, *Recherches*, #23. December 28, 1827:

"What I have to say to your lordship is that before this we sent your highness a letter dated the 27th of Rabi'ettani in which we informed you that an American schooner had arrived from Malta that day and had brought the news that the English, the French and the Russians (God exterminates them!) had attacked the ships of our Lord the Sultan (may God help him!) and the ships of Sid Mehmed-Ali Pasha, in the harbor Navarino; that they had given them a great battle, and that, according to their assertions, the Moslem fleet was entirely destroyed; that the English ships had entered Malta in the most dilapidated state, and that they had 755 wounded and 40 killed.

After that, we heard that the three nations mentioned had a considerable number of dead and wounded in countless quantities, and that they had raised quarantine in Malta in order to bring down the wounded.

It has also come down to us that about thirty of the ships of the Muslims are safe and sound. The Muslims had 22 warships, namely: 5 vessels, 15 large frigates, 30 corvettes; the overhang consisted of brigs and schooners; with them were 41 merchant ships, in all 107 vessels. The ships of the Christians who took part in the battle were 27 according to their statements, including 12 ships with three decks; the surplus consisted of small vessels and frigates.

It is said that at the time of the fight, Ibrahim Pasha was not in Navarino, that he was traveling on land and that he took a city named Meniteha and killed most of the inhabitants. When the Christians learned this, they wanted to avenge the Greeks and did what was just told; but (God knows!) they have received: a big blow, and they do not want to admit it. When Captain Loubi arrived here from Livorno, I wanted to charter him to send him to Navarino to obtain certain news, even at my expense. But he told us: "'Before my departure from Livorno, the English, the French, and the Russians informed all the merchantmen that they were forbidden to go to Turkey, and that those who were to be sailed for that destination would be brought back to Malta.'—Loubi also told us:—'My sailors have imposed the condition to make no trip to Turkey, otherwise I would venture to leave, but it is impossible for me to find other sailors.'"

35 A. De Voulx, *Recherches*, #22. September 28, 1827.
36 Weiss, *Captives and Corsairs*, 152–4.
37 A. De Voulx, *Recherches*, #23. December 28, 1827.
38 Weiss, *Captives and Corsairs*, 166–7.
39 Ibid., 162.
40 Thomas W. Gallant, *The Edinburgh History of the Greeks, 1768 to 1913: The Long Nineteenth Century* (Edinburgh University Press, 2015), 104.
41 Laskarina Bouboulina was another great admiral of the revolution. She perished in 1825, not in combat with the Ottomans, but in a feud with other Greeks on the island of Spetses. See, Sakis Gekas, "From the Nation to Emancipation: Greek Women Warriors from the Revolution (1820s) to the Civil War (1940s)," in *Women Warriors and National Heroes: Global Histories*, ed. Cothran, Boyd, Joan Judge, and Adrian Shubert (Bloomsbury Publishing, 2020).
42 Christopher Montague Woodhouse, *Capodistria: The Founder of Greek Independence* (Oxford University Press, 1973), 501.
43 Kostis Konstantinides, *Η ληστεία και η πειρατεία στη Σκύρο, Σκιάθο και Σκόπελο κατά τη διάρκεια της επανάστασης του 1821 μέχρι της αντιβασιλείας του Όθωνα, Ιστορική μελέτη βασισμένη αποκλειστικά επί εγγράφων, τόμος πρώτος* [*Brigandage and Piracy in Skyros, Skiathos, and Skopelo during the 1821 revolution until the reign of Otho*] (Athens: The Skyros Society, 1988).
44 "Ωστόσο ο Καποδίστριας γνώριζε ότι για να εξαλειφθεί η πειρατεία έπρεπε να εκλείψουν τα γενεσιουργά αίτιά της, δηλαδή τα οικονομικά και κοινωνικά προβλήματα που την προξενούσαν και τη συντηρούσαν. Για τον λόγο αυτό προσπάθησε να εντάξει στις ένοπλες δυνάμεις ή να απασχολήσει στην καλλιέργεια της γης τους άνεργους ναυτικούς και άτακτους στρατιωτικούς, και τους πρόσφυγες. Οι οικονομικές όμως δυσχέρειες του κράτους, απέτρεπαν την αξιοποίηση όλων αυτών των ανέργων, γεγονός που προκαλούσε τη δυσαρέσκειά τους εναντίον του Κυβερνήτη. Έτσι σιγά—σιγά η πειρατεία άρχισε να επανεμφανίζεται. Όσο λοιπόν καθυστερούσε η αποκατάσταση των ανέργων, τόσο δύσκολη ήταν η παντελής εξάλειψη της πειρατείας. Μετά τη δολοφονία

του Καποδίστρια τα πειρατικά κρούσματα πολλαπλασιάστηκαν. Ήταν δε τέτοιο το θράσος τους που δεν δίστασαν να αιχμαλωτίσουν πλοίο του πολεμικού ναυτικού. Ακόμα στις πηγές αναφέρεται και η περίπτωση ενός πολεμικού πλοίου που μεταπήδησε σε πειρατικό. Χρειάστηκε να περάσουν αρκετά χρόνια και οι συντονισμένες ενέργειες των επόμενων κυβερνήσεων για την καταπολέμηση του φαινομένου. Ωστόσο όποτε εξασθενούσε η κεντρική διοίκηση με αφορμή τις κυβερνητικές, συνταγματικές και πολιτειακές μεταβολές που έλαβαν χώρα μέχρι τα μέσα του δευτέρου μισού του 19ου αιώνος, η δράση των πειρατών αυξανόταν." George Kolovos, "Η πειρατεία στα χρόνια της Ελληνικής Επαναστάσεως και η αντιμετώπισή της από τον Καποδίστρια [Piracy in the years of the Greek Revolution and the Confrontation of Kapodistrias]," https://perialos.blogspot.com/2011/05/blog-post_09.html (accessed May 9, 2011).

45 Dimitris G. Fokas, *Χρονικά του Ελληνικού Β. Ναυτικού, 1833–1873* [*Chronicles of the Hellenic Royal Navy 1833–1873*] (Documents of the General Headquarter of the Royal Navy, 1923), 23–4.

46 See chapter four in, Peter T. Leeson, *The Invisible Hook: The Hidden Economics of Pirates* (Princeton: Princeton University Press, 2009), 82–106.

47 White, *Piracy and Law*, 24–5.

48 The Hijaz is the west coast of the Arabian Peninsula. It includes Jeddah and the holy cities of Mecca and Medina.

49 This newspaper was published in both a *Katharevousa* form of Cretan-dialect Greek and Ottoman Turkish. Some Greek references to the newspaper mistakenly identify the latter language as Arabic, which shares a common script. Each issue covers both domestic and international events, as well as providing barometric readings. The copies kept in Crete and Alexandria have been lost, so all that remains are scans of the version archived in İstanbul. Unfortunately, many issues of this periodical are forever lost.

50 Issue 71, *Vaka-yı Giridiyye* [*Events of Crete*] (Herakleion: Vikelaia Municipal Library, 1832), September 6, 1832.

51 Issue 67, *Vaka-yı Giridiyye*, August 4, 1832.

Chapter 3

1 This period of reforms was known as the *Tanzimat*. For the classic tome on the subject, see, Roderic H. Davison, *Reform in the Ottoman Empire, 1856–1876* (Princeton University Press, 1963). Marinos Sariyannis has shown that the

Tanzimat was an extension of longstanding Ottoman political thought and couched in Islamic rhetoric. It was less an example of Westernization than the New Order reforms instituted by Selim III. Marinos Sariyannis, "Ottoman Political Thought up to the Tanzimat: A Concise History," *Research Project, Institute for Mediterranean Studies, Greece* 173 (2015).

2   The main source for piracy in Greece during the revolution is not the Ministry of Foreign Affairs, which had not been yet fully setup during the revolution, but rather sources such as the Kapodistrian Naval Courts and foreign naval records like those of Admiral Codrington as recorded in *Piracy in the Levant*. See, Despina Themeli-Katifori, Αἱ ἀποφάσεις τοῦ Θαλάσσιου Δικαστηρίου 1828–1829 [*The decisions of the naval court, 1828–1829*] (Athens, 1976); and, Jones, *Piracy in the Levant*.

3   Hobsbawm, *Primitive Rebels*. Hobsbawm's understanding of banditry has sparked much debate on the topic. While at this point, academics generally refute his understanding of banditry as not reflecting reality, it does reflect folk understanding of banditry and social resistance. Thus, it is worth using his frameworks when discussing how different societies understood banditry as part of their social fabric.

4   Ypourgeio Exoterikon (Archives of the Greek Ministry of Foreign Affairs, YE) 1840/55/1, #4227, pp. 35–6.

5   Haydar Çoruh, "Moralı Korsanların Kıbrıs Çevresindeki Faaliyetleri (1821–1828) [Activities of Mora Pirates around Cyprus (1821–1828)]," *Atatürk Üniversitesi Türkiyat Araştırmaları Enstitüsü Dergisi* 61 (2018): 304.

6   YE 1840/55/1, #4227, pp. 37–8.

7   For a summary of how Greece and the Ottoman Empire cooperated to secure their land borders over the nineteenth century, see, George Gavrilis, *The Dynamics of Interstate Boundaries* (Cambridge University Press, 2008).

8   Fokas, *Chronicles*, 109. During the Crimean war, documents from 1854 to 1855 show that Samos once again became a center of Greek insurgents whom the state accused of piracy. BOA Hariciye Nezareti Tercüme Odası (HR.TO) 418/276 and 481/60.

9   See the letter from Mavrokordatos to Baron Forth-Rouen promising "more precise and severe orders relating to the hunt for pirates." YE 1854/55/1B, #6874, pp. 176–7.

10 Thomas W. Gallant, *Modern Greece: From the War of Independence to the Present*, second edition (Bloomsbury Academic, 2016), 71.

11 YE 1854/55/1 B, #3434 (Translation of #4551 into French), pp. 26–7. P. Kalligas, Minister of Justice, to the General Procurers of the Royal Court.
12 YE 1854/55/1 B, #2297, pp. 28–9. Athens, May 31, 1854.
13 YE 1854/55/1 B, #337, pp. 189–91. The Captain of the Frigate *Solon* writing to the commander of the goletta *Mathilde*. Skiathos, December 27, 1854.
14 YE 1854/55/1 A, #148423, pp. 96–9. Letter in English from Thomas Wyse to M. Argyropoulos, Minister of Foreign Affairs. Athens, July 25, 1854.
15 YE 1854/55/1 B, p. 99. Letter in French from the Hellenic Ministry of the Royal House to Thomas Wyse and Baron Rouen (English and French Ambassadors). Athens, July 30, 1854.
16 YE 1854/55/1 A, #4964, pp. 116–30. Athens, August 30, 1854. Letter in English from Thomas Wyse, the British Ambassador, to Mr. A. Mavrokordatos, Minister of Foreign Affairs. This is the first document where the Minister of Foreign Affairs changes from Argyropoulos to Mavrokordatos.
17 Gøbel, "Danish Algerian Sea Passes," 164–89.
18 YE 1854/55/1B, #6813, p. 166. Athens December 9/21, 1854. Document in French from Mavrokordatos addressed to Baron Forth-Rouen.
19 YE 1854/55/1 B, #6879, pp. 174–5. Athens December 22, 1854. Letter in French from Baron Forth-Rouen to Mavrokordatos.
20 YE 1854/55/1 B, #6899, pp. 176–7. Athens December 14/26, 1854. Letter in French from Mavrokordatos to Baron Forth-Rouen.
21 YE 1854/55/1 B, #2297, pp. 28–9. Athens, May 31, 1854.
22 Thomas W. Gallant, *Experiencing Dominion: Culture, Identity, and Power in* the British Mediterranean (Notre Dame, Indiana: University of Notre Dame Press, 2002), 1–55.
23 "Tutti queste Pirati sono Greci, e da essi conossero uno di nome Pietro Leucaditi da Sta Maura. Tanto esposero col loro giuramento, ed io siccome ho rilevato che hanno communicato con pirati i quali non si puo conoscere da quale parte crano partiti; o dalla Grecia ovvero dalla Turchia." YE 1846/55/1, #14359, pp. 9–11. Eussamia, September 14, 1846. Letter in Italian from Fermiato Antonio F. Pana, Incaricato di Pamita to the Local Director of Cefalonia.
24 In the case of this particular document, a summary in Greek from the Ministry of Foreign Affairs asserts that other than one of the pirates whose origin was unknown, the remainder in this instance was subjects of Greece. YE 1846/55/1, #14713, p. 3.
25 For some examples, see, Eythimios Papataxiarchis and Socrates D. Petmezas, "The Devolution of Property and Kinship Practices in Late-and Post-Ottoman

Ethnic Greek Societies: Some Demo-Economic Factors of Nineteenth and Twentieth Century Transformations," *Mélanges de l'Ecole française de Rome. Italie et Méditerranée* 110, no. 1 (1998): 217–41, and Irini Renieri, "Household Formation in 19th-Century Central Anatolia: The Case Study of a Turkish-Speaking Orthodox Christian Community," *International Journal of Middle East Studies* 34, no. 3 (2002): 495–517.

26 YE 1854/55/1 A, #6599, pp. 12–13. Athens, November 23/December 9, 1854. Letter in French from Baron Forth-Rouen to Mavrokordatos.

27 Thomas W. Gallant, "Greek Bandit Gangs: Lone Wolves or a Family Affair?," *Journal of Modern Greek Studies* 6 (1988): 283–4.

28 In the early modern era, ship crews were ethnically and religiously diverse. Knowing the flag that a vessel flew or the background of its captain does not indicate the background of the rest of the crew, who may have signed up or been taken aboard as forced labor at different points along the voyage. White, *Piracy and Law*, 246.

29 BOA HR.TO 481/60. Constantinople, December 1, 1855. Letter in French from Ion Ghica to Fuad Pasha, Ottoman Minister of Foreign Affairs, concerning piracy on Samos.

30 YE 1855/55/1A, #3917, pp. 56–7. Syros, March 8, 1855. Council report on suspects of piracy off the coast of Syros and Andros.

31 BOA Sadâret Mektubî Kalemi Belgeleri (A.MKT) 148/12. September 13, 1848. Document in Ottoman Turkish to the Vali of Egypt.

32 Kalligas was a very common name on Kefalonia, one of the Ionian Islands.

33 For a study of attacks upon Muslim pilgrims undertaking the Hajj and the steps that Islamic states took to prevent them in the early modern period, see Naim R. Farooqi, "Moguls, Ottomans, and Pilgrims: Protecting the Routes to Mecca in the Sixteenth and Seventeenth Centuries," *The International History Review* 10, no. 2 (1988): 198–220.

34 YE 1854/55/1 B, #337, pp. 189–91. The Captain of the Frigate *Solon* writing to the commander of the goletta *Mathilde*. Skiathos, December 27, 1854.

35 Pirates, whether real or fictional, are popular figures in the collective memories of coastal societies. Even today, residents of the Datça Peninsula recall giving aid to pirates whose names do not match any historical record. See, Tülay Artan, "Journeys and Landscapes in the Datça Peninsula: Ali Agaki of Crete and the Tuhfezâde Dynasty," in *Halcyon Days in Crete VI*, ed. Antonis Anastasopoulos (Rethymno: Crete University Press, 2009): 362.

36 Rather than attributing peasant heroification of outlaws to the belief in social bandits giving their goods to the poor, Nicholas Curott offers an explanation of how bandit activities can provide less direct, but still valuable services to peasant communities. "Bandits routinely flout inefficient laws, raise the opportunity cost of state predation, and in some cases directly provide an alternative to official protection and adjudication services." See, Nicholas A. Curott and Alexander Fink, "Bandit Heroes: Social, Mythical, or Rational?," *American Journal of Economics and Sociology* 71, no. 2 (2012): 489. While the Ottoman Empire had once allowed nomadic societies to flourish, by the nineteenth century it, like other modern states, was attempting to settle its populace. Nomadic tribes and pastoral subjects evaded state efforts at centralization and counting its populace. See, Reşat Kasaba, *A Moveable Empire: Ottoman Nomads, Migrants, and Refugees* (Seattle: University of Washington Press, 2009). Since shepherds' ways of life were often in conflict with the goals of the modern state, they often found themselves at odds with the law and needing to look elsewhere for protection.

37 Pirates frequently would claim that they were abducted and pressed into service to avoid the gallows. Lauren Benton shows us that such alibis in case of capture were common among pirates who were navigating multiple imperial legal spaces. See chapter 3 of, Benton, *A Search for Sovereignty*, 104–61.

38 Maneuver could be interpreted as gambit or manipulation.

39 YE 1854/55/1 B, #5145, pp. 126–7. Athens. 9/21 September 1854. Letter from the Hellenic Royal House to Baron Forth-Rouen of France.

40 Women such as Koutzoukos's mother often participated in Mediterranean piracy "not only as victims, but as resisters, mitigators, and collaborators." See, Judith E. Tucker, "She Would Rather Perish: Piracy and Gendered Violence in the Mediterranean," *Journal of Middle East Women's Studies* 10, no. 3 (2014): 8. Even when women were not aboard the ships as raiders or victims, they played key roles in piratical societies. Wendy Bracewell argues that Uskok women were seen as symbols, as mediators between Uskoks and the outside world, and as members of the Uskok community. Uskoks were a group of Christian naval marauders that inhabited the city of Senj and plundered the coasts of Dalmatia during the sixteenth century. Venetian sources either cast the Uskok women as immoral criminals or as crusaders desperately defending Christendom from the Ottoman-Muslim threat. The former claimed Uskok marriage practices were immoral, as women from well-to-do families were abducted by Uskok raiders to coerce their family into a marriage alliance. When their husbands died, women would immediately remarry, probably to ensure that they obtained economic

support. Venetian naysayers also claimed that Uskok women bore arms, viewed themselves as part of a violent honor society, and even resorted to witchcraft to conjure up storms to aid their husbands on raids. Contrasting with these accounts, Giovanni of Fermo, a local merchant, casted the Uskoks as driven by "poverty, want, and the short-sighted self-interests of Venice." He claimed that much like the Knights of St. John at Malta, Uskok raiders distinguished between illicit Christian goods and licit booty from Muslims and their business associates. When speaking of Uskok women in particular, he held them up as a beacon of morality who should be looked up to by Italian women.

While Venetian writers looking to extol or slander the Dalmatian raiders distorted many of the details about Uskok society, they agree that Uskok women played an important role in both Uskok and broader society. One Venetian source abandoned all hope of luring a man who had married into an Uskok family out of a life of crime, noting that the bonds of Uskok marriage were stronger than the freedom granted by a state pardon. Uskok women would invest heavily in their husbands' raiding activities, even joining syndicates to provide supplies and share in the rewards. When their husbands were captured, they would either attempt to free them through bribes, or buy the rights to Ottoman prisoners in order to exchange them for their husbands. Because Uskok women were not guilty of any crime except by association, they could circulate in Venetian and Ottoman society to act as intermediaries, to collect ransom, and to gather information. See, Wendy Bracewell, "Women among the Uskoks of Senj: Literary Images and Realities," in *Bandits at Sea: A Pirates Reader*, ed. C. R. Pennel (New York: New York University Press, 2001): 323–5, 329–31. The relation between women and piracy extended into the Mediterranean beyond Uskok society. Judith Tucker shows that, on one hand, the gendered masculine violence of pirates made the sea an existentially unsafe space for women. Violent competition between men would place victors on the masculine end of the patriarchal hierarchy and feminize the subordinated groups. On the other hand, women participated in piracy "not only as victims, but as resisters, mitigators, and collaborators." See, Tucker, "She Would Rather Perish," 8, 33–4. Tucker joins Gillian Weiss in showing how gendered images of piracy were used by European powers to depict a violent, backward orient as an area which required European intervention. See chapters seven and eight in, Weiss, *Captives and Corsairs*, 131–69. This shows how understanding gendered aspects of piracy is important not simply for its own sake, but it helps to show how piracy fit with other developments such as nationalization, imperialism, and colonialism.

41 In 1790, there was a similar case where the Algerian fleet captured a foreign privateering vessel filled with Greek crew and captives claiming various subjecthoods, primarily Ottoman, Venetian, and Russian. In a break of policy with his predecessor, Sultan Selim III initially ordered the entire crew to be executed. He amended the order to spare foreign subjects to not harm diplomatic relations, but extended capital punishment to any Ottoman subject onboard, including the captives who he feared were attempting to disguise their involvement to avoid punishment. Smiley, *From Slaves to Prisoners of War*, 169–70.

42 YE 1854/55/1 B, #1047 pp. 128–30. Ermoupoli, July 21, 1854. Letter in Greek from the Limnarch Milaras of Ermoupoli to the Hellenic Ministry of the Navy.

Chapter 4

1 "Declaration Respecting Maritime Law," Paris, April 16, 1856, *British State Papers 1856*, Vol. LXI: 155–8.

2 The United States refused to sign the treaty, as Article 1, Section 8 of the US Constitution clearly invested Congress with the ability "to declare War, grant letters of Marque and Reprisal and make Rules concerning Capture on Land and Water." The Northern States began to regret this decision when the Southern Confederacy deployed privateers during the Civil War. The United States was among the last states to adhere to the Treaty of Paris and its ban on privateering, doing so at the century's end during the 1898 Spanish-American war. See, Heller-Roazen, *Enemy of All*, 89–90.

3 Until the Battle of Navarino during the Greek War of Independence, governments could only legally declare blockades during times of war. While giving their support for Greek rebels, the Great Powers theoretically maintained neutrality with the Ottoman Empire and never formally declared war, even when they destroyed the Ottoman fleet. This "pacific blockade" set a precedent for international military intervention for humanitarian or other reasons. See, Will Smiley, "War without War: The Battle of Navarino, the Ottoman Empire, and the Pacific Blockade," *Journal of the History of International Law* 18 (2016): 42–5.

4 Poverty has been credited with being a key cause of piracy from ancient times. The Greco-Roman historian Strabo, for example, identified poverty, geographic characteristics like mountains, absence of strong leadership, and corruption as key factors in causing piracy in a region. Philip De Souza, *Piracy in the Graeco-Roman World* (Cambridge University Press, 2002), 202.

5   This halving is when examining rates of piracy by decade, as seen in Figure 1.4 in Chapter 1.
6   Hershenzon, *Captive Sea*, 84.
7   This information is according to the deposition of Miridine Lindi to the British Ionian colonial authorities. He claimed that he met Strati in Salonica in 1860. YE 1868/55/1, #5066, pp. 53–4, 73–5. Salonica is present-day Thessaloniki.
8   Piracy in the Mediterranean during the nineteenth century did not mirror what was happening in the Chinese seas during the same period. Joseph MacKay argues that large numbers of pirates were able to create "escape societies" that would contest the rule of the Qing in late imperial China. See, Joseph MacKay, "Pirate Nations: Maritime Pirates as Escape Societies in Late Imperial China," *Social Science History* 37, no. 4 (2013): 551–73.
9   Ginio, "Piracy and Redemption," 135–47.
10 TNA, FO 78/1534, Campbell to Russell, Rhodes, December 17, 1860.
11 Martin Blinkhorn, "Liability, Responsibility and Blame: British Ransom Victims in the Mediterranean Periphery, 1860–81," *Australian Journal of Politics & History* 46, no. 3 (2000): 336.
12 Hobart-Hampden's autobiography has been published under two titles. See, Augustus Charles Hobart-Hampden, *Hobart Pasha: Blockade-Running, Slaver-Hunting, and War and Sport in Turkey* (Outing Publishing Company, 1915); and Hobart Pasha, *Sketches from My Life, by Hobart Pasha* (Longmans, Green, & Company, 1886). The contents of both works are identical.
13 See chapter 17, "I Enter the Turkish Navy," in, Hobart-Hampden, *Hobart Pasha*.
14 The National Archives of the United Kingdom at Kew, London (TNA), Foreign Office (FO) 78/1534, Campbell to Russell, Rhodes, May 16, 1862. No 25.
15 TNA, FO 78/1534, Campbell to Russell, Rhodes, May 16, 1862. No 26. Cape Crio was the location of Knidos, an ancient settlement on the far western end of the Datça peninsula. The source used the name Scio, the Italian name for the island of Chios. The Turkish name for the island is Sakız. The Oxford English Dictionary defines trabaccolo as "an Italian ship of medium size; a small coasting vessel." A trabaccolo is a sailing vessel typically found in the Adriatic, usually around twenty meters in length.
16 TNA, FO 78/1534, Campbell to Hobart, Rhodes, May 26, 1862.
17 Benerson Little, *Pirate Hunting: The Fight against Pirates, Privateers, and Sea Raiders from Antiquity to the Present* (Potomac Books, Inc., 2010), 283.
18 Daniel Panzac, *La marine ottomane: De l'apogée à la chute de l'Empire, 1572–1923* (CNRS, 2009), 330–40.

19 Until the nineteenth century, domestic drydocks were responsible for the production of the Ottoman war fleet. The dominance of ironclad over wooden ships was irrefutable, but rapid advances in that technology were expensive to keep up with. In the midcentury, the Sublime Porte had ceased upgrading its domestic naval production capabilities and opted instead to import ironclads from Britain. In the 1880s, the Ottoman Empire largely abandoned its drydocks and instead relied on naval and arms imports from Germany. See, Jonathan Grant, "The Sword of the Sultan: Ottoman Arms Imports, 1854–1914," *The Journal of Military History* 66, no. 1 (2002): 17–28.

20 Bernd Langensiepen and Ahmet Güleryüz, *The Ottoman Steam Navy, 1828–1923* (Conway Maritime Press, 1995), 3.

21 Panzac, *La marine ottomane,* 330.

22 K. Paizis-Paradelis, *Hellenic Warships, 1829–2001* (Society for the Study of Greek History, 2002).

23 The *Megali Idea,* or Great Idea, was Greece's irredentist ambitions. Depending on the context, Greece's borders were to be expanded to include all coasts of the Aegean, all places once settled by ancients Greeks (which could potentially expand throughout the Mediterranean and Black Sea), or the borders of the Eastern Roman Empire. Usually the goal was expansion north into the Balkans or east into the Aegean islands and Anatolian mainland.

24 Gallant, *Edinburgh History of the Greeks,* 141–3.

25 See the Hellenic Navy website, Ekaterini Fakalou, http://www.hellenicnavy.gr/el/istoria/istoria-tou-pn.html; and Kaitē Arōnē-Tsichlē, *Αγροτικές εξεγέρσεις στην Παλιά Ελλάδα* [*Rural Revolt in Old Greece*] (Papazēsēs, 1989), cited in Gallant, *Edinburgh History of the Greeks,* 123.

26 Fokas, *Chronicles,* 216.

27 The archives of the Hellenic Navy would likely offer evidence of the piracy claimed in their chronicles. Unfortunately, I was unable to attain access to that archive while I was conducting research in Greece.

28 Fokas, *Chronicles,* 240.

29 "Greece and Turkey," Times [London, England] July 1, 1867: 5. *The Times Digital Archive.* Web. April 14, 2017.

30 Fokas, *Chronicles,* 239–40.

31 See Hobart-Hampden, *Hobart Pasha,* 200; and, Fokas, *Chronicles,* 240–1.

32 Francis Raymond Stark, *The Abolition of Privateering and the Declaration of Paris. Vol. 8. No. 3* (Columbia University, 1897), 153–60.

33 "Greece and Turkey," *The Times Digital Archive.*

34 Ibid.
35 Hobart-Hampden, *Hobart Pasha*, 200–1. It should be noted that the *Enossis* is titled after the Greek word for "union." It seems that both the *Enossis* and the *Arkadi* were christened with provocative names involving a Greek conquest of Crete.
36 Ibid., 204–7.
37 Ibid., 208–10.
38 Langensiepen and Güleryüz, *The Ottoman Steam Navy*, 4.
39 The last chapters of his memoir display specifically Turkish, not Ottoman, nationalism. He denies any Turkish wrongdoing in massacres of Bulgarians and says things such as "Always take up your quarters in a Turkish village, if possible, in preference to a Greek village. At the former you will find the traditional hospitality of the Oriental, even among the very poor people, practised in every sense of the word; whilst in the latter you will be exploité… to the last degree, even to the pilfering of your cartridges." Hobart-Hampden, *Hobart Pasha*, 228, 248.
40 John Dickie, "A Word at War: The Italian Army and Brigandage 1860–1870," *History Workshop Journal* 33, no. 1 (1992): 1–24.
41 Baris Cayli, "Peasants, Bandits, and State Intervention: The Consolidation of Authority in the Ottoman Balkans and Southern Italy," *Journal of Agrarian Change* 18, no. 2 (2018): 425–43.
42 YE 1863/55/1, #5133, pp. 32–3; #6003, pp. 42–4.
43 BOA HR.TO 277/35. Bertinatti (who also appears as Butinatti) was the former *charge d'affairs* of the Kingdom of Sardinia who had conducted diplomacy as far away as with the United States in 1860. He found his position as a diplomat continued in the unified Kingdom of Italy.
44 Ulqin/Ulcinj, a largely Albanian port city on the southern border of present-day Montenegro was a hub of pirates and smugglers in the nineteenth century. After Montenegro gained independence in 1878, black market trade intensified as smugglers seeking to avoid taxes sought to evade customs at official ports in Ottoman Albania. The Ottoman state held a monopoly on salt, so that commodity was frequently trafficked southward into the Ottoman domains. Isa Blumi, "Illicit Trade and the Emergence of Albania," in *Understanding Life in the Borderlands: Boundaries in Depth and in Motion*, ed. I. William Hartman (Athens: University of Georgia Press, 2010), 70.
45 Ibid., 78–9.
46 Yahya Yeşilyurt, "Yemen Karasularında Korsanlık ve Osmanlı Devleti'nin Aldığı Tedbirler (1869–1914) [Piracy in the Territorial Waters of Yemen and

the Measures Taken by the Ottoman Empire (1869–1914)]," *Bilig, Turk Dunyası Sosyal Bilimler Dergisi* 85 (2018): 75.

47 While Greek economic success in the period is largely attributable to currant exports, the tertiary industry of shipping created invisible earnings comparable to those brought in by the agriculture bubble. When the currant-bubble popped, the shipping sector was able to adapt and continue growing. See, Gelina Harlaftis and George Kostelenos, "International Shipping and National Economic Growth: Shipping Earnings and the Greek Economy in the Nineteenth Century," *The Economic History Review* 65, no. 4 (2012): 1426.

Chapter 5

1 Steamships were more easily able to transit through the Suez Canal than comparably sized sailing vessels, which added further pressure to international shippers to adopt steam technology. Alexis Wick, *The Red Sea: In Search of Lost Space* (University of California Press, 2016), 152.

2 For an example of piracy in the Red Sea, see BOA Yıldız Sadaret Hususi Maruzat (Y.A.HUS) 164/130 concerning the British capture of a pirate ship in Ottoman territorial waters in the Red Sea in 1880.

3 The *phylloxera* outbreak devastated vineyards as far east as the Dalmatian coastline (present-day Croatia). Barbara Jelavich, *History of the Balkans: Twentieth Century,* Vol. 2 (Cambridge University Press, 1983), 58.

4 Georges Progoulakis and Eugenia Bournova, "Le monde rural grec, 1830–1912," *Ruralia* 8 (2001).

5 Faruk Tabak, *The Waning of the Mediterranean, 1550–1870: A Geohistorical Approach* (Johns Hopkins University Press, 2008).

6 Gallant, *Modern Greece,* 141.

7 BOA Yıldız Perakende Evrakı Askeri Maruzat (Y.PRK.ASK) 19/54.

8 BOA Y.PRK.ASK 22/66.

9 BOA Y.PRK.ASK 42/46.

10 Matthew Hopper discusses two cases of piracy in the Persian Gulf during 1876 and 1887. In both cases, pirates were targeting pearls and the African slaves who were trained to dive for them. Matthew S. Hopper, *Slaves of One Master: Globalization and Slavery in Arabia in the Age of Empire* (Yale University Press, 2015), 87. The sources he uses are from British registers. As part of its efforts to achieve global abolition, Great Britain declared that any vessel transporting slaves was guilty of piracy. Any vessels in regions where slavery was legal were

suspect and subject to search and seizure. This created a constant interruption of maritime trade that greatly damaged the economies of the Indian Ocean. Isa Blumi, *Ottoman Refugees, 1878–1939: Migration in a Post-Imperial World* (Bloomsbury Academic, 2013), 100.

11 For the 1847 case, see BOA A.MKT 79/36. It is worth remembering the limits of this archive. The Ottoman Prime Ministry archives, much like those of the Greek Ministry of Foreign Affairs, are more likely to track major incidents that draw international attention. Purely domestic affairs that solely involve Ottoman subjects are unlikely to appear in this archive. Study of local piracy and other crimes requires access to regional archives and archives of the proper authorities, be that navy, coast guard, police, or gendarmerie.

12 Johan Mathew, *Margins of the Market: Trafficking and Capitalism across the Arabian Sea* (University of California Press, 2016), 88–9.

13 YE 1877/55/1, #255, p. 24.

14 YE 1879/55/1, #2188, p. 27. Berguz, or Bergos, is present-day Umurbey and is located on the eastern shores of the Dardanelles roughly 30 kilometers northeast of the city of Çanakkale, Turkey.

15 See chapter 3 of, Gavrilis, *Interstate Boundaries*, 37–65.

16 Ibid., 86–9.

17 Britain treated Greece during this time as a crypto-colony, granting legal autonomy but retaining economic dominance. See, Kalliopi Kefalas, "Amnesty and Conflict of Interest in the Dilessi Murders (1870)," *Chronica Mundi* 11, no. 1 (2016): 120–45.

18 See, Gallant, *Edinburgh History of the Greeks*, 152; Romilly Jenkins, *The Dilessi Murders* (Prion Books, 1998); Koliopoulos, *Brigands with a Cause*; Rodanthi Tzanelli, "The 'Greece' of Britain and the 'Britain' of Greece: Performance, Stereotypes, Expectations and Intermediaries in 'Neohellenic' and Victorian Narratives (1864–1881)" (PhD diss., Lancaster University, 2009).

19 Gavrilis, *Interstate Boundaries*, 87.

20 YE 1879/55/1, p. 11. October 3/15, 1879.

21 YE 1880/55/1, #5155, pp. 23–8.

22 Theodore A. Couloumbis, John Anthony Petropoulos, and Harry J. Psomiades, *Foreign Interference in Greek Politics: An Historical Perspective* (Pella Publishing Company, 1976), 29.

23 This would not always be the case. For a historical moment when Greece would be willing to encourage criminality in the lands and seas of the Ottoman Empire, see the following chapter on piracy during the 1897 war.

24 Gallant, *Edinburgh History of the Greeks*, 256.

25 Tabak, *Waning,* 290.
26 Chris Gratien, "The Ottoman Quagmire: Malaria, Swamps, and Settlement in the Late Ottoman Mediterranean," *International Journal of Middle East Studies* 49, no. 4 (2017): 583–604.
27 Tabak, *Waning,* 129.
28 For a table of the type and amount of annual care required to tend to currant vines, see table V.1 in Alexis Franghiadis, "Peasant Agriculture and Export Trade: Currant Viticulture in Southern Greece, 1830–1893" (PhD diss., Florence: European University Institute, 1990), 221.
29 Gallant, *Edinburgh History of the Greeks,* 258–9.
30 Thanasis Kalafatis, "Η αγροτική οικονομία: Όψεις της αγροτικής ανάπτυξης [The Agriculture Economy: Aspects of Rural Development]," in *Ιστορία του νέου ελληνισμού* [History of New Greek Hellenism] 1770–2000. Vol. 5, 1871–1909 (Athens: Greek Letters, 2003), 71–8.
31 Gallant, *Edinburgh History of the Greeks,* 243.
32 To be specific, the Greek state footed the bill for French and English companies to come in and drain Lake Kopais. While the change from wetlands to plains eliminated a major source of malaria and increased arable lands, the regional ecology was destroyed, along with local industries that had relied on harvesting eel and fish from the lake. See, David Idol, "The 'Peaceful Conquest' of Lake Kopais: Modern Water Management and Environment in Greece," *Journal of Modern Greek Studies* 36, no. 1 (May 2018): 71–95.
33 Faruk Tabak, "Imperial Rivalry and Port-Cities: A View from Above," *Mediterranean Historical Review* 24, no. 2 (2009): 88.
34 Tabak, *Waning,* 240.
35 David Idol, "Commercial Agriculture and the Landscape of Capitalism in Nineteenth-Century Greece," *EuropeNow* 7 (2017).
36 See figures 7.14 and 7.17 in Gallant, *Edinburgh History of the Greeks,* 256, 261.
37 For a comparison of the value of currant exports compared to the value of all exports in Greece, see Appendix V in Franghiadis, *Peasant Agriculture,* 320.
38 Kalafatis, "Agriculture Economy," 74. See Table 2.
39 Socrates D. Petmezas, "Export-dependent Agriculture, Revenue Crisis and Agrarian Productivity Involution. The Greek Case (1860s–1930s)," *Histoire & Mesure* (2000): 331–2.
40 For a discussion of the Ottoman path to bankruptcy, see chapter 4 of Roger Owen, *The Middle East in the World* Economy, *1800–1914* (I.B. Tauris, 1993), 100–21.

41 Each of these states also backed banks in the Ottoman Empire, funneling capital to projects in the interests of those states. The French controlled the Imperial Ottoman bank, which in addition to issuing banknotes and credit also promoted granting railway construction contracts to French firms. The Deutsche Bank, back unambiguously by Germany, promoted sales of German armaments from manufacturers like Krupp. The National Bank of Turkey, backed by Britain, worked with the other two banks to ensure they would not undercut each other when offering extortionist interest rates on loans to the Ottomans. Ibid., 195.
42 Ibid., 192–3, 197.
43 Ibid., 118–19.
44 Reşat Kasaba, *The Ottoman Empire and the World Economy: The Nineteenth Century* (SUNY Press, 1988), 105.
45 See Table A1, ibid., 120–1.
46 See Table A2, ibid., 122–3.
47 Donald Quataert, *The Ottoman Empire, 1700–1922* (Cambridge University Press, 2005), 120.
48 For Western figures on the adoption of steamships, see Gelina Harlafti, *Η ιστορία της ελληνόκοτητης ναυτιλίας το 19ο και 20ό αι.* [*The History of the Hellenic Merchant Marine in the 19th and 20th Centuries*] (Nefeli, 2001), cited in Gelina Harlafti, "Η εμπορική ναυτιλία: Η μετάβαση από τα ιστιοφόρα στα ατμόπλοια. [The Merchant Fleet: The Transition from Sailboats to Steamships]," in *Ιστορία του νέου ελληνισμού* [History of New Greek Hellenism] 1770–2000. Vol. 5, 1871–1909 (Athens: Greek Letters, 2003), 96.
49 Harlaftis and Kostelenos, "International Shipping," 1426.
50 Kemal H. Karpat, "The Ottoman Emigration to America, 1860–1914," *International Journal of Middle East Studies* 17, no. 2 (1985): 181.
51 Even with a surplus of labor, an illicit slave trade continued its presence in Ottoman domestic shipping, which prompted intervention on behalf of Austrian and British ships which conducted most of the tramp shipping in the Eastern Mediterranean. See, Alison Frank, "The Children of the Desert and the Laws of the Sea: Austria, Great Britain, the Ottoman Empire, and the Mediterranean Slave Trade in the Nineteenth Century," *The American Historical Review* 117, no. 2 (2012): 410–44. In the Ottoman Empire and the New World, there was a demand for cheap labor to staff expanding plantation and mining operations in the late nineteenth and early twentieth centuries. Blumi, *Ottoman Refugees*, 92.
52 Oktay Özel, "Migration and Power Politics: The Settlement of Georgian Immigrants in Turkey (1878–1908)," *Middle Eastern Studies* 46, no. 4 (2010): 477–96.

53 Christoph Herzog, "Migration and the State: On Ottoman Regulations Concerning Migration since the Age of Mahmud II," in *The City in the Ottoman Empire: Migration and the Making of Urban Modernity*, ed. Ulrike Freitag, Malte Fuhrmann, Nora Lafi, and Florian Riedler (Routledge, 2011).
54 Alexis Franghiadis, "Land Tenure Systems, Peasant Agriculture and Bourgeois Ascendancy in Greece, 1830–1914," in *The Economic Development of Southeastern Europe in the 19th Century*, ed. Edhem Eldem and Socrates Petmezas (Athens: Alpha Bank, 2011), 101–36.
55 Catherine Zara Raymond, "Piracy and Armed Robbery in the Malacca Strait: A Problem Solved?," *Naval War College Review* 62, no. 3 (2009): 40. This solution matches the diagnosis by Gonçal López Nadal that the emergence of corsairing and piracy often coincide with periods of economic crisis. See, López Nadal, Gonçal, "Corsairing as a Commercial System: The Edges of Legitimate Trade," in *Bandits at Sea: A Pirates Reader*, ed. C. R. Pennell (New York: New York University Press, 2001), 128.

Chapter 6

1 As the scale of trade increased, seafarers could invest in military ships to protect a large merchant convoy, or ultimately have a navy effectively patrol an entire area to ensure the safety of unarmed maritime traffic. See, John L. Anderson, "Piracy and World History: An Economic Perspective on Maritime Predation," *Journal of World History* 6, no. 2 (1995): 182.
2 Starkey, "Pirates and Markets," 107–24.
3 BOA Y.PRK.ASK 42/46.
4 Present-day Al-Faw, Iraq, situated on the Persian Gulf. BOA Y.PRK.ASK 62/22.
5 Gallant, *Edinburgh History of the Greeks*, 158–9.
6 He was also known as Kabaağaçlızade Ahmet Cevat Pasha. After his reign in Crete, he would go on to become grand vizier to Sultan Abdülhamid II.
7 For a local and imperial level study of the 1895–8 crisis on Crete, see, Pinar Şenışık, *The Transformation of Ottoman Crete: Revolts, Politics and Identity in the Late Nineteenth Century* (I.B. Tauris, 2011).
8 Gallant, *Edinburgh History of the Greeks*, 291–7.
9 Ibid., 297–300.
10 Kaori Komatsu, "Financial Problems of the Navy during the Reign of Abdülhamid II," *Oriente Moderno* 20, no. 1 (2001): 209–19.
11 Langensiepen and Güleryüz, *The Ottoman Steam Navy*, 8–9.

12 Hedley Paul Willmott, *The Last Century of Sea Power: From Port Arthur to Chanak, 1894–1922*, Vol. 1 (Indiana University Press, 2009), 35.
13 Fatma Şimşek, "Blockading an Island: Collective Punishment, Islanders, and the State in the 'Largest' Island at the End of the Nineteenth Century," in *Islands of the Ottoman Empire*, ed. Antonis Hadjikyriacou (Princeton: Markus Wiener, 2018), 112–13.
14 Langensiepen and Güleryüz, *The Ottoman Steam Navy*, 9.
15 Willmott, *Sea Power*, 32–3.
16 BOA Yıldız Perakende Evrakı Posta Telgraf Nezareti Maruzatı (Y.PRK.PT) 12/10.
17 Great Britain, Parliament, *Correspondence Respecting the Negotiations for the Conclusion of Peace between Turkey and Greece*, 1898, #29.
18 Ibid., #53.
19 Ibid., #56. Inclosure 2. May 25, 1897.
20 Ibid., #78. Inclosure.
21 Ibid., #163. June 30, 1897. Inclosure: Detailing the State of the Turkish Occupation of Thessaly.
22 BOA Yıldız Mütenevvi Maruzat (Y.MTV) 157/91.
23 *Correspondence*, 1898, #29.
24 Ibid., #48. June 6, 1897. Terms of the Armistice at Sea.
25 Talbot, "Ill-Treated by Friends."
26 In the present day, we have returned to considering territorial water to being a certain distance from controlled land. Exactly how far that distance is has caused fierce debate and tension between Greece and Turkey, almost leading to war in the Aegean in several instances. The reach of territorial waters has been considered 6, 10, or 12 nautical miles at various points over the twentieth and twenty-first centuries. Currently, further reach from the shoreline favors Greece as it controls almost all the Aegean islands.
27 BOA Y.MTV 164/253.
28 See article 2 of the *Preliminaires de Paix* in appendix V of Theodore George Tatsios, *The Megali Idea and the Greek-Turkish War of 1897: The Impact of the Cretan Problem on Greek Irredentism, 1866–1897* (New York, 1984), 253. The terms agreed upon during the preliminary peace negotiations were considered binding in the final peace treaty.
29 Maria Mandamadiotou, *The Greek Orthodox Community of Mytilene: Between the Ottoman Empire and the Greek State, 1876–1912* (Oxford; Berlin: Lang, 2013).

30 See, Martin Strohmeier, "Economy and Society in the Aegean Province of the Ottoman Empire, 1840–1912," *Turkish Historical Review* 1, no. 2 (2010): 185–8; Fatma Şimşek, "19. Yüzyılın İkinci Yarısında Cezayir-i Bahr-i Sefid Vilayetinde Kaçak Gemi Yapımı [Illegal Shipbuilding in the Archipelago Province in the Second Half of the 19th Century]," *Belleten* 83, no. 296 (2019): 201–27.

31 Strohmeier, "Economy and Society in the Aegean," 164–95. This is comparable to Ussama Makdisi's argument that there was an internal Ottoman Orientalism that developed parallel to Western Oriental discourse that viewed the minorities in the peripheries of the empire, particularly the Arab lands, to be the Other against which the idea of *osmanlılık* and later Turkish nationalism were formed. See, Ussama Makdisi, "Ottoman Orientalism," *The American Historical Review* 107, no. 3 (2002): 768–96.

32 Mandamadiotou, *The Greek Orthodox Community of Mytilene*.

33 Baris Cayli, "Crime, Bandits, and Community: How Public Panic Shaped the Social Control of Territory in the Ottoman Empire," *Territory, Politics, Governance* 8, no. 3 (2020): 356–71.

34 Jenkins, *The Dilessi Murders*, 14.

35 Gallant, *Modern Greece*, 103–5.

36 Nathan Brown, "Brigands and State Building: The Invention of Banditry in Modern Egypt," *Comparative Studies in Society and History* 32 (April 1990): 258–81.

37 Jenkins, *The Dilessi Murders*, 183–5.

38 Batalas, "Send a Thief."

39 Andrew G. Gould, "Lords or Bandits? The Derebeys of Cilicia," *International Journal of Middle East Studies* 7, no. 4 (1976): 494.

40 Yakup Bektas, "The Sultan's Messenger: Cultural Constructions of Ottoman Telegraphy, 1847–1880," *Technology and Culture* 41, no. 4 (2000): 669–96.

41 Stephen Kern, *The Culture of Time and Space, 1880–1918* (Harvard University Press, 2003), 188, 214.

42 The inscription can be found on the statue in the municipal gardens in Rethymno, Crete. In Greek, the text reads "ΕΥΑΓΓΕΛΟΣ ΚΥΡ. ΦΡΑΝΓΚΙΑΔΑΚΗΣ / 1869 – 1951 / ΠΕΝΤΑΚΟΣΙΑΡΧΟΣ ΚΡΗΤΙΚΟΝ ΑΓΩΝΩΝ / ΑΡΗΓΟΣ ΜΑΚΕΔΟΝΙΚΟΥ ΚΑΙ / ΕΛΛΗΝΟΤΟΥΡΚΙΚΟΥ ΠΟΛΕΜΟΥ / Η ΜΑΤΩΜΕΝΗ ΛΕΥΤΕΡΙΑ / ΠΕΤΑ ΨΗΛΑ ΚΑΙ ΚΡΙΝΕΙ / ΚΑΙ ΣΤΕΦΑΝΩΝΕΙ ΚΑΘΕ ΠΙΟ / ΠΟΥ ΜΑΧΕΤΑΙ ΓΙΑ ΕΙΡΗΝΗ."

43 Dimitris Livanios, "'Conquering the Souls': Nationalism and Greek Guerrilla Warfare in Ottoman Macedonia, 1904–1908," *Byzantine and Modern Greek Studies* 23, no. 1 (1999): 195–221.

44 Bülent Özdemir, *Ottoman Reforms and Social Life: Reflections from Salonica, 1830–1850* (Istanbul: Isis Press, 2003), 1–7.
45 Willmott, *Sea Power*, 34.
46 Livanios, "Conquering the Souls."
47 Ali Arslan, "Greek—Vlach Conflict in Macedonia," *Etudes Balkaniques* 39, no. 2 (2003): 78–102.
48 İpek K. Yosmaoğlu, *Blood Ties: Religion, Violence and the Politics of Nationhood in Ottoman Macedonia, 1878–1908* (Cornell University Press, 2013), 71.
49 See article 8 of *traité de paix définitif* in appendix V in Tatsios, *The Megali Idea*, 265.
50 Greece's traumatic loss in this war led the government to more seriously pursue the modernization and strengthening of its military. Rather than grow docile, Greece undertook four major military operations in the following twenty-five years: the two Balkan Wars, the First World War, and the 1919–22 Greco-Turkish War, the last of which resulted in even greater catastrophe. See, Stefanos Katsikas and Anna Krinaki, "Reflections on an 'Ignominious Defeat': Reappraising the Effects of the Greco-Ottoman War of 1897 on Greek Politics," *Journal of Modern Greek Studies* 38, no. 1 (2020): 125.
51 While Greece effectively doubled in size from these territorial acquisitions, its grasp on these territories remained tenuous. During the First World War, Greece nearly split in two during a political divide that placed royalist supporters, located primarily in "Old Greek" territories that were incorporated in Greece since the nineteenth century, against supporters of Eleftherios Venizelos, located primarily in the "New Greek" territories acquired from the Ottomans in the twentieth century. Venizelos was elected Greek prime minister in 1910. He hailed from Crete, which formally unified with Greece during the Balkan Wars after achieving autonomy in 1898 as a result of the 1897 Greco-Ottoman War. While the union between Old and New Greece wound up lasting, the cement did not dry quickly.

Epilogue

1 For the incident where a shepherd received those basic items as his share of the loot for supporting piracy, see YE 1854/55/1 B, #337, pp. 189–91. The Captain of the Frigate *Solon* writing to the commander of the goletta *Mathilde*. Skiathos, December 27, 1854.
2 Thomson, *Mercenaries, Pirates, and Sovereigns*, 144–6.

3   See, Artan, "Journeys and Landscapes," 405–6. Like the other scholars discussed in this chapter, Artan does not contextualize this raid within the broader history of piracy in the Mediterranean, and her contribution has eluded citation by scholars of the subject.
4   BOA Dahiliye Nazareti İdare (DH.İD) 78/2.
5   BOA Dahiliye Nezareti Asayiş Şubesi (DH.EUM.AYŞ) 4/92.
6   For an example of mid-nineteenth-century industrial development creating economic equality that impoverished farmers while enriching railways workers, thus causing the peasants to turn to banditry, see, Basil C. Gounaris, "Peasants, Brigands, and Navvies: Railways Dreams and Realities in the Ottoman Balkans," *European Journal of Economic History* 34, no. 1 (2006): 215–45.
7   "The literature on honor in the Mediterranean is vast. The major works consulted were J. Davis, *People of the Mediterranean: An Essay in Comparative Social Anthropology* (London, 1977); Anton Blok, 'Rams and Billy-Goats: A Key to the Mediterranean Code of Honour,' in *Religion, Power and Protest in Local Communities: The Northern Shore of the Mediterranean*, ed. Eric R. Wolf (Amsterdam, 1984), 51–70; David D. Gilmore, ed., *Honor and Shame and the Unity of the Mediterranean* (Washington, DC, 1987). Those arguing against such a view include Michael Herzfeld, 'Honour and Shame: Problems in the Comparative Analysis of Moral Systems,' *Man* 15 (1980): 339–51; Herzfeld, 'The Horns of the Mediterraneanist Dilemma,' *American Ethnologist* 11 (1984): 439–54; Josep R. Llobera, 'Fieldwork in Southwestern Europe: Anthropological Panacea or Epistemological Straightjacket?' *Critique of Anthropology* 6 (1986): 25–33; Victoria A. Goddard, 'From Mediterranean to Europe: Honour, Kinship and Gender,' in *The Anthropology of Europe: Identity and Boundaries in Conflict*, ed. Josep R. Llobera Goddard and Cris Shore (Providence, R.I., 1994), 57–92." See, Thomas W. Gallant, "Honor, Masculinity, and Ritual Knife Fighting in Nineteenth-Century Greece," *The American Historical Review* 105, no. 2 (2000): 375. Also see, Gallant, *Experiencing Dominion*, 95–148.
8   Gallant, "Greek Bandit Gangs," 269–90.
9   See, Frederick Anscombe, "Albanians and 'Mountain Bandits,'" in *The Ottoman Balkans 1750–1830*, ed. Frederick Anscombe (Markus Wiener Publishers, 2006), 87–113.
10 Hobsbawm's chapter on social banditry in *Primitive Rebels* is widely credited as having opened the banditry debate in academia. Hobsbawm, *Primitive Rebels*, 13–29.
11 Barkey, *Bandits and Bureaucrats*, 152–3.

12 Brown, "Brigands and State Building," 258–81.
13 In his historiography on debates in naval history, Richard Harding has questioned the emphasis placed upon the role of navies in enacting larger changes such as the elimination of piracy or the ushering in of strong economies. He maintains the efficacy of British and French navies in attaining desired diplomatic results. Harding, *Modern Naval History*, 28, 112.
14 Guy Chet, *The Ocean Is a Wilderness: Atlantic Piracy and the Limits of State Authority, 1688–1856* (University of Massachusetts Press, 2014). David Starkey and Matthew McCarthy published research in the same year that also extended piracy in the Atlantic to the nineteenth century, ending with the Treaty of Paris. Rather than emphasize economic factors, they focus on shifts in British grand strategy leading to a policy of suppressing piracy and discouraging British warships to seize neutral prizes. David J. Starkey and Matthew McCarthy, "A Persistent Phenomenon: Private Prize-taking in the British Atlantic World, c.1540–1856," in *Persistent Piracy: Maritime Violence and State-Formation in Global Historical Perspective*, ed. Stefan Eklöf Amirell and Leos Müller (Palgrave Macmillan, 2014).
15 Martin Strohmeier, for example, identifies a number of cases of piracy in the 1860s, and briefly discusses piracy as part of the Aegean economy during those years. He did not, however, realize the importance of these cases upending the historiography of Mediterranean piracy. See, Strohmeier, "Economy and Society in the Aegean," 189–90.
16 Paizis-Paradelis only spent four sentences on piracy after Otto's reign began. "Τα κρούσματα ληστοπειρατείας συνεχίστηκαν για πολλά ακόμη χρόνια. Ακόμη και το 1850 αναφέρεται δράση πειρατών στο Αιγαίο κυρίως κοντά στα Τουρκικά παράλια. Η δράση αυτών των ομάδων μικρών συνήθως αυξανόταν κάθε φορά που εξασθενούσε η Κεντρική Διοίκηση, και αυτό γινόταν πολλές φορές με αφορμή τις Κυβερνητικές, συνταγματικές και πολιτειακές μεταβολές που έλαβαν χώρα μέχρι τα μέσα του δευτέρου ημίσεως του 19ου αιώνα. Συντέλεσε επίσης ότι μέρος του Αιγαίου ήταν υπό Ελληνική κυριαρχία, ενώ το λοιπό ήταν υπό Τουρκικό έλεγχο." See, K. Paizis-Paradelis, "Η πειρατεία κατά τους χρόνους της Ελληνικής Επανάστασης και τα πρώτα μεταεπαναστατικά χρόνια [Piracy during the Years of the Greek Revolution and the Immediate Post-Revolutionary Years]," *Nautiki Epitheorisi* 133, no. 469 (1991): 393.
17 Fokas, *Chronicles*, 216.
18 Spyridon F. Argyros, *Η Πειρατεία από του 1500 Π.Χ. Εως το 1860, Ιστορία και Θρύλος* [*Piracy from 1500 B.C. to 1860, History and Legend*] (Athens, 1963), 267.

19 Judith Tucker echoes this sentiment for the Mediterranean in particular. "The Mediterranean has lent itself equally to the development of different themes in various historical contexts; those who study ancient, medieval, early modern, or modern periods are preoccupied with distinct topics, some of which may or may not travel well over time." Judith E. Tucker, "Introduction," in *The Making of the Modern Mediterranean: Views from the South*, ed. Judith E. Tucker (University of California Press, 2019), 9.

20 For an overview of these broad historical trends over the long nineteenth century, See Eric Hobsbawm's trilogy: Eric Hobsbawm, *Age of Revolution: 1789–1848* (Hachette UK, 2010); Eric Hobsbawm, *Age of Capital: 1848–1875* (Hachette UK, 2010); Eric Hobsbawm, *Age of Empire: 1875–1914* (Hachette UK, 2010).

21 Mostafa Minawi, *The Ottoman Scramble for Africa: Empire and Diplomacy in the Sahara and the Hijaz* (Stanford University Press, 2016), 2–3.

22 For an excellent example of this, see, Ilham Khuri-Makdisi, *The Eastern Mediterranean and the Making of Global Radicalism, 1860–1914* (University of California Press, 2010).

23 Phanariots like Stephanos Vogorides remained ignored by history until very recently because they could not be easily claimed by nationalist history. Vogorides became a high-ranking *dragoman* in the Ottoman Empire who was instrumental in forming the failed Ottoman nationalism, *osmanlılık*. He was from a Bulgarophone village, spoke Greek among family, and governed in Ottoman Turkish. He is perhaps the quintessential example of someone who was prominent and influential but lost by the distortion of modern nationalisms. Christine M. Philliou, *Biography of an Empire: Governing Ottomans in an Age of Revolution* (University of California Press, 2011). Likewise, the poets and intellectuals of Ionian islands often get distorted from nationalist Greek and Italian histories. Konstantina Zanou's transnational framework allows us to understand their importance not just to Greek or Italian national identity, but seeing regional developments and ideas as a whole. Konstantina Zanou, *Transnational Patriotism in the Mediterranean, 1800–1850: Stammering the Nation* (Oxford University Press, 2018).

24 Janice Thomson considers filibustering to be a uniquely American phenomena, where independent expedition leaders from a young United States launched attacks aimed at conquering territories from a weak Spanish empire and nascent successor states during the nineteenth century. To support this American exceptionalism, Thomson argues that "individuals from Western Europe, for example, did not launch private military expeditions to seize territory from the

decaying Ottoman Empire." Thomson, *Mercenaries, Pirates, and Sovereigns,* 118. The Greek organization National Society did just that that during the late nineteenth century, recruiting non-state military entrepreneurs to cross the Ottoman border and take territory for the Greek state.

25 During the Macedonia conflict, the *Teşkilat-ı Mahsusa* records show that they would often discipline those among their ranks who would commit atrocities. At the same time, Bulgarian records complain of massacres and rapes committed by entire companies of the Special Organization. Benjamin C. Fortna, *The Circassian: A Life of Eşref Bey, Late Ottoman Insurgent and Special Agent* (Oxford University Press, 2016), 103. Janice Thomson has suggested that states using clandestine or covert operations to advance their territorial interests could be considered as "neofilibustering." Thomson, *Mercenaries, Pirates, and Sovereigns,* 145.

26 Erik J. Zürcher, "The Ottoman Conscription System in Theory and Practice," *International Review of Social History* 43 (1998): 449.

27 Ryan Gingeras, *Sorrowful Shores: Violence, Ethnicity, and the End of the Ottoman Empire, 1912–1923* (Oxford: Oxford University Press, 2009), 169.

Bibliography

Archives

BOA   Başbakanlık Osmanlı Arşivi. Ottoman Prime Ministry Archive
    A.MKT   Sadâret Mektubî Kalemi Belgeleri
    BEO   Bab-ı Ali Evrak Odası
    DH.EUM.AYŞ   Dahiliye Nezareti Asayiş Şubesi
    DH.İD   Dahiliye Nezareti İdare
    HR.TO   Hariciye Nezareti Tercüme Odası
    MF.MKT   Maarif Nezareti Mektubî Kalemi
    Y.A.HUS   Yıldız Sadaret Hususi Maruzat
    Y.MTV   Yıldız Mütenevvi Maruzat
    Y.PRK.ASK   Yıldız Perakende Evrakı Askeri Maruzat
    Y.PRK.EŞA   Yıldız Perakende Evrakı Elçilik ve Şehbenderlik Maruzâtı
    Y.PRK.PT   Yıldız Perakende Evrakı Posta Telgraf Nezareti Maruzatı
    ZB   Zabtiye Nezareti Evrakı

GAK   Genika Archeia tou Kratous. Greek General State Archives

TNA   The National Archives of the United Kingdom at Kew, London
    FO   Foreign Office
        78   Political and Other Departments: General Correspondence before 1906, Ottoman Empire

YE   Ypourgeio Exoterikon. Archives of the Greek Ministry of Foreign Affairs
    55/1 Peirateia. Piracy

Published Primary and Secondary Sources

Abdullah Fréres, photographers. "[The Cannon Drill on the Imperial Ironclad Frigate Mes'udiye]/Constantinople, Abdullah Frères." Photographic print. Constantinople: [between 1880 and 1893], no known restrictions on publication. From Library of Congress: *Abdul Hamid II Collection*. https://www.loc.gov/pictures/item/2003671378/ (accessed May 1, 2020).

Anderson, John L. "Piracy and World History: An Economic Perspective on Maritime Predation." *Journal of World History* 6, no. 2 (1995): 175–99.

Anscombe, Frederick. "Albanians and 'Mountain Bandits'." In *The Ottoman Balkans 1750–1830*, edited by Frederick Anscombe, 87–113. Markus Wiener Publishers, 2006.

Anscombe, Frederick F. *State, Faith, and Nation in Ottoman and Post-Ottoman Lands*. Cambridge University Press, 2014.

Argyros, Spyridon F. *Η Πειρατεία από του 1500 Π.Χ. Εως το 1860, Ιστορία και Θρύλος* [*Piracy from 1500 B.C. to 1860, History and Legend*]. Athens, 1963.

Arōnē-Tsichlē, Kaitē. *Αγροτικές εξεγέρσεις στην Παλιά Ελλάδα* [*Rural Revolt in Old Greece*]. Papazēsēs, 1989.

Arslan, Ali. "Greek—Vlach Conflict in Macedonia." *Etudes Balkaniques* 39, no. 2 (2003): 78–102.

Artan, Tülay. "Journeys and Landscapes in the Datça Peninsula: Ali Agaki of Crete and the Tuhfezâde Dynasty." In *Halcyon Days in Crete VI*, edited by Antonis Anastasopoulos, 339–411. Rethymno: Crete University Press 2009.

Atauz, Ayşe Devrim. "Trade, Piracy, and Naval Warfare in the Central Mediterranean: The Maritime History and Archaeology of Malta." PhD diss., Texas A & M University, 2004.

Barkey, Karen. *Bandits and Bureaucrats: The Ottoman Route to State Centralization*. Cornell University Press, 1994.

Başaran, Betül. *Selim III, Social Control and Policing in Istanbul at the End of the Eighteenth Century: Between Crisis and Order*. Brill, 2014.

Batalas, Achilles. "Send a Thief to Catch a Thief: State Building and the Employment of Irregular Military Formations in Mid-Nineteenth-Century Greece." *Irregular Armed Forces and Their Role in Politics and State Formation* (2003): 149–77.

Beek, Aaron. "Freelance Warfare and Illegitimacy: The Historians' Portrayal of Bandits, Pirates, Mercenaries and Politicians." PhD diss., University of Minnesota, 2015.

Bektas, Yakup. "The Sultan's Messenger: Cultural Constructions of Ottoman Telegraphy, 1847–1880." *Technology and Culture* 41, no. 4 (2000): 669–96.

Benton, Lauren A. *A Search for Sovereignty: Law and Geography in European Empires, 1400–1900*. Cambridge: Cambridge University Press, 2010.

Bevan, Andrew, and James Conolly. *Mediterranean Islands, Fragile Communities and Persistent Landscapes: Antikythera in Long-Term Perspective*. Cambridge University Press, 2013.

Blinkhorn, Martin. "Liability, Responsibility and Blame: British Ransom Victims in the Mediterranean Periphery, 1860–81." *Australian Journal of Politics & History* 46, no. 3 (2000): 336–56.

Blumi, Isa. "Illicit Trade and the Emergence of Albania." In *Understanding Life in the Borderlands: Boundaries in Depth and in Motion*, edited by I. William Hartman, 58–84. Athens: University of Georgia Press, 2010.

Blumi, Isa. *Ottoman Refugees, 1878–1939: Migration in a Post-Imperial World*. Bloomsbury Academic, 2013.

Bracewell, Wendy. "Women among the Uskoks of Senj. Literary Images and Reality." In *Bandits at Sea: A Pirates Reader*, edited by C. R. Pennell, 321–34. New York: New York University Press, 2001.

Braudel, Fernand. *The Mediterranean and the Mediterranean World in the Age of Philip II*. University of California Press, 1995.

Brewer, David. *The Greek War of Independence: The Struggle for Freedom from Ottoman Oppression*. Overlook Duckworth, 2011.

Brown, Nathan. "Brigands and State Building: The Invention of Banditry in Modern Egypt." *Comparative Studies in Society and History* 32 (April 1990): 258–81.

Campo, JNFM À. "Asymmetry, Disparity and Cyclicity: Charting the Piracy Conflict in Colonial Indonesia." *International Journal of Maritime History* 19, no. 1 (2007): 35–62.

Cayli, Baris. "Crime, Bandits, and Community: How Public Panic Shaped the Social Control of Territory in the Ottoman Empire." *Territory, Politics, Governance* 8, no. 3 (2020): 356–71.

Cayli, Baris. "Peasants, Bandits, and State Intervention: The Consolidation of Authority in the Ottoman Balkans and Southern Italy." *Journal of Agrarian Change* 18, no. 2 (2018): 425–43.

Chet, Guy. *The Ocean Is a Wilderness: Atlantic Piracy and the Limits of State Authority, 1688–1856*. University of Massachusetts Press, 2014.

Colley, Linda. *Captives: Britain, Empire and the World 1600–1850*. Random House, 2003.

Couloumbis, Theodore A., John Anthony Petropoulos, and Harry J. Psomiades. *Foreign Interference in Greek Politics: An Historical Perspective*. Pella Publishing Company, 1976.

Çoruh, Haydar. "Moralı Korsanların Kıbrıs Çevresindeki Faaliyetleri (1821–1828) [Activities of Mora Pirates around Cyprus (1821–1828)]." *Atatürk Üniversitesi Türkiyat Araştırmaları Enstitüsü Dergisi* 61 (2018): 297–312.

Curott, Nicholas A., and Alexander Fink. "Bandit Heroes: Social, Mythical, or Rational?" *American Journal of Economics and Sociology* 71, no. 2 (2012): 470–97.

Davis, Robert C. *Christian Slaves, Muslim Masters: White Slavery in the Mediterranean, the Barbary Coast, and Italy, 1500–1800*. New York: Palgrave Macmillan, 2003.

Davison, Roderic H. *Reform in the Ottoman Empire, 1856–1876*. Princeton University Press, 1963.

"Declaration Respecting Maritime Law." Paris, April 16, 1856. *British State Papers 1856*. Vol. LXI: 155–8.

Delis, Apostolos. "A Hub of Piracy in the Aegean: Syros during the Greek War of Independence." In *Corsairs and Pirates in the Eastern Mediterranean, Fifteenth-Nineteenth Centuries*, edited by Gelina Harlaftis, 41–54. Athens: Sylvia Ioannou Foundation, 2016.

De Souza, Philip. *Piracy in the Graeco-Roman World*. Cambridge University Press, 2002.

De Voulx, A. *Recherches sur la cooperation de la Regence d'Alger a la guerre de l'independance grecque d'apres des documents inedites*. Paris, 1856.

Dickie, John. "A Word at War: The Italian Army and Brigandage 1860–1870." *History Workshop Journal* 33, no. 1 (1992): 1–24.

Dimitropoulos, Dimitris. "Pirates during a Revolution: The Many Faces of Piracy and the Reaction of Local Communities." In *Corsairs and Pirates in the Eastern Mediterranean, Fifteenth-Nineteenth Centuries*, edited by Gelina Harlaftis, 29–40. Athens: Sylvia Ioannou Foundation, 2016.

Dumas, Alexandre. *Le Comte de Monte-Cristo*. Vol. 2. Paris: Michel Levy Freres, Libraires Editeurs, 1861.

Emrence, Cem. *Remapping the Ottoman Middle East: Modernity, Imperial Bureaucracy and Islam*. I.B. Tauris, 2015.

Erdem, Hakan. "'Do Not Think of the Greeks as Agricultural Labourers': Ottoman Responses to the Greek War of Independence." In *Citizenship and the Nation-state in Greece and Turkey*, edited by Thalia Dragonas, and Faruk Birtek, 67–84. Routledge, 2004.

Fahmy, Khaled. *All the Pasha's Men: Mehmed Ali, His Army and the Making of Modern Egypt*. Cambridge University Press, 1997.

Fakalou, Ekaterini. "Ιστορία του ΠΝ [History of the War Fleet]." http://www.hellenicnavy.gr/el/istoria/istoria-tou-pn.html (accessed March 10, 2018).

Farooqi, Naim R. "Moguls, Ottomans, and Pilgrims: Protecting the Routes to Mecca in the Sixteenth and Seventeenth Centuries." *The International History Review* 10, no. 2 (1988): 198–220.

Finkel, Caroline. *Osman's Dream: The History of the Ottoman Empire*. Hachette UK, 2007.

Finlay, George. *History of the Greek Revolution*. Vol. 2. Cambridge University Press, 2014.

Fokas, Dimitris G. *Χρονικά του Ελληνικού Β. Ναυτικού, 1833–1873* [*Chronicles of the Hellenic Royal Navy 1833–1873*]. Documents of the General Headquarter of the Royal Navy, 1923.

Fontenay, Michel. *La Méditerranée entre la Croix et le Croissant: Navigation, commerce, course et piraterie (xvie-xixe siècle)*. Paris: Classiques Garnier, 2010.

Fortna, Benjamin C. *The Circassian: A Life of Eşref Bey, Late Ottoman Insurgent and Special Agent*. Oxford University Press, 2016.

Franghiadis, Alexis. "Land Tenure Systems, Peasant Agriculture and Bourgeois Ascendancy in Greece, 1830–1914." In *The Economic Development of Southeastern Europe in the 19th Century*, edited by Edhem Eldem and Socrates Petmezas. Athens: Alpha Bank, 2011.

Franghiadis, Alexis. "Peasant Agriculture and Export Trade: Currant Viticulture in Southern Greece, 1830–1893." PhD diss., Florence: European University Institute, 1990.

Frank, Alison. "The Children of the Desert and the Laws of the Sea: Austria, Great Britain, the Ottoman Empire, and the Mediterranean Slave Trade in the Nineteenth Century." *The American Historical Review* 117, no. 2 (April 2012): 410–44.

Galani, Katerina. "The Napoleonic Wars and the Disruption of Mediterranean Shipping and Trade: British, Greek and American Merchants in Livorno." *The Historical Review/La Revue Historique* 7 (2011): 179–98.

Gallant, Thomas W. "Brigandage, Piracy, Capitalism, and State-Formation: Transnational Crime from a Historical World Systems Perspective." In *States and Illegal Practices*, edited by Josiah McC. Heyman, 25–61. New York: Berg, 1999.

Gallant, Thomas W. *Experiencing Dominion: Culture, Identity, and Power in the British Mediterranean*. Notre Dame, Indiana: University of Notre Dame Press, 2002.

Gallant, Thomas W. "Greek Bandit Gangs: Lone Wolves or a Family Affair?" *Journal of Modern Greek Studies* 6 (1988): 269–90.

Gallant, Thomas W. "Honor, Masculinity, and Ritual Knife Fighting in Nineteenth-Century Greece." *The American Historical Review* 105, no. 2 (2000): 359–82.

Gallant, Thomas W. *Modern Greece: From the War of Independence to the Present*. Rev. edn. Bloomsbury Academic, 2016.

Gallant, Thomas W. *The Edinburgh History of the Greeks, 1768 to 1913: The Long Nineteenth Century*. Edinburgh University Press, 2015.

Gauci, Liam. *In the Name of the Prince: Maltese Corsairs 1760–1798*. Heritage Malta Publishing, 2016.

Gavrilis, George. *The Dynamics of Interstate Boundaries*. Cambridge University Press, 2008.

Gekas, Sakis. "From the Nation to Emancipation: Greek Women Warriors from the Revolution (1820s) to the Civil War (1940s)." In *Women Warriors and National Heroes: Global Histories*, edited by Boyd Cothran, Joan Judge, and Adrian Shubert, 113–30. Bloomsbury Publishing, 2020.

Gingeras, Ryan. *Sorrowful Shores: Violence, Ethnicity, and the End of the Ottoman Empire, 1912–1923*. Oxford: Oxford University Press, 2009.

Ginio, Eyal. "Piracy and Redemption in the Aegean Sea during the First Half of the Eighteenth Century." *Turcica* 33 (2001): 135–47.

Gøbel, Erik. "The Danish 'Algerian Sea Passes', 1747–1838: An Example of Extraterritorial Production of 'Human Security'/Die 'Algerischen Seepässe' Dänemarks, 1747–1838: Ein Beispiel der extraterritorialen Produktion humaner Sicherheit." *Historical Social Research/Historische Sozialforschung* 35, no. 4 (2010): 164–89.

Gould, Andrew G. "Lords or Bandits? The Derebeys of Cilicia." *International Journal of Middle East Studies* 7, no. 4 (1976): 485–506.

Gounaris, Basil C. "Peasants, Brigands, and Navvies: Railways Dreams and Realities in the Ottoman Balkans." *European Journal of Economic History* 34, no. 1 (2006): 215–45.

Grant, Jonathan. "The Sword of the Sultan: Ottoman Arms Imports, 1854–1914." *The Journal of Military History* 66, no. 1 (2002): 9–36.

Gratien, Chris. "The Ottoman Quagmire: Malaria, Swamps, and Settlement in the Late Ottoman Mediterranean." *International Journal of Middle East Studies* 49, no. 4 (2017): 583–604.

Great Britain Parliament. *Correspondence Respecting the Negotiations for the Conclusion of Peace between Turkey and Greece*. 1898.

Greene, Molly. *A Shared World: Christians and Muslims in the Early Modern Mediterranean*. Princeton University Press, 2000.

Greene, Molly. *Catholic Pirates and Greek Merchants: A Maritime History of the Early Modern Mediterranean*. Princeton University Press, 2010.

Gürkan, Emrah Safa. "Batı Akdeniz'de osmanlı korsanlığı ve gaza meselesi [The Issue of Ottoman Piracy and Gaza in the Western Mediterranean]." *Kebikeç: İnsan Bilimleri İçin Kaynak Araştırmaları Dergisi* 33 (2012): 173–204.

Gürkan, Emrah Safa. *Sultanın Korsanları: Osmanlı Akdenizi'nde Gazâ, Yağma ve Esaret, 1500–1700* [*Pirates of the Sultan: Holy War, Looting, and Captivity in the Ottoman Mediterranean*]. İstanbul: Kronik Kitap, 2018.

Hallwood, C. Paul, and Thomas J. Miceli. *Maritime Piracy and Its Control: An Economic Analysis*. Singapore: Springer, 2014.

Hanna, Mark G. *Pirate Nests and the Rise of the British Empire, 1570–1740*. Chapel Hill: UNC Press, 2015.

Harding, Richard. *Modern Naval History: Debates and Prospects*. Bloomsbury Publishing, 2015.

Harlafti, Gelina. "Η εμπορική ναυτιλία: Η μετάβαση από τα ιστιοφόρα στα ατμόπλοια. [The Merchant Fleet: The Transition from Sailboats to Steamships]." In *Ιστορία του νέου ελληνισμού* [History of New Greek Hellenism] 1770–2000. Vol. 5, 1871–1909. Athens: Greek Letters, 2003.

Harlafti, Gelina. *Η ιστορία της ελληνόκοτητης ναυτιλίας το 19ο και 20ό αι.* [*The History of the Hellenic Merchant Marine in the 19th and 20th Centuries*]. Nefeli, 2001.

Harlaftis, Gelina. "The 'Eastern Invasion': Greeks in Mediterranean Trade and Shipping in the Eighteenth and Early Nineteenth Centuries." In *Trade and Cultural Exchange in the Early Modern Mediterranean: Braudel's Maritime Legacy*, edited by Colin Heywood, Mohamed-Salah Omri, and Maria Fusaro, 223–52. London and New York: Tauris Academic Studies, 2010.

Harlaftis, Gelina, and George Kostelenos. "International Shipping and National Economic Growth: Shipping Earnings and the Greek Economy in the Nineteenth Century." *The Economic History Review* 65, no. 4 (2012): 1403–27.

Harlaftis, Gelina, and Sophia Laiou. "Ottoman State Policy in Mediterranean Trade and Shipping, c. 1780–c.1820: The Rise of the Greek Owned Ottoman Merchant Fleet." In *Networks of Power in Modern Greece: Essays in Honor of John Campbell*, edited by Mark Mazower, 1–31. New York, 2008.

Hatzopoulos, Konstantinos. "The U.S. Navy in the Aegean during the Greek War of Independence, 1821–1829." In *Southeast European Maritime Commerce and Naval Policies from the Mid-Eighteenth Century to 1914*, edited by Apostolos E. Vacalopoulos, Constantinos D. Svolopoulos, and Béla K. Király, 343–61. Highland Lakes, NJ: Atlantic Research Publications, 1988.

Heller-Roazen, Daniel. *The Enemy of All: Piracy and the Law of Nations*. New York: Zone Books, 2009.

Hershenzon, Daniel. "Towards a Connected History of Bondage in the Mediterranean: Recent Trends in the Field." *History Compass* 15, no. 8 (2017).

Hershenzon, Daniel. *The Captive Sea: Slavery, Communication, and Commerce in Early Modern Spain and the Mediterranean*. University of Pennsylvania Press, 2018.

Herzog, Christoph. "Migration and the State: On Ottoman Regulations Concerning Migration since the Age of Mahmud II." In *The City in the Ottoman Empire: Migration and the Making of Urban Modernity*, edited by Ulrike Freitag, Malte Fuhrmann, Nora Lafi, and Florian Riedler, 117–34. Routledge, 2011.

Hobart, Pasha. *Sketches from My Life, by Hobart Pasha*. Longmans, Green, & Company, 1886.

Hobart-Hampden, Augustus Charles. *Hobart Pasha: Blockade-Running, Slaver-Hunting, and War and Sport in Turkey*. Outing Publishing Company, 1915.

Hobsbawm, Eric. *Age of Capital: 1848–1875*. Hachette UK, 2010.

Hobsbawm, Eric. *Age of Empire: 1875–1914*. Hachette UK, 2010.

Hobsbawm, Eric. *Age of Revolution: 1789–1848*. Hachette UK, 2010.

Hobsbawm, Eric. *Bandits*. Hachette UK, 2010.

Hobsbawm, Eric. *Primitive Rebels: Studies in Archaic Forms of Social Movement in the 19th and 20th Centuries*. Manchester University Press, 1971.

Hopper, Matthew S. *Slaves of One Master: Globalization and Slavery in Arabia in the Age of Empire*. Yale University Press, 2015.

Horden, Peregrine, and Nicholas Purcell. *The Corrupting Sea: A Study of Mediterranean History*. Wiley-Blackwell, 2000.

Howarth, David Armine. *The Greek Adventure: Lord Byron and Other Eccentrics in the War of Independence*. HarperCollins, 1976.

Huntington, Samuel P. *The Clash of Civilizations and the Remaking of World Order*. Penguin Books India, 1996.

Idol, David. "Commercial Agriculture and the Landscape of Capitalism in Nineteenth-Century Greece." *EuropeNow* 7 (2017).

Idol, David. "The 'Peaceful Conquest' of Lake Kopais: Modern Water Management and Environment in Greece." *Journal of Modern Greek Studies* 36, no. 1 (May 2018): 71–95.

Işıksel, Güneş. "Imperial Limits and Early Modernity: Borderland Clients of the Ottoman Empire and the 'Well-Protected Dominions'." *Journal of the Ottoman and Turkish Studies Association* 7, no. 1 (2020): 49–51.

Jelavich, Barbara. *History of the Balkans: Twentieth Century*. Vol. 2. Cambridge University Press, 1983.

Jenkins, Romilly. *The Dilessi Murders*. Prion Books, 1998.

Jones, C. G. Pitcairn, ed. *Piracy in the Levant, 1827–8*. Navy Records Society, 1934.

Kalafatis, Thanasis. "Η αγροτική οικονομία: Όψεις της αγροτικής ανάπτυξης [The Agriculture Economy: Aspects of Rural Development]." In *Ιστορία του νέου ελληνισμού* [History of New Greek Hellenism] 1770–2000. Vol. 5, 1871–1909. Athens: Greek Letters, 2003.

Karabelias, Gerassimos. "From National Heroes to National Villains: Bandits, Pirates and the Formation of Modern Greece." In *Subalterns and Social Protest: History from below in the Middle East and North Africa*, edited by Stephanie Cronin, 277–97. Routledge, 2008.

Karpat, Kemal H. "The Ottoman Emigration to America, 1860–1914." *International Journal of Middle East Studies* 17, no. 2 (1985): 175–209.

Kasaba, Reşat. *A Moveable Empire: Ottoman Nomads, Migrants, and Refugees*. Seattle: University of Washington Press, 2009.

Kasaba, Reşat. "Dreams of Empire, Dreams of Nations." In *Empire to Nation: Historical Perspectives on the Making of the Modern World*, edited by Joseph W. Esherick, Hasan Kayali, and Eric Van Young, 198–225. Rowman & Littlefield Publishers, 2006.

Kasaba, Reşat. *The Ottoman Empire and the World Economy: The Nineteenth Century.* SUNY Press, 1988.

Katsikas, Stefanos, and Anna Krinaki. "Reflections on an 'Ignominious Defeat': Reappraising the Effects of the Greco-Ottoman War of 1897 on Greek Politics." *Journal of Modern Greek Studies* 38, no. 1 (2020): 109–30.

Kefalas, Kalliopi. "Amnesty and Conflict of Interest in the Dilessi Murders (1870)." *Chronica Mundi* 11, no. 1 (2016): 120–45.

Kern, Stephen. *The Culture of Time and Space, 1880–1918.* Harvard University Press, 2003.

Khuri-Makdisi, Ilham. *The Eastern Mediterranean and the Making of Global Radicalism, 1860–1914.* University of California Press, 2010.

Koliopoulos, John S. "Brigandage and Irredentism in Nineteenth-Century Greece." *European History Quarterly* 19, no. 2 (1989): 193–228.

Koliopoulos, John S. *Brigands with a Cause: Brigandage and Irredentism in Modern Greece, 1821–1912.* Clarendon Press, 1987.

Kolovos, Elias. "Insularity and Island Society in the Ottoman Context." *Turcica* 39 (2007): 49–122.

Kolovos, Elias, Yorgos Vidras, and Aris Kydonakis. *A Database of the Ottoman Documents in the Kaireios Library of the Island of Andros.* http://androsdocs.ims.forth.gr/

Kolovos, George. "Η πειρατεία στα χρόνια της Ελληνικής Επαναστάσεως και η αντιμετώπισή της από τον Καποδίστρια [Piracy in the Years of the Greek Revolution and the Confrontation of Kapodistrias]." https://perialos.blogspot.com/2011/05/blog-post_09.html (accessed May 9, 2011).

Komatsu, Kaori. "Financial Problems of the Navy during the Reign of Abdülhamid II." *Oriente Modern* 20, no. 1 (2001): 209–19.

Konstantinides, Kostis. *Η ληστεία και η πειρατεία στη Σκύρο, Σκιάθο και Σκόπελο κατά τη διάρκεια της επανάστασης του 1821 μέχρι της αντιβασιλείας του Όθωνα, Ιστορική μελέτη βασισμένη αποκλειστικά επί εγγράφων, τόμος πρώτος [Brigandage and Piracy in Skyros, Skiathos, and Skopelo during the 1821 Revolution until the Reign of Otho].* Athens: The Skyros Society, 1988.

Lambert, Frank. *The Barbary Wars: American Independence in the Atlantic World.* Macmillan, 2005.

Langensiepen, Bernd, and Ahmet Güleryüz. *The Ottoman Steam Navy, 1828–1923.* Conway Maritime Press, 1995.

Leeson, Peter T. *The Invisible Hook: The Hidden Economics of Pirates.* Princeton: Princeton University Press, 2009.

Lev, Yaacov. *Charity, Endowments, and Charitable Institutions in Medieval Islam.* University Press of Florida, 2005.

Lewis, Martin W., and Kären E. Wigen. *The Myth of Continents: A Critique of Metageography*. University of California Press, 1997.

Linebaugh, Peter, and Marcus Rediker. *The Many-Headed Hydra: Sailors, Slaves, Commoners, and the Hidden History of the Revolutionary Atlantic*. Beacon Press, 2013.

Little, Benerson. *Pirate Hunting: The Fight against Pirates, Privateers, and Sea Raiders from Antiquity to the Present*. Potomac Books, Inc., 2010.

Liu, Sandy J. C. "Violence and Piratical/Surreptitious Activities Associated with the Chinese Communities in the Melaka–Singapore Region (1780–1840)." In *Piracy and Surreptitious Activities in the Malay Archipelago and Adjacent Seas, 1600–1840*, edited by Tedd Y. H. Sim, 51–76. Singapore: Springer, 2014.

Livanios, Dimitris. "'Conquering the Souls': Nationalism and Greek Guerrilla Warfare in Ottoman Macedonia, 1904–1908." *Byzantine and Modern Greek Studies* 23, no. 1 (1999): 195–221.

López Nadal, Gonçal. "Corsairing as a Commercial System: The Edges of Legitimate Trade." In *Bandits at Sea: A Pirates Reader*, edited by C. R. Pennell, 125–36. New York: New York University Press, 2001.

MacKay, Joseph. "Pirate Nations: Maritime Pirates as Escape Societies in Late Imperial China." *Social Science History* 37, no. 4 (2013): 551–73.

Makdisi, Ussama. "Ottoman Orientalism." *The American Historical Review* 107, no. 3 (2002): 768–96.

Mandamadiotou, Maria. *The Greek Orthodox Community of Mytilene: Between the Ottoman Empire and the Greek state, 1876–1912*. Oxford; Berlin: Lang, 2013.

Mathew, Johan. *Margins of the Market: Trafficking and Capitalism across the Arabian Sea*. University of California Press, 2016.

Mazower, Mark. *Salonica, City of Ghosts: Christians, Muslims and Jews 1430–1950*. Vintage, 2007.

Minawi, Mostafa. *The Ottoman Scramble for Africa: Empire and Diplomacy in the Sahara and the Hijaz*. Stanford University Press, 2016.

Moalla, Asma. *The Regency of Tunis and the Ottoman Porte, 1777–1814: Army and Government of a North-African Eyâlet at the End of the Eighteenth Century*. Routledge, 2005.

Oliver, Steven, Ryan Jablonski, and Justin V. Hastings. "The Tortuga Disease: The Perverse Effects of Illicit Foreign Capital." *International Studies Quarterly*, Vol. 61, Issue 2, no. 1 (June 2017): 312–27.

Orfali, Moisés. "Ragusa and Ragusan Jews in the Effort to Ransom Captives." *Mediterranean Historical Review* 17, no. 2 (2002): 14–31

Owen, Roger. *The Middle East in the World Economy, 1800–1914*. I.B. Tauris, 1993.

Özdemir, Bülent. *Ottoman Reforms and Social Life: Reflections from Salonica, 1830–1850*. Istanbul: Isis Press, 2003.

Özel, Oktay. "Migration and Power Politics: The Settlement of Georgian Immigrants in Turkey (1878– 1908)." *Middle Eastern Studies* 46, no. 4 (2010): 477–96.

Paizis-Paradelis, K. *Hellenic Warships, 1829–2001*. Society for the Study of Greek History, 2002.

Paizis-Paradelis, K. "Η πειρατεία κατά τους χρόνους της Ελληνικής Επανάστασης και τα πρώτα μεταεπαναστασττικά χρόνια [Piracy during the Years of the Greek Revolution and the Immediate Post-Revolutionary Years]." *Nautiki Epitheorisi* 133, no. 469 (1991): 377–94.

Papataxiarchis, Eythimios, and Socrates D. Petmezas. "The Devolution of Property and Kinship Practices in Late-and Post-Ottoman Ethnic Greek Societies: Some Demo-Economic Factors of Nineteenth and Twentieth Century Transformations." *Mélanges de l'Ecole française de Rome. Italie et Méditerranée* 110, no. 1 (1998): 217–41.

Panzac, Daniel. "International and Domestic Maritime Trade in the Ottoman Empire during the 18th Century." *International Journal of Middle East Studies* 24, no. 2 (1992): 189–206.

Panzac, Daniel. *La marine ottomane: de l'apogée à la chute de l'Empire, 1572–1923*. CNRS, 2009.

Panzac, Daniel. *The Barbary Corsairs: The End of a Legend, 1800–1820*. Brill, 2005.

Petmezas, Socrates D. "Export-Dependent Agriculture, Revenue Crisis and Agrarian Productivity Involution. The Greek Case (1860s–1930s)." *Histoire & Mesure* (2000): 321–37.

Philliou, Christine M. *Biography of an Empire: Governing Ottomans in an Age of Revolution*. University of California Press, 2011.

Policante, Amedeo. "Barbary Legends on the Mediterranean Frontier: Corsairs, Pirates and the Shifting Bounds of the International Community." In *Corsairs and Pirates in the Eastern Mediterranean, Fifteenth-Nineteenth Centuries*, edited by Gelina Harlaftis, 141–50. Athens: Sylvia Ioannou Foundation, 2016.

Progoulakis, Georges, and Eugenia Bournova. "Le monde rural grec, 1830–1912." *Ruralia* 8 (2001).

Prousis, Theophilus C. "Bedlam in Beirut: A British Perspective in 1826." *Chronos: Revue d'Histoire de l'Université de Balamand*, no. 15 (2007): 89–106.

Quataert, Donald. *The Ottoman Empire, 1700–1922*. Cambridge University Press, 2005.

Raymond, Catherine Zara. "Piracy and Armed Robbery in the Malacca Strait: A Problem Solved?" *Naval War College Review* 62, no. 3 (2009): 31–42.

Rejeb, Lotfi Ben. "'The General Belief of the World': Barbary as Genre and Discourse in Mediterranean History." *European Review of History—Revue européenne d'histoire*, 19, no. 1 (2012): 15–31.

Renieri, Irini. "Household Formation in 19th-Century Central Anatolia: The Case Study of a Turkish-Speaking Orthodox Christian Community." *International Journal of Middle East Studies* 34, no. 3 (2002): 495–517.

Rodogno, Davide. *Against Massacre: Humanitarian Interventions in the Ottoman Empire, 1815–1914*. Princeton University Press, 2012.

Rubin, Alfred P. *The Law of Piracy*. Newport, Rhode Island: US Naval War College Press, 1988.

Said, Edward W. *Culture and Imperialism*. New York: Alfred A Knopf, Inc, 1993.

Said, Edward W. *Orientalism*. New York: Vintage, 1979.

Salzmann, Ariel. "A Travelogue Manqué? The Accidental Itinerary of a Maltese Priest in the Seventeenth Century Mediterranean." In *A Faithful Sea: The Religious Cultures of the Mediterranean, 1200–1700*, edited by Adnan Ahmed Husain and Katherine Elizabeth Fleming, 149–72. Oneworld Publications Limited, 2007.

Sariyannis, Marinos. "Ottoman Political Thought Up to the Tanzimat: A Concise History." *Research Project, Institute for Mediterranean Studies, Greece* 173 (2015).

Sicking, Louis H. J. et al. "Islands, Pirates, Privateers and the Ottoman Empire in the Early Modern Mediterranean." In *Seapower, Technology and Trade: Studies in Turkish Maritime History*, edited by Couto, Dejanirah, Feza Günergun, and Maria Pia Pedani Fabris, 239–52. Piri Reis University Publications, 2014.

Smiley, Will. *From Slaves to Prisoners of War: The Ottoman Empire, Russia, and International Law*. Oxford University Press, 2018.

Smiley, Will. "War without War: The Battle of Navarino, the Ottoman Empire, and the Pacific Blockade." *Journal of the History of International Law* 18 (2016): 42–69.

Stark, Francis Raymond. *The Abolition of Privateering and the Declaration of Paris. Vol. 8. No. 3*. Columbia University, 1897.

Starkey, David J. "Pirates and Markets." In *Bandits at Sea: A Pirates Reader*, edited by C. R. Pennell, 107–24. New York: New York University Press, 2001.

Starkey, David J., and Matthew McCarthy, "A Persistent Phenomenon: Private Prize-taking in the British Atlantic World, c.1540–1856." In *Persistent Piracy: Maritime Violence and State-Formation in Global Historical Perspective*, edited by Stefan Eklöf Amirell, and Leos Müller, 131–51. Palgrave Macmillan, 2014.

Strohmeier, Martin. "Economy and Society in the Aegean Province of the Ottoman Empire, 1840–1912." *Turkish Historical Review* 1, no. 2 (2010): 164–95.

Şenışık, Pinar. *The Transformation of Ottoman Crete: Revolts, Politics and Identity in the Late Nineteenth Century*. I.B. Tauris, 2011.

Şimşek, Fatma. "Blockading an Island: Collective Punishment, Islanders, and the State in the 'Largest' Island at the End of the Nineteenth Century." In *Islands of the Ottoman Empire*, edited by Antonis Hadjikyriacou, 107–19. Princeton: Markus Wiener, 2018.

Şimşek, Fatma. "19. Yüzyılın İkinci Yarısında Cezayir-i Bahr-i Sefid Vilayetinde Kaçak Gemi Yapımı [Illegal Shipbuilding in the Archipelago Province in the Second Half of the 19th Century]." *Belleten* 83, no. 296 (2019): 201–27.

Tabak, Faruk. "Imperial Rivalry and Port-Cities: A View from Above." *Mediterranean Historical Review* 24, no. 2 (2009): 79–94.

Tabak, Faruk. *The Waning of the Mediterranean, 1550–1870: A Geohistorical Approach*. Johns Hopkins University Press, 2008.

Talbot, Michael. "'Ill-Treated by Friends': Ottoman Responses to British Privateering in the Mid-18th Century." Presentation, Sylvia Ioannou Foundation Conference: Corsairs and Pirates in the Eastern Mediterranean, 15th–19th *c*., Athens, Greece October 18, 2014.

Talbot, Michael. "Ottoman Seas and British Privateers: Defining Maritime Territoriality in the Eighteenth-Century Levant." In *Well-Connected Domains: Towards an Entangled Ottoman History*, edited by Pascal Firges, Tobias Graf, Christian Roth, and Gülay Tulasoğlu, 54–70. Brill, 2014.

Talbot, Michael. "Separating the Waters from the Sea: The Place of Islands in Ottoman Maritime Territoriality during the Eighteenth Century." *Princeton Papers: Interdisciplinary Journal of Middle Eastern Studies* 18 (2018): 61–86.

Tatsios, Theodore George. *The Megali Idea and the Greek-Turkish War of 1897: The Impact of the Cretan Problem on Greek Irredentism, 1866–1897*. New York, 1984.

The Times Digital Archive. "Greece and Turkey." Times [London, England] July 1, 1867: 5. Web. April 14, 2017.

Themeli-Katifori, Despina. *Η δίωξις της πειρατείας και το θαλάσσιον δικαστήριον: κατά την πρώτην Καποδιστριακή περίοδον: 1828–1829* [The Persecution of Pirates and the Naval Courts during the First Kapodistrian Period: 1828–1829], 1/2. Athens: National Kapodistrian University—School of Philosophy, 1973.

Themeli-Katifori, Despina. *Αἱ ἀποφάσεις τοῦ Θαλάσσιου Δικαστηρίου 1828–1829* [The Decisions of the Naval Court, 1828–1829]. Athens, 1976.

Thomson, Janice E. *Mercenaries, Pirates, and Sovereigns: State-building and Extraterritorial Violence in Early Modern Europe*. Princeton University Press, 1996.

Tlili-Sellaouti, Rachida. "La France revolutionnaire et les populations musulmanes de la Turquie d'Europe au moment de l'expedition d'Egypte: une mise a l'epreuve du cosmopolitisme." In *Ottoman Rule and the Balkans, 1760–1850*, edited by Antonis

Anastasopoulos and Elias Kolovos, 95–120. Rethymno, Greece: Department of History and Archaeology of the University of Crete, 2007.

Tröster, Manuel. "Roman Hegemony and Non-State Violence: A Fresh Look at Pompey's Campaign against the Pirates." *Greece & Rome* 56, no. 1 (2009): 14–33.

Tucker, Judith E. "Introduction." In *The Making of the Modern Mediterranean: Views from the South*, edited by Judith E. Tucker, 1–15. University of California Press, 2019.

Tucker, Judith E. "She Would Rather Perish: Piracy and Gendered Violence in the Mediterranean." *Journal of Middle East Women's Studies* 10, no. 3 (2014): 8–39.

Tzanelli, Rodanthi. "Haunted by the 'Enemy' Within: Brigandage, Vlachian/Albanian Greekness, Turkish 'Contamination,' and Narratives of Greek Nationhood in the Dilessi/Marathon Affair (1870)." *Journal of Modern Greek Studies* 20, no. 1 (2002): 47–74.

Tzanelli, Rodanthi. "The 'Greece' of Britain and the 'Britain' of Greece: Performance, Stereotypes, Expectations and Intermediaries in 'Neohellenic' and Victorian Narratives (1864–1881)." PhD diss., Lancaster University, 2009.

Vaka-yı Giridiyye [*Events of Crete*]. Herakleion: Vikelaia Municipal Library, 1832.

Wadsworth, James E. *Global Piracy: A Documentary History of Seaborne Banditry*. Bloomsbury Publishing, 2019.

Weiss, Gillian. *Captives and Corsairs: France and Slavery in the Early Modern Mediterranean*. Stanford: Stanford University Press, 2011.

White, Joshua M. *Piracy and Law in the Ottoman Mediterranean*. Stanford: Stanford University Press, 2017.

White, Joshua M. "Piracy of the Ottoman Mediterranean: Slave Laundering and Subjecthood." In *The Making of the Modern Mediterranean: Views from the South*, edited by Judith E. Tucker, 95–122. University of California Press, 2019.

Wick, Alexis. *The Red Sea: In Search of Lost Space*. University of California Press, 2016.

Willmott, Hedley Paul. *The Last Century of Sea Power: From Port Arthur to Chanak, 1894–1922*. Vol. 1. Indiana University Press, 2009.

Wilson, Peter Lamborn. *Pirate Utopias: Moorish Corsairs & European Renegadoes*. Autonomedia, 2003.

Woodhouse, Christopher Montague. *Capodistria: The Founder of Greek Independence*. Oxford University Press, 1973.

Yaycioglu, Ali. *Partners of the Empire: The Crisis of the Ottoman Order in the Age of Revolutions*. Stanford University Press, 2016.

Yeşilyurt, Yahya. "Yemen Karasularında Korsanlık ve Osmanlı Devleti'nin Aldığı Tedbirler (1869–1914) [Piracy in the Territorial Waters of Yemen and the Measures Taken by the Ottoman Empire (1869–1914)]." *Bilig* 85 (2018): 57–82.

Yosmaoğlu, İpek K. *Blood Ties: Religion, Violence and the Politics of Nationhood in Ottoman Macedonia, 1878–1908.* Cornell University Press, 2013.

Zanou, Konstantina. *Transnational Patriotism in the Mediterranean, 1800–1850: Stammering the Nation.* Oxford University Press, 2018.

Zarinebaf, Fariba. *Mediterranean Encounters: Trade and Pluralism in Early Modern Galata.* University of California Press, 2018.

Zürcher, Erik Jan. "The Ottoman Conscription System in Theory and Practice 1844–1914." *International Review of Social History* 43, no. 3 (1998): 437–49.

Index

Abdülaziz (Ottoman sultan) 66, 73, 82, 91
Abdülhamid II (Ottoman sultan) 91, 100, 113, 164n6
Abdülmecid (Ottoman sultan) 73, 91
Abode of Islam (*darülislam*) 3, 32
Adriatic Sea 10, 80–2, 157n15
Agriovotani 54
Albania 57, 159n44
Albanians 27, 59, 81, 115; as irregular soldiers 103, 107, 145n10
Algiers (Algeria) 6, 9, 13–16, 23, 134n28, 137n43, 142n70, 156n41; French colonization of 1, 3, 16–17, 39–40, 45, 48, 136n33, 142n71; giving humanitarian aid to Crete 28, 36, 45; in the Greek War of Independence 35–40, 148n34; resettling refugees from Morea 37
Ali Pasha Tepedelenli 2, 27, 112
Amalia (Greek corvette) 49
Andros 138–9n44, 153n30
Angelo dell' Abbondanza (Italian merchant ship) 81
Antikythera (Cerigotto) 76–7
Archipelago Province (*Eyalet-i Cezayir-i*) archives 10, 17–23, 43, 47, 67, 81, 86–8, 97–9, 105, 122, 124
Argyros, Spyridon 121
Arkadi (Greek blockade-runner) 75–9, 159n35
Artan, Tülay 119–20, 168n3
Attica 43
Austria-Hungary 9, 49, 65, 123, 163n51
Aydın 120

Bahr-i Sefid 9–11, 28, 35, 43, 108, 115
Balkan Peninsula 9–10, 25, 27, 57, 81, 87, 134n27, 143–4n4, 158n23
Balkan Wars (1912–13) 116, 123, 167n50, 167n51

bankruptcy 97; in Greece 49, 91, 99; in the Ottoman Empire 24, 73, 91, 100–1
Batalas, Achilles 111, 144n4
Battle of Navarino 33, 37–9, 147n27, 148–9n34, 156n3
Beirut 29
Benghazi 13
Berkefşan (Ottoman torpedo boat) 101
Bertinatti, Joseph 81, 159n43
Black Sea 9–11, 112, 120, 158n23
blockade 15, 74, 83, 106–7; blockade runners 70, 73, 75–80; criteria of legality established by Treaty of Paris 65; French blockade of Algiers 17, 40; illegal blockades 66; in times of war vs peace 156n3
Boeotia 90
Bouboulina, Laskarina 149n41
boundary regimes 4, 49, 159n44; border disputes 130n7; Greece allowing pirates to escape its maritime borders 50–1, 54–7; in the Greco-Ottoman borderlands 49, 87–8, 123, 171n24
brigands 88, 110; and state formation 25, 69, 111–12, 114–15, 120, 131n17, 132–3n20, 143–4n4; released from prison 24, 98, 104–5, 117; terrestrial versus amphibious 6, 69, 109
Brown, Nathan 120
Bulgaria 115, 159n39, 170n23, 171n25

Cairo 35
Cape Crio (Deveboynu) 70, 157n15
Caribbean Sea 6, 8–9
Cayli, Baris 109
Çeşme 103
Cevat Şakir Pasha 99, 164n6
Chalcis (Chalkida) 58
Chania 36–8, 44–5, 75
Charles X (king of France) 17, 40

Chet, Guy 121
Chios 68, 70, 103, 107
civilizing mission 17, 39
climate change 85–6, 136n34
Cockatrice (British steamer) 86
Codrington, Edward 29, 32–3, 146–7n17, 151n2
constitutional reforms in Greece: in the first Hellenic Republic 41; 1844 constitutional monarchy 23, 42, 47; 1864 constitutional reforms 42, 121
Corbatzi 54
corsairs 3, 25, 38, 68, 83, 122, 131n12, 164n55; definitions of 5–8; Greek 23, 32–4, 38, 63, 87, 145n10; Maltese 6, 12–14, 141n61; North African (Barbary) 3, 6, 10, 12–13, 15, 17, 23, 28, 30, 35–6, 39–40, 45, 62. (*See also* privateers).
covert operations 70–3, 171n25
Crete 31, 110, 130n7, 150n49, 167n51; Algerian aid to 36; in the Greek War of Independence 23, 28, 31–2; under Egyptian rule 23, 28, 31, 43–5, 99; under Venetian rule 10, 31–2; 1866–9 rebellion 66, 70, 75–80, 83, 99, 159n35; 1875–8 rebellion 99; 1895–8 rebellion 99–101, 113–15, 164n6, 166n42
Crimean War 10, 19, 21, 23–4, 64–6, 79, 88, 91, 93, 110, 112; Greek role in 49–50
Crotone (Cotrone) 81
Cyprus 48–9

Dardanelles 9, 29, 87, 161n14
Datça Peninsula 120, 153n35, 157n15
Deliyannis, Theodoros 88, 99–100, 102
Deval, Pierre 17, 40
devşirme, end of 34
Dilessi (Marathon) Murders 88, 111
Dumas, Alexandre 2–3, 69

Egypt 11, 23, 27–8, 32, 35–9, 47, 60, 85, 111, 136n33, 140n59; military reforms 30, 35–6; rule over Crete 23, 31, 44–5, 99; uprising against the Ottoman Empire 23, 28, 44–5, 47
emigration 86, 94–5
enosis (unification with Greece) 114, 117

Enossis (Greek blockade-runner) 79, 159n35
Epiros 49, 51, 54, 61
Ethniki Etaireia (National Society) 99–100, 104, 170–1n24
Euboea 50–2, 58
export-oriented agriculture 85–6, 89–95, 97, 160n47

false flag operations 68, 71, 76–7
Fao (Al-Faw) 99
filibusters 5, 25, 119; from Greece 123, 135n32
Forth-Rouen, Baron Alexandre 53, 55, 62, 151n9
Foxhound (British warship) 70–2
France 2–3, 13–14, 50, 54, 63, 65, 76, 89–91, 107, 113, 129n2, 134n29, 138n43, 139n46, 140n59, 141n61; colonization of Algiers 1, 3, 16–17, 39–40, 45, 48, 136n33, 142n71; in the Greek War of Independence 33, 40
Frangiadakis, Evangelos 114
Fuad Pasha 73, 79, 81

Gallant, Thomas 58, 132n20
Gavrilis, George 87, 151n7
George of Denmark (King of Greece) 74, 81, 100
George Washington (US warship) 14–5
Gökçeada (İmroz) 86
Gramvousa 31–4, 44–5, 49, 119
Great Britain 14, 16, 19, 23, 48, 76, 78–9, 82, 97, 103–5, 7, 109, 145n10, 158n19, 160n10, 163n41, 163n51; colonies of 14, 57, 68, 111, 120, 141n61, 161n17; in the Crimean War 50, 52–6, 65, 88, 112; in the Greek War of Independence 30, 32–3, 38–9; privateers of 5, 15, 86, 88, 91, 107; Royal Navy 3, 8, 10, 16, 24, 49, 60–1, 66, 70–4, 87, 121, 169n13, 169n14
Great Powers 10, 32–3, 45, 51, 54, 74, 76–7, 80, 104, 156n3
Greco-Ottoman War (1897) 24, 97–117; causes of 97–100; piracy during the armistice 105–6, 108; piracy during the war 103; preparation for 100–2; outcomes of 106–7, 116–17, 167n51

Greek War of Independence 2, 16, 23, 27–44, 48, 99, 136n33, 142n71, 144n4, 146n16, 150n44, 156n3
Greene, Molly 13, 130n11
Gürkan, Emrah Safa 14

Halepa Pact 99
Halki 71
Hellas (Greek frigate) 30
Herakleion 75
Hobart-Hampden, Augustus Charles (Hobart Pasha) 66; in the British Navy 70–3, in the Ottoman Navy 79–80
Hobsbawm, Eric 54, 59, 122, 132n20, 151n3, 168n10, 170n20
Holland 14, 16
human trafficking 38, 68–70
humanitarianism 16, 142n71, 156n3; Algiers giving humanitarian aid to Crete 28, 36, 45; Algiers resettling refugees from Morea 37
Hussein *Dey* 16–17, 38, 40
Hydra (Greek coastal defense ship) 102
Hydra 29, 61

Ibrahim Pasha 32, 35, 37–9, 44–5, 147n27, 148n34
Indian Ocean 10, 85, 95, 161n10
Indonesia 95–6, 146n13
Ionian Islands 56–60, 68, 71, 153n32, 157n7
Ionian Sea 81
Iraklia 88
irregular soldiers 24–5, 28–30, 41, 49, 98, 103–5, 133n20, 144n4, 145n10; categories of 5–6; in the Macedonia conflict 99–100, 108–17; legislation against 65–6, 106–7; shift from using irregulars to special forces 123–4, 171n25; trafficked to Crete to aid rebels 75–6
İstanbul 11, 14–15, 35, 38, 105, 108, 113, 134n29, 135n32, 135n33, 150n49
İstanköy (Kos) 28
Italy 2, 59, 66, 80–2, 88–9, 131n15, 143n78, 155n40, 159n43; ambiguous ethnicity 57–9, 170n23; captives from 16–17, 40; Italian language 6, 18, 58–9, 131n16, 157n15; suppressing brigandage and piracy 24, 80

İzmir 38, 92–3, 120, 148n30
İzzeddin (Ottoman warship) 79

janissaries 29–30, 34–5, 133n20, 145n10
Jefferson, Thomas 15
journalism: *London Times* 75–8; pirated newspapers and printed materials 143n76; *Vaka-yı Giridiyye* 44, 150n49

Kalas 86
Kalligas, Giorgios 60–1
Kalligas, Paulos 50
Kanaris, Konstantinos 51, 56
Kapodistrias, Ioannis 33–4, 41, 49, 146n17; assassination of 41–2
Karaağaç 105
Karteria (Greek steamer) 30–1
Kasteli Kissamou 44
Kastellorizo 71
Kefalonia 68, 153n32
Kerochori 52–4
Kitros 103, 109
Knights of Saint John 6, 13–14, 141n61, 155n40
Koliopoulos, John 27, 143–4n4
Kolovos, George 41–2
Kostis Konstantinides 41
Koumoundouros, Alexandros 90
Koutzoukos, Dimitris 62–4

Lake Kopais 90, 162n32
Lakonia 34
land reform in Greece 85–6, 90–1
language 4; creating ethnic ambiguity 59–60, 81, 170n23; Greek 6–7, 18, 58–9, 99, 132n18, 150n49, 131n15, 132n18; pidgin 7; Turkish 6–7, 18, 21, 58–9, 131n15, 134n27, 150n49
Larissa 104
Law of Release (concerning prisoners of war) 38
Leander (British frigate) 53
Limnos 108–11, 113–14, 121
littoral 4, 15, 31–2, 102, 105–6
loans 30, 90–1, 163n41

Macedonia (region) 52, 61; conflict in 98, 100, 114–16, 123, 171n25
Mahmoud ben Amin Essekka 38, 138n34

Mahmud II (Ottoman sultan) 2, 16, 29, 35, 44, 145n8
Malay Peninsula 8, 96
Malta 6, 12–14, 32–3, 39, 86, 141n61, 148–9n34, 155n40
Mandamadiotou, Maria 109
Mani 34, 37, 147–8n27
Marie Joë (French brig) 48–9
Marmaris 71
Mathilde (Greek schooner) 52, 55
Mavrokordatos, Alexandros 53–6, 152n16
Mavromichalis, Petrobey 32–4, 41
megali idea (Greek irredentism) 74, 88, 100, 158n23
Mehmed Ali 23, 28, 31–2, 35, 39, 44–5, 105, 136n33, 148n34
Messinia 34
Mesudiye (Ottoman ironclad) 101
Methoni (Greek corvette) 49
Miaoulis, Andreas 34
Minawi, Mostafa 122
monopoly on violence 3, 6, 111, 133n20
Morea (the Peloponnese) 13, 27, 32, 34–5, 37, 39, 43, 45, 49, 57, 147n27
Moustafa ben Gabes 37
Murad V (Ottoman sultan) 91
Mykonos 32
Mytilene (Lesbos) 37, 108–9, 114

Napoleon 14–15, 141n61
Narval (French steamer) 53
nationalism in Greece and the Ottoman Empire 109, 140n59, 170n23; spread through education 115; Turkish vs Ottoman 159n39, 166n31
naval courts 7, 151n2. *See also* prize tribunals
Naxos 88
Neçm-i Şevket (Ottoman ironclad) 101
New Order military (*nizam-ı cedid*) 29, 35, 151n1
North Africa 6, 10–17, 28, 30–40, 48, 107, 122, 134n29, 136n34, 137n40, 141n61, 146n16

Odessa 86
olive production 89–90

orientalism 2–3, 17, 119; "Barbary" as an orientalist trope 11–12; internal Ottoman orientalism 166n31
Otto of Bavaria (king of Greece) 27, 41–3, 48, 90, 169n16; expulsion of 66, 74
Ottoman constitution 109, 112
Ottoman Land Code (1858) 89–90, 92

Paizis-Paradelis, K 121, 169n16
Paris Declaration Respecting Maritime Law. *See* Treaty of Paris (1856)
Peleng-i Derya (Ottoman torpedo boat) 101
Persian Gulf 10, 87, 160n10
phylloxera 24, 85, 89, 93, 160n3
Piraeus 74, 77, 86
pirates: attacking warships 41–3; allowed to flee into Ottoman waters 23–4, 47, 50–1, 54–7, 98, 103, 105, 108, 111, 114, 117; and state-building 3–4, 8–10, 24, 33–4, 123–4, 144n4, 145n10; as a label for enemies 8, 11–12, 23; definitions of 4–8, 45, 131n17; determining ethnicity of 57–62, 81; in the Western imagination 1–3, 69; protected as *Rum* rebels 51–4, 146n16; transitioning to licit professions 95–6
Policante, Amadeo 11
Port Said 11
primitive rebellion 48, 54, 120, 122, 132n20, 151n3
privateers 4, 10, 12, 45, 67–8, 107, 131n12, 156n2; abolition of 3, 21, 24, 45, 64–6, 82–3, 97, 119, 124; ambiguous situations 47, 70–2, 106, 143n76, 156n41; definitions of 5–8; of Greece 29, 33, 48–9, 86, 145n10; of the Great Powers 13, 15, 86, 107
prizes 5, 8, 14, 29, 65, 68, 105, 107, 110, 120, 169n14; prize tribunals 32–3, 45
Psara (Greek coastal defense ship) 102
Psara 61
Public Debt Administration (PDA) 86, 92

Ragusa 138n44
Rallis, Dimitrios 100, 116
ransom 48, 104, 120; after ransom networks dismantled 24, 45, 62–4, 67–9; early modern ransom networks

8, 12–15, 122, 137n43, 138n44, 139n46, 155n40
Raymond, Catherine Zara 96
Red Sea 10–11, 21, 82, 85, 87, 143n78, 160n2
refugees 37, 41, 95, 100
Rejeb, Lotfi Ben 11–12
religions: as identity 59; bias against Islam 11–12, 76–8, 80; coexistence of 12, 28, 36–7, 44–5, 47, 60, 78, 109, 114, 121, 135n33, 138n44; conflict between 6, 11, 13, 16, 27–8, 32, 37–8, 45, 60–1, 130n11, 153n33, 154n40; conflict within 14–15, 44–5, 131n12; conversion 32, 34, 137n43; in nation-building 113, 116, 151n1; Jewish community 17, 37, 40, 104, 114, 138n44
Rethymno 75, 114
Rhodes 13, 63–4, 70–1, 87, 108, 113
Risorgimento 66, 80
Romania (Danubian Principalities) 9
Rum (Ottoman Greeks) 7, 13–14, 58–60, 116–17, 121, 130n11, 131n15; between Greek and Ottoman nationalism 108–110, 116–17; rebelling after formation of Greece 75, 98, 120
Russia 9, 13, 49, 57, 65, 74, 76, 78, 94, 101, 107, 143n76, 145n10, 156n41; Greek-Russian notables 27, 33, 41; in the Greek War of Independence 3, 27, 33, 40–1

Saint Nicholas (Ottoman ship) 87
Salonica (Thessaloniki) 61, 68, 102, 120, 157n7
Samos (Greek warship) 42–3
Samos 32, 49, 151n8, 153n29
Samothrace 52, 86, 98
Schoinoussa 88
Selim III (Ottoman sultan) 29, 35, 145n7, 151n1, 156n41
Seskli 71
shepherds aiding pirates 61–2, 88, 154n36, 167n1
Sicily 32–3, 81
Sicking, Louis 5
Skiathos 52

Skopelos 52
Skyros 62
slavery 12, 64, 129n2, 137n43; abolition of slave trade 14, 70, 160n10, 163n51; captives sold at slave markets 8, 12–13, 62–4, 68; saturated of slave markets 38; slave raids 13; white slavery debates 39–40
smuggling 1–2, 5, 82, 102, 120, 139n44, 143n78, 159n44; of arms 75–6, 79, 82
social banditry 109, 132n20, 154n36, 168n10
Solon (Greek schooner) 52
Souda 32, 44, 75
Spain 89, 146n16
Spetsai (Greek coastal defense ship) 102
Spetses 29, 149n41
Spinalonga 32, 75
steamships 49, 52–3, 72, 76–7, 85–7, 101, 105, 146n13; introduction of 30–1, 93–4, 160n1, 163n48; upgrading war fleets to 73–4, 108, 115
Strati, Giovanni 68–9, 157n7
Strohmeier, Martin 109, 169n15
Suez Canal 11, 67, 82, 85, 87, 141n61, 160n1
Suzanna (Greek merchant brigantine) 81
Symi 70–1
Syria 44–5, 89, 135n33
Syros (Syra) 32, 58, 62–3, 68, 77–9, 88

Tanzimat 23, 67, 99, 150n1
telegraphy 112–3
Tevfik Pasha 88
Thasos 52
the auspicious incident 29–30, 35
Themeli-Katifori, Despina 34, 147n20
Thessaly 49, 53, 88, 98, 100, 103–5, 107–8, 111
Thomson, Janice 119–20, 131n17, 170n24, 171n25
Tirekili 105
Treaty of Berlin (1878) 99
Treaty of Paris (1856) 3, 21, 24, 64–7, 69, 77, 82–3, 97, 121, 156n2, 169n14
Trikoupis, Harilaos 86, 91, 97, 99
Tripoli 6, 10, 14, 17; war with United States 12, 14–15

Tripolitsa 37
Triton (British steamer) 52
Tunis 6, 10, 14–15, 17, 137n43; in the Greek War of Independence 35, 37–8

Ulcinj (Ulqin) 159n44
Umurbey (Berguz) 87, 161n14
United States 27, 30, 48, 94, 99, 129, 146n16, 159n43, 170n24; Civil War 77, 156n2; wars in North Africa 14–16
Uskoks 154–5n40

Varese (Italian corvette) 81
Venice 10, 14, 31–2, 38, 57 134n29, 138n43, 138–9n44, 141n61, 154–5n40, 156n41
Versaci, Raffaelo and Salvadore 81

Victorious Soldiers of Muhammad (*Asâkir-i Mansûre-i Muhammediye Ordusu*) 29, 145n8
Vlavianos, Spiros 88
Volos 52, 104

Wadsworth, James 4, 134n30
wetlands 86; draining of 89–90, 162n32
women 16–17, 38, 75, 132n20, 149n41; participation in piracy 55, 63–4, 154–5n40
Wyse, Thomas 52–4

Young Turk revolution 109, 112

Zante currants 24, 66, 86, 89–90, 95–7, 99, 160n47, 162n28

www.ingramcontent.com/pod-product-compliance
Lightning Source LLC
Chambersburg PA
CBHW061829300426
44115CB00013B/2310